W9-BNN-952

CONTENTS

MAP LIST

Suzy Gershman's

BORN TO SHOP

NEW YORK

The Ultimate Guide for
People Who Love to Shop

12th Edition

WILEY
Wiley Publishing, Inc.

For ~~...~~ ...e and Janet, our New York team.

Published by:

Wiley Publishing, Inc.
111 River St.
Hoboken, NJ 07030-5774

ISBN: 978-0-470-25714-2
Editor: Jennifer Polland
Production Editor: Suzanna R. Thompson
Cartographer: Elizabeth Puhl
Production by Wiley Indianapolis Composition Services

This revision reported and written by Suzy Gershman and Sarah Lahey.

For information on our other products and services or to obtain technical support, please contact our Customer Care Department within the U.S. at 800/762-2974, outside the U.S. at 317/572-3993 or fax 317/572-4002.

Wiley also publishes its books in a variety of electronic formats. Some content that appears in print may not be available in electronic formats.

Manufactured in the United States of America

5   4   3   2   1

ABOUT THE AUTHORS

Suzy Gershman is a journalist, author, and honest-to-goodness shopping goddess who has worked in the fashion and fiber industry for more than 35 years. The Born to Shop series, which is over 25 years old, is translated into eight languages, making Gershman an international expert on retail and trade. Her essays on retailing have been used by the Harvard School of Business; her reportage on travel and retail has appeared in *Travel + Leisure, Travel Holiday, Travel Weekly,* and most of the major women's magazines.

Suzy's guide to world shopping, *Where to Buy the Best of Everything: The Outspoken Guide for World Travelers and Online Shoppers,* was published in April 2008. When not in an airport, Gershman divides her time between her homes in Provence and San Diego, California, where she lives with her long-hair dachshund, Toffee.

Suzy also gives lectures and shopping tours. Visit www.suzygershman.com or write to suzy@suzygershman.com for details.

Sarah Lahey is the Editorial Director of Born to Shop. She travels extensively to research and rewrite Born to Shop editions and still finds time to show and sell English smalls at several northern California antiques fairs and on eBay. Sarah lives in Tiburon, California, with her husband, Tom, and two dogs, Bentley and Beckham.

Aaron and Jenny Gershman got their jobs through nepotism, but they happen to be very good shoppers. While they did not do a lot of reporting on this edition, their tips for the under-30 crowd are woven throughout.

TO START WITH

As the author of several international travel guides and a woman with property and bank accounts in France, I have taken to wondering why anyone else would travel to Europe in these days of expensive everything and low dollar returns. Yes, Asia is still great, but anyone who needs a shot of shopping adrenalin might just want to stay stateside and head to Manhattan.

Now that I am back living in the U.S., it's more fun than ever to visit New York—I can't imagine why anyone wouldn't schedule an annual trip, just to soak up the energy. Prices are high these days, but bargains are hidden and ready to be claimed. There's more and more luxury every day (wait till you see Ivanka Trump's new store), while at the same time there are more and more chances to buy cut-rate.

This is deal city, and the deals are thriving. Deal or No Deal? The whole point of this game is to make the deal. Sarah Lahey and I will show you the way.

As always, I look for what can't be found elsewhere in the world—and, of course, I look for great prices. Since the laws on sales tax and the regulations on luggage allowance have both gotten stricter in the past years, I made a lot of trips to the post office to mail home many boxes. The shoes will be here any day now. Can't wait!

Special thanks go to New York correspondent Paul Baumrind, who does a lot of cutting, clipping, calling, and schlepping on my behalf, as well as Janet Rodgers and Michele Peck, who whisper their secrets into my phone and e-mail.

Note: If you are shopping from Europe and the euro is your currency, lucky you. At press time, the euro is 50% stronger than the dollar, making most of America one big bargain for you. By the time you read this, who knows what the rate of exchange will be. My advice to you? *Bienvenue* and *bien vendu.*

Manhattan Neighborhoods

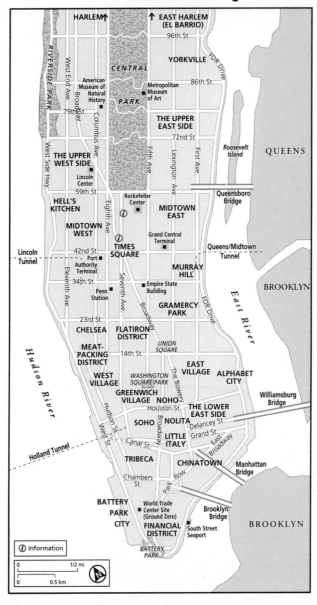

Manhattan: 14th Street & Below

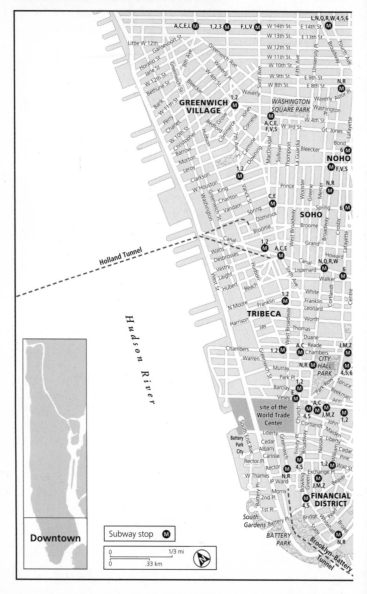

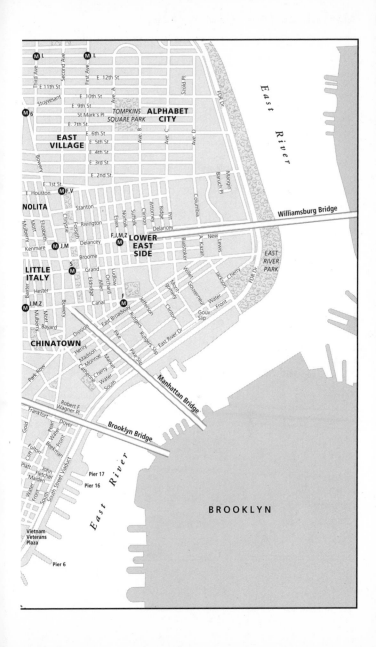

Manhattan: 14th Street & Above

Manhattan Subways

Herald Square, Garment District, Times Square, Rockefeller Center & More

SHOPS ●
Aaron Faber **44**
Abercrombie & Fitch **30**
Alfred Dunhill **39**
American Girl Place **53**
Anne Fontaine **3**
Ann Taylor **5**
Anya Hindmarch **7**
Ascot Chang **26**
Aveda **44**
A/X Armani Exchange **39**
Baccarat **11**
Bally **6**
Banana Republic **54**
Bauman Rare Books **40**
Belgian Shoes **32**
Bergdorf Goodman **25**
Bergdorf Goodman Men **25**
Bernardaud/Limoges **8**
Best of Scotland **59**
Billabong **62**
B&J Fabrics **74**
Blanc de Chine **45**
Bloomingdale's **14**
Borders **19**
Bottega Veneta **6**
Bridge Kitchenware Corporation **42**
Brooks Brothers **39, 67**
Brookstone **27, 52**
Bulgari **24**
Burberry **24**
Calvin Klein **2**
Capezio **50**
Cartier **39**
Caswell-Massey **56**
Celine **3**
Chanel **23**
Christian Dior **23**
Christian Lacroix **23**
Christie's **53**
Club Monaco **24, 39**
Concord Chemists **47**
Crabtree & Evelyn **44, 54**
Crate & Barrel **6**
Crouch & Fitzgerald **57**
Daffy's **17, 70, 81**
Dean & DeLuca **53**
Destination Maternity **21**
Diesel **11**
DKNY **5**

Drama Book Shop **74**
Dylan's Candy Bar **12**
Eileen Fisher **44**
Eres **18**
Ermenegildo Zegna **46**
FAO Schwarz **22**
Felissimo **29**
Fendi **45**
Fortunoff **24**
Frédéric Fekkai **34**
Gale Grant **43**
Gucci **30**
Hammacher Schlemmer **15**
Harry Winston **30**
Henri Bendel **30**
H&M **46**
H. Stern **46**
H2O Plus **5**
Hyman Hendler & Sons **76**
Ivanka Trump **1**
Janet Sartin Institute **18**
J. Crew **68**
Jean-Claude Biguine **60**
Jos. A. Bank **66**
Kate's Paperie **28**
Laila Rowe **10**
Lana Marks **5**
L'Occitane **43**
Lord & Taylor **77**
Louis Vuitton **24**
Lush **81**
M&M's World **51**
Mackenzie-Childs **27**
Macy's **82**
Manolo Blahnik **38**
Maurice Badler **59**
Michael C. Fina **65**
M&J Trimming **80**
Mokuba New York **78**
MoMA Design and Book Store **48**
Nicole Farhi **5**
Niketown **21**
Nine West **16**
Old Navy **83**
Oliviers & Co. **71**
Original Levi's Store **11**
Origins **71**
Orvis **65**
Paul Stuart **66**
Porthault **8**

Pottery Barn **13**
Prada **20**
Rare Vintage **23**
Reem Acra **4**
Rizzoli Bookstore **27**
Rochester Big & Tall **49**
Saks Fifth Avenue **54**
Salvatore Ferragamo **45**
Sermoneta **22**
Sharper Image **27**
Sherpa Shop **57**
Smythson of Bond Street **24**
Sony Style **31**
Sports Authority **42**
St. John **45**
Stitches East **47**
Strawberry **70**
Suarez **30**
Takashimaya **39**
Talbots **40**
Talbots Mens **40**
Tall Girl Shop **78**
Taryn Rose **1**
Tiffany & Co. **24**
Tinsel Trading Co. **79**
Tom Austin **72**
Tourneau **6**
Trump Tower Atrium **30**
Urban Zen **36**
Van Cleef & Arpels **24**
Yves St. Laurent **24**
Zara **39**

WHERE TO STAY ■
The Alex **69**
The Benjamin **55**
Four Seasons Hotel **20**
The Millennium Broadway **63**
The Peninsula **35**
The Warwick **37**

WHERE TO DINE ◆
Adour **34**
Burger Heaven **33, 45, 58, 75**
DB Bistro Moderne **64**
ESPN Zone **73**
Gino **9**
Ollie's Noodle Shop **61**
Vong **41**

SoHo, NoHo, Nolita & the Lower East Side

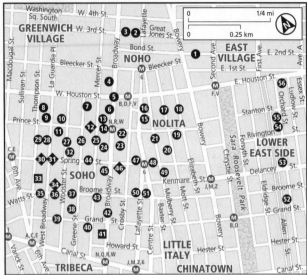

Flatiron, Union Square, Chelsea, Ladies' Mile & the Village

SHOPS ●

ABC Carpet & Home **28**
Aerosoles **21**
Alexander McQueen **38**
Anthropologie **26**
A/X Armani Exchange **22**
Banana Republic **25**
Barnes & Noble **16, 31**
Barneys Co-Op **9**
Bed Bath & Beyond **18**
Belly Dance Maternity **58**
Best Buy **6**
Burlington Coat Factory **5**
Canine Styles **45**
Chelsea Market **37**
Club Monaco **21**
Condomania **57**
The Container Store **17**
Corniche Furs & Luxury
  Outerwear **1**
Cynthia Rowley **59**
DSW **35**
Dulken & Derrick **19**
Eileen Fisher **51**
Filene's Basement **18, 35**
Fishs Eddy **28**
Forbidden Planet **48**
Forever 21 **35**
Gabay's Outlet **32**

Greenmarket **29**
H&M **24**
Home Depot **7**
Housing Works
  Thrift Shop **14**
Intermix **23**
J. Crew **25**
James Perse **59**
Jean-Claude Biguine **4**
Jean Shop **38**
Jensen-Lewis **12**
Jo Malone **20**
Keni Valenti
  Retro-Couture **2**
Kiehl's **49**
Kleinfeld **15**
Kmart **53**
Le Fanion **44**
Les Pierre Antiques **59**
L'Occitane **56**
Loehmann's **11**
Lucky Brand Jeans **20**
Lulu Guinness **60**
Old Navy **18**
Origins **20**
Otte **43**
Paragon **28**
Paul Smith **26**
Petco **30**

Poleci **40**
Pottery Barn Bed & Bath **11**
Restoration Hardware **20**
Ricky's **8, 46, 54**
Rothman's of
  Union Square **31**
Rugby **47**
Shooz **10**
St. Mark's Comics **52**
Strand Book Store **48**
T.J. Maxx **18**
Tracy Reese **41**
Trina Turk **42**
Trader Joe's **33**
Trash and Vaudeville **52**
Urban Outfitters **36, 50, 55**
Virgin Megastore **34**
Waterworks **27**
Whole Foods/
  Whole Body **3, 35**
Zara **25**

WHERE TO DINE ◆

Cafeteria **13**
Coffee Shop **29**
Cornelia St. Café **56**
Magnolia Bakery **60**
Pastis **39**

Chapter One

....

THE BEST OF NEW YORK

Best this, best that, best, best, best—editors and list makers are obsessed with the best. In fact, I've just published a book called *Where to Buy the Best of Everything,* so I guess I too am obsessed. If you are dashing about in a New York Minute, or thinking that all the possibilities in these pages are overwhelming, this at-a-glance chapter might help you get started quickly and easily.

This chapter features some easy-to-locate shops where you can find what you need if you're short on time, as well as some easy-to-make choices when in a hurry. Each store mentioned here is explained in greater depth in later chapters, and, of course, there are plenty more shops discussed inside.

Addresses in all listings are given with cross streets so that you can find your destination more easily. When taking a taxi, tell the driver the cross streets as soon as you get in the car so there is no confusion.

The subway is your best bet—especially for long hauls, which can get tedious (and expensive) in traffic. Never take the uptown or downtown bus when you are in a hurry unless it's an express bus; crosstown buses, however, are worth the effort.

Note: I use 34th Street as the dividing line between uptown and downtown. This is not a traditional dividing line (many people use 14th St. or 23rd St. as the official dividing point and consider 34th St. as Midtown), but I find it very handy and use it throughout this text.

YOU HAVE ONLY 1 HOUR TO SHOP

If you have only an hour to shop, your choices really depend on what part of town you're in, what your goals are, and how frequently you get to New York. Sometimes I'm willing to blow my single hour in town on something totally nontraditional, and sometimes I'm forced to look for something as specific as a matching button. But let's concentrate on location in this chapter, since time is so tight here.

Upper East Side

I can walk from 57th Street to 90th Street along Madison Avenue in a little over 2 hours, poking into whatever stores interest me (but not doing serious shopping). You can do this same stroll in less time if you stick to window-shopping. Few districts of the city give you a better overview of why New York is so special.

Midtown Fifth Avenue

Do you want an hour's worth of visual stimulation and excitement or do you want to do some serious shopping? If it's inspiration you seek (and maybe not that much in terms of durable goods), poke in quickly at **Takashimaya** (693 Fifth Ave., at 54th St.) and **Henri Bendel** (712 Fifth Ave., at 56th St.). Then stop by **Felissimo** (10 W. 56th St.), a shop filled with whimsy and wonder. **Gucci**'s new flagship (675 Fifth Ave., at 56th St.) is a must-see. If you really need something and need it fast, do what I do and spend an hour at **Saks Fifth Avenue** (611 Fifth Ave., at 50th St.).

Meatpacking District & Chelsea

Take a taxi to **Jeffrey** (449 W. 14th St., near Tenth Ave.) and step on it. Walk east across 14th Street to see all the new stuff and then hop over to **Barneys Co-Op** (236 W. 18th St., near Seventh Ave.) if you have time. From there, well, if you're game, let's go to **Loehmann's** Chelsea store.

SoHo & Nolita

Sure, you can spend an hour breezily and easily in SoHo, but take time out and head for nearby Nolita! No doubt about it, these two neighborhoods are bursting with new stores—some original shops and some branches of big names. The big money (**Chanel,** 139 Spring St., at Wooster; **Louis Vuitton,** 116 Greene St., between Prince and Spring sts.; **Armani Casa,** 97 Greene St., between Prince and Spring sts.) continues to move here, so if you're looking for funky, hunt for it on the fringes. The best shopping is on Wooster, Greene, and Mercer streets, between Prince and Spring streets. Stores open late, so make a day of it by adding on dinner at one of the hot restaurants in the vicinity.

YOU WANT TO SEE SOMETHING *VERY* NEW YORK

If you're visiting from Europe, much of American retail will seem new and fresh to you. If you're visiting from another American city, you'll find that many Manhattan versions of your favorite chain stores are bigger and better but fundamentally the same. Therefore, visiting those stores that are the epitome of New York style (even if they have stores in other cities as well) will give you supreme pleasure, whether you buy anything or not. For those reasons, check out:

ABC CARPET & HOME
888 Broadway, at 19th St. (Subway: R or W to 23rd St.).

EILEEN FISHER
521 Madison Ave., near 53rd St. (Subway: E or V to Fifth Ave./53rd St.).

TAKASHIMAYA
693 Fifth Ave., at 54th St. (Subway: E or V to Fifth Ave./53rd St.).

YOU WANT SOME PLACE NEW TO DISCOVER

Union Square

Union Square offers tons of stores, lots of energy, and the chance to hit the **Greenmarket** (held Mon, Wed and Fri–Sat 8am–6pm). Check out **Whole Foods** (40 E. 14th St., between Broadway and University Place), then go upstairs to **Filene's Basement** (4 Union Sq. S., at 14th St.), **DSW** (40 E. 14th St., 3rd floor, between Broadway and University Place), and **Forever 21** (49 E. 14th St., between Broadway and University Place). To keep with the foodie theme, head to **Trader Joe's** (142 E. 14th St., between Third and Fourth aves.).

Midtown

Head for Columbus Circle and the **Time Warner Center,** which houses a hotel, a large mall, and a huge **Whole Foods.** The mall is sort of overglitzy, but you'll find good **Borders** and **Williams-Sonoma** stores.

YOU WANT ONE ADDRESS TO TELL FRIENDS ABOUT

Get your fix at **Dylan's Candy Bar** (1011 Third Ave., near 60th St.), operated by none other than Ralph Lauren's daughter. This place has two floors of goodies and items not found anywhere else. There's a basement floor as well as an old-fashioned soda fountain. You'll see plenty of gift ideas, including beautiful ready-made and custom-made gift baskets.

ONE ADDRESS YOU CAN'T BELIEVE YOU DON'T KNOW

Speaking of Ralph Lauren, you probably think you know it all and there's not much more to say. So, have you been to **Rugby** (99 University Place, at 12th St.) yet? This store near the NYU campus is very Ralph, but has been tweaked just so for the college set. There's clothing and gear for all of life's needs, from active sportswear to dress-up.

BEST HAUTE HOME STYLE

Dress up, pretend you live in the neighborhood, and head to **Ankasa** (135 E. 65th St., at Lexington Ave.) to gush over the India-inspired textile, furniture, and accessory collections. A couple of blocks away, **Charlotte Moss** (20 E. 63rd St., between Fifth and Sixth aves.) flaunts her impeccable design talent in a new, five-story town-house showroom. You'll want to buy it all or just move in.

SOMETHING FOR THE YOUNG ONES

Toys "R" Us is all over the U.S., but the best one is at Times Square—you ain't seen nuthin' like it, I promise you. I'll give you a hint: indoor Ferris wheel. Also in Midtown are the **Disney Store** (711 Fifth Ave., at 55th St.), **M&M's World** (1600 Broadway, between 48th and 49th sts.), and the **Metropolitan Museum of Art Store** at Rockefeller Center, which has a wonderful kids' department. **F.A.O. Schwarz** (767 Fifth Ave., at 58th St.) has scaled down a bit, but it's still a treat for everyone in the family. Yes, you can play the foot-piano as in the movie *Big*.

BEST BLING

Ivanka Trump (683A Madison Ave., between 61st and 62nd sts.) just opened a jewelry store, showcasing her Deco-inspired designs, where you can sip a coffee and be shown diamonds by the mile.

BEST DOWN-&-DIRTY BARGAINS

It's got to be **Ladies' Mile** (Sixth Ave., around 18th St.). And no, it's not just for ladies anymore. Off-pricers **T.J. Maxx** and **Filene's Basement** are located in the same building at 620 Sixth Ave., at 18th Street.

Although it's not in this stretch, **Loehmann's** (101 Seventh Ave., at 16th St.) is only a block away, and should definitely be included in this neighborhood.

BEST STUFF FOR YOUR APARTMENT OR HOME

You won't believe you read this here, and I can't believe I'm writing it, but here goes: the East Side, mostly around the East 50s and 60s!

Move over to Madison for **Crate & Barrel** (650 Madison Ave., at 59th St.). Or head straight for **The Conran Shop** (407 E. 59th St.) and **Bed Bath & Beyond** (410 E. 61st St.), both under the 59th Street Bridge.

Not too far away, there's also a big department store at 59th Street and Lexington Avenue called **Bloomingdale's** (yep, you've heard of it before!), which has a terrific bed-linen selection that, when it goes on sale, equals discount prices. And for the final flourishes, head to **Gracious Home** (1217 Third Ave. and 1220 Third Ave., both at 70th St.).

You should also check out Lower Broadway and Ladies' Mile. Start at **ABC Carpet & Home** (888 Broadway, at 19th St.) and **Fishs Eddy** (889 Broadway, at 19th St.); then wander the side streets east of Broadway and look for the upholsterers and quiet fabric and furniture sources nestled in and around 20th Street. Or just head straight over to Seventh Avenue to the new **Pottery Barn Bed and Bath** (100–104 Seventh Ave., between 16th and 17th sts.).

BEST GIFTS

Need to pick up a few quick gifts for friends? Here are a few ideas:

- Soap or a Dead Sea beauty treatment from **Sabon.**
- Something from **Tiffany & Co.** Small leather goods, scarves, and items in sterling silver are reasonably priced.
- Health, beauty, or well-being products from a brand with limited distribution—browse the selection at **Space.NK** (99 Greene St., between Prince and Spring sts.).
- Art or folk art from any of the museum stores—or even the street. The **Metropolitan Museum of Art** has a shop in Macy's and one at Rockefeller Center; notebooks and stationery items are in the $9-to-$12 price range and make useful, stylish gifts.
- A Lady Liberty M&M dispenser from **M&M's World** (1600 Broadway, between 48th and 49th sts.), for the kids.
- A fabric-covered hatbox full of chocolates from **La Maison du Chocolat** (1018 Madison Ave., between 78th and 79th sts.)—for a very good friend.
- A gift for the pet—pet boutiques are the rage in New York. Try **Canine Styles** (43 Greenwich Ave., near Charles St.); the Cheeky Squeaky toy made of tennis-ball material is a winner for $12. The **Sherpa Shop** (400 Madison Ave., near 48th St.), inside Crouch & Fitzgerald, is where you'll find high-quality totes for cats and dogs.

CHEAP THRILLS

- NYC makeup brush set from **Duane Reade** ($2)
- A bag of gourmet popcorn from **Garrett Popcorn Shops** ($5–$10)
- Bath bombs from **Lush** ($5)
- Silk flower hairclips from **Dulken & Derrick** ($12)
- Mini gel eye masks from **Waterworks** ($10)

BEST QUICKIE SHOPPER'S LUNCH

Burger Heaven. Yummy burgers. See p. 63 for locations.

BEST HOTEL LUNCH

Fancy hotels can offer very competitively priced luncheons, served in restaurants that are true hidden gems. The **Surrey** is home to **Café Boulud** (20 E. 76th St., near Madison Ave.), which has a fixed-price lunch. **Sarabeth's** is located in the **Hotel Wales** (1295 Madison Ave., at 92nd St.). Famous for Sunday brunch (arrive early!), it's a great midpriced lunch stop at the top of Madison Avenue.

BEST AFTERNOON TEA

The **Peninsula's Gotham Lounge** serves legendary afternoon tea from 2:30 to 5:30pm every afternoon (700 Fifth Ave., at 55th St.). **The Pierre** (2 E. 61st St., at Fifth Ave.) has been totally redone, so pop in for tea and a gawk.

BEST OVERALL DEPARTMENT STORE

Saks Fifth Avenue (611 Fifth Ave., at 50th St.) has it all.

BEST SALES

Nothing beats **Saks Fifth Avenue** (611 Fifth Ave., at 50th St.) when the sale merchandise gets marked down an additional 30% to 40%. **Barneys'** warehouse sale (255 W. 17th St., between Seventh and Eighth aves.) is usually held in February, when prices are slashed 50% to 75%.

BEST OFF-PRICER

New York is suddenly teeming with off-pricers and discounters, so a new and better resource could pop up at any time. I left my heart at **Century 21,** which has locations in Manhattan (22 Cortlandt St., near Church St.) and Brooklyn (472 86th St., between Fourth and Fifth aves.).

BEST RESALE SHOPS

Try **Encore** (1132 Madison Ave., near 84th St., 2nd floor), **Michael's** (1041 Madison Ave., near 80th St., 2nd floor), and neighbor **La Boutique** (1045 Madison Ave., near 80th St., 2nd floor). Remember, though, you have to get lucky.

BEST PLACE FOR A WEDDING GOWN

Filene's Basement now holds its famous bridal sale twice a year in New York, too! See p. 293 for details.

If you time it right, you can get to the **Vera Wang** sample sale, usually held at the Hotel Pennsylvania. Check **Daily Candy** online or call © **212/628-3400** for the dates and details. Vera also does a bridal-event-cum-sale with Barneys.

Should you be willing to wear a used gown (of course you are), **Michael's** (1041 Madison Ave., near 80th St., 2nd floor) has one of the best selections in town.

If nothing but the full regalia will do, and your mom wants to sip tea while you try on your train, **Saks Fifth Avenue** (611 Fifth Ave., at 50th St.) has been doing this for years and remains the last of the full-service wedding belles.

And finally, I have to remind you that **Kleinfeld** of Brooklyn has come to Manhattan (110 W. 20th St., near Sixth Ave.). It has over 1,000 gowns on hand and all sorts of insider information, tips, and services for the bride and her entourage.

BEST HANDBAGS

I'd head straight for **Suarez** (5 W. 56th St., at Fifth Ave.), which sells a variety of designer-style handbags made in the same Italian factories as the big names (Gucci, Prada).

If you have the scratch and want the best wow bag in the world, head to **Anthony Luciano** (347 W. 36th St., Ste. 1400; ☎ **212/563-2225,** by appointment; www.anthonyluciano.com). He uses vintage frames and exotic skins and fabrics to create the best bags in the city. They're also among the priciest; expect to pay $1,500 and way up.

BEST "REGULAR" DRUGSTORE

Manhattan is dotted with drugstores. **CVS, Duane Reade,** and **Rite Aid** are fighting it out for the hearts and minds and teeth of New Yorkers, even in the best business districts in Midtown. They carry all the basics, from bottled water to beauty aids to condoms. Please note that prices on sundries in Manhattan are more expensive than anyplace else in the U.S., so you'll almost always pay less at home. Unless home is overseas.

Best for beauty supplies is **Ricky's,** which also sells wigs, jewelry, and funky gifts. See p. 241 for details and locations.

BEST FANCY DRUGSTORE

Go straight to **Clyde's** (926 Madison Ave., near 74th St.). Wait here please, James. ☎ **212/744-5050.**

BEST MUSEUM STORE

METROPOLITAN MUSEUM OF ART STORE
Fifth Ave., at 82nd St. (Subway: 4, 5, or 6 to 86th St.).

The flagship inside the museum itself is the best, but there are multiple branches around town, including one inside Macy's and one at Rockefeller Center. © **212/570-3894.** www.met museum.org/store.

BEST TRENDY SHOP

JEFFREY NEW YORK
449 W. 14th St., between Ninth and Tenth aves. (Subway: A, C, E, or L to 14th St./Eighth Ave.).

This place has trendsetting clothes and the attitude to go with them. There's an excellent service policy as well as a DJ. Time to rock 'n' roll. © **212/206-1272.**

TRENDY WITH ARCHITECTURE

ADIDAS
610 Broadway, at Houston St. (Subway: B, D, F, or V to Broadway/Lafayette St.).

Not as large as Niketown, but the store is sleek and black and minimalist and functional all at once. © **212/529-0081.** www. adidas.com.

PRADA
575 Broadway, near Prince St. (Subway: N, R, or W to Prince St.).

There are other Prada stores in Manhattan, but this is the one for style freaks and architecture buffs to check out. You don't have to buy anything; just bring a tissue in case you start to drool. In keeping with Miuccia's devotion to outstanding architecture statements, this store could be a museum. © **212/ 334-8888.** www.prada.com.

BEST STORES IN NEW YORK

In alphabetical order:

ABC CARPET & HOME
888 Broadway, at 18th St. (Subway: R or W to 23rd St.).

Even if you buy nothing, step into this beautifully dressed showcase for tabletop, linens, fabrics, and, oh yeah, carpets. © 212/473-3000. www.abchome.com.

BLANC DE CHINE
673 Fifth Ave., at 53rd St. (Subway: E or V to Fifth Ave./53rd St.).

This Hong Kong maker of luxury men's and women's clothing combines Chinese classic styles with Armani palette and makes expensive tailored clothes that will outlast fashion and rest in your world of style forever. © 800/228-2322.

CENTURY 21
22 Cortlandt St., between Church St. and Broadway (Subway: R or W to Cortlandt St.); 472 86th St., between Fourth and Fifth aves., Brooklyn (Subway: R to 86th St. in Brooklyn).

If you crave the biggest designer names at discount prices, it's worth the subway ride to downtown Manhattan, the schlep to Brooklyn, and maybe even the trip to New York! Note that the Brooklyn branch is better than ever (with a new home store). © 212/227-9092 for Manhattan; © 718/748-3266 for Brooklyn. www.c21stores.com.

CHARLOTTE MOSS
20 E. 63rd St., between Fifth and Madison aves. (Subway: 6 to 68th St.).

This five-story town house is filled to the rafters with style, substance, and beautiful home furnishings and accessories. © 212/308-3888. www.charlottemoss.com.

EILEEN FISHER
521 Madison Ave., near 53rd St. (Subway: E or V to Fifth Ave./53rd St.).

Several branches around town offer droopy chic for women. Love those elastic waists! Silks and linens, bouclé wools, and a soft color palette a la Armani—but affordable. © 212/759-9888. www.eileenfisher.com.

KATE'S PAPERIE
561 Broadway, near Prince St. (Subway: N, R, or W to Prince St.); 140 W. 57th St., between Sixth and Seventh aves. (Subway: N, Q, R, or W to 57th St./Seventh Ave.).

You'll find an eye-popping choice of papers, wraps, and ribbons here. © 212/941-9816 for Broadway; © 212/459-0700 for West 57th Street. www.katespaperie.com.

MUJI SOHO
455 Broadway, at Grand St. (Subway: N or R to Canal St.).

Sarah and I disagree on this. I know Muji from around the world and am not impressed with the new U.S. flagship. Sarah likes this lifestyle store's no-frills basics in timeless designs and neutral colors that will work with any decor or lifestyle. © 212/334-2002. www.muji.com.

TAKASHIMAYA
693 Fifth Ave., near 54th St. (Subway: E or V to Fifth Ave./53rd St.).

This place has gorgeous flowers and drop-dead lifestyle designs to gawk at. © 212/350-0100.

UNIQLO
546 Broadway, between Prince and Spring sts. (Subway: N, R, or W to Prince St.).

Uniqlo features an endless assortment of value-priced colorful clothing: cashmere, knits, outerwear, and more. Everything is inexpensive and disposable; if you're bored with something after a few wearings, toss it. © 212/966-5374. www.uniqlo.com.

Chapter Two

· · · · · · · · · · · · · · · · · · · ·

NEW YORK DETAILS

BIG APPLE CIRCUS

· ·

This is the place that never sleeps, so why be naked when you can shop 24/7? Where you can almost always get it wholesale? Subway strike? Just keep walking and shopping. Disgruntled taxi drivers? Ask 'em how they like your smile. No matter what the work conditions, New York has so much to offer that you won't be able to stop grinning.

There are lots of new stores and many, many arrivals from international shores. Luxury keeps outdoing itself here; big-box stores and suburban retailing styles have been blossoming as well—wait till you get down to Union Square. East 57th Street, east of Fifth Avenue, has practically reinvented itself. Street vendors sell fake Bottega Veneta and Goyard bags from Midtown corners; sample sales and showrooms are popping up everywhere while SoHo is always more, more, and more more.

Read on for more on what's new.

WHAT'S NEW, PUSSYCAT?

· ·

- Suburbia has invaded Manhattan. **The Container Store** has added a new location at 725 Lexington Ave., a couple of blocks from Bloomingdale's. There's a new **Pottery Barn Bed**

& **Bath** in Chelsea and **Pottery Barn Kids'** newest boutique, **Threads,** has opened on the Upper East Side.

- Suburban style has also come to **Union Square,** the hottest destination in town. There's everything from **Filene's Basement** to **DSW.** And **Sephora, Virgin Megastore,** and **Barnes & Noble** have been here for several years.

- Mass-market has gotten bigger and bolder. Check out a chain called **Forever 21,** the poor gal's H&M. SoHo is home to newcomer **Uniqlo,** where you'll find floors of inexpensive casual clothes.

- Being a Broadway baby no longer means you're bound for the Theater District. Retail on Broadway from the West 60s on up to the mid-70s is hot. **Loehmann's** has opened a new megastore at 2101 Broadway between 73rd and 74th streets. **Sephora** has moved into a new space at 2164 Broadway between 76th and 77th streets, and the **Pottery Barn** at 67th Street and Broadway has revamped and emerged as a fresh new face.

- This is not to imply that the only thing that's new in town is low-end or mass-market—oh no, sirree. For one, **De Beers** is here. And wait 'til you see the bling at **Ivanka Trump's** new Madison Avenue boutique.

- **SoHo** (short for "South of Houston") has turned out to be uptown in a downtown location. Recent arrivals include luxe mattress maker **Hastens, Kiki De Montparnasse** with sexy lingerie (sexy toys, too), and **M Missoni,** the slightly more affordable line of zigzag knits. LA's **True Religion** has opened a denim boutique, and the best of Italian tabletop can be found at **Alessi. Muji** just opened on Broadway between Grand and Howard streets.

- **Nolita** (short for "North of Little Italy") has become the new SoHo, sort of, but it's real and small and intimate and fabulous. This is where small stores are an art form and the retailer is the curator—and maybe the designer as well. Check out **Laces,** a women's-only sneaker boutique, and **SOHO** for enameled jewelry.

- The **Meatpacking District** (very far west on 14th St. and into Chelsea), though still working on the smells, is fast becoming a restaurant scene, while hip department store **Jeffrey** continues to offer edgy fashion. The area has everything from art galleries to warehouse spaces to the **Comme des Garçons** boutique, which marries retail with a gallery feel and redefines the borders of Chelsea. **Diane von Furstenberg** has opened a boutique on the ground floor of her DVF Studio, and you won't want to miss newcomers **Trina Turk** and **Tracy Reese** while you're in the 'hood.

- **TriBeCa** (short for "Triangle below Canal Street") has big-name retailers including **Issey Miyake** and **Baker Furniture,** and small boutiques are sprouting all over. Check out **LuLuLemon** for active wear, **Rogan** for jeans, and **Moulin Bleu** for home style. Watch this neighborhood.

- **Fifth Avenue** at its midpoint has become one giant mall, with a wider range of retail than ever before. You'll find this brave shopping world right around Rockefeller Center, with flagships representing everyone from **Banana Republic** to **Kenneth Cole.**

- But Fifth Avenue is not all down-market or mass-market. The new **Gucci** flagship in Trump Tower is the largest boutique in the world. **Armani** plans to open a new bigger-and-better store at the corner of Fifth Avenue and 56th Street in early 2009.

- **Columbus Circle,** considered dead for the past decade, is now the address to boast about—it's become home to a chic hotel, apartments, and a luxury mall, all contained in the **Time Warner Center,** New York's latest architectural wonder. The building anchors a hot eating and shopping district. The mall is rather ho-hum; but the **Whole Foods** in the basement is a big hit, and **Borders** is one of the best-stocked bookstores in the city.

- **Middle Madison Avenue** (in the 40s) is getting classier—first the rebirth of Grand Central Terminal (with great stores, including **Oliviers & Co.** for imported olive oil) and an enormous branch of **J. Crew.**

- **Ladies' Mile,** the section of Sixth Avenue where the first department stores in New York opened more than 100 years ago, has turned into superstore, discounter, and off-pricer heaven. Try the blocks from 17th to 20th streets for some rather amazing sights and discounts for all members of the family—yep, even the kids.
- **Wall Street**'s rebirth has added big-name shopping, as well. **Tiffany & Co.**'s and **Hermès**'s new stores are stunning, as is **Borders.**
- Need to look, feel, or shop like a New Yorker? Log on to **www.dailycandy.com** to find out what's hot, what's new, and where to find the sample sales.

THE NEW YORK RULE OF NATURAL SELECTION

New York offers more selection than any other marketplace in the United States, and probably in the world—and that includes Tokyo. (Okay, Tokyo may have more merchandise, but it won't all fit you.)

One of the things that makes New York great is the fact that you can find things here that aren't available elsewhere or haven't yet been introduced in other parts of the country. Shopping in this city offers the biggest mental challenges of all time—can you bear to see this much stuff and not buy it all? Can you possibly choose the best thing for you at the best price? Shopping in New York is like living a game show.

Even though Midtown is populated by stores that you may have back home (even if home is Paris), the New York Rule of Natural Selection is simple: If it's new, it comes to New York first.

WINDOW-SHOPPING 101

To me, the biggest bargains in New York are the education that you get from wandering around and the high that comes from absorbing so much energy and so many creative ideas.

Look at the men and women who rush past on their way to work—study what they're wearing and the shopping bags they're carrying, and learn from them. Look at the store windows and displays; stare at mannequins and even at ads in the *New York Times*. But the windows are easy. The bargains take work. (See chapter 11 for more on bargains.)

GETTING THERE

Because it is the international hub city of the United States, just about every domestic and international carrier—and then some—serves New York. The trick is to realize that there are several airports and to know that you can avoid a traffic jam or even get a bargain by using an alternative airport.

John F. Kennedy International Airport (JFK) is the best-known airport, especially for international flights, but it's not the only game in town. **LaGuardia Airport (LGA)** takes mostly domestic flights, but it does serve cities in Canada, Bermuda, and a few other destinations outside the continental U.S. **Newark Liberty International Airport (EWR)**, in New Jersey,

Business Deals

It's glamorous, it's indulgent, and, yes, there's value, too. If you're considering a business-class flight from Europe or the U.K. to New York, you'll want to make the most of your time and money.

Open Skies, an offshoot of British Airways, started service from Brussels and Paris to New York in June 2008. Their 757s are designed to carry only 82 passengers. Beginning in 2009, **British Airways** will fly all-business-class A318s from London City Airport to JFK and Newark.

American Airlines and **United** are both redesigning their business-class seats and promise new cabins on all aircrafts by 2009.

has grown dramatically as an international hub; new AirTrain service can get you from Newark to Manhattan in less than a half-hour.

Westchester County Airport (HPN), in White Plains, serves the suburbs directly north of New York. **Long Island Macarthur Airport (ISP)** is in Islip, on the south shore of Long Island. Upstate in the Hudson Valley, **Stewart International Airport (SWF)** hopes to become an international hub to take some of the pressure off JFK. The outer-fringe airports might not be convenient, but frequent promotions are available to encourage traffic through them. Maybe you wanted to see Westchester after all?

ARRIVAL & DEPARTURE

A few tricks of the trade:

- If you arrive at JFK, prepare for a long wait to collect your bags. Suzy and I flew in on separate American flights; both planes arrived on time, but we waited over an hour for our luggage (from both flights) to be delivered.
- United (and other carriers now too) has limited the free bag check-in to one per passenger on domestic flights. If you have a nonrefundable domestic ticket, you'll be charged $25 to check a second bag. Look for more airlines to follow with both domestic and international baggage restrictions and fees.
- For international arrivals, luggage carts are free; for domestic, they are not. Use the machine, which takes credit cards and dispenses carts.
- There are porters at the airport, and you should pay them as you see fit—there is no fixed charge for baggage service in New York, as there is in many other cities. A dollar per bag is the going rate.
- Illegal taxi drivers will hustle you; ignore them and get in line for a real, legit New York City yellow cab.

- The city has implemented flat-rate fees for taxi service to and from JFK and the city ($45). This rate does not include tips or tolls. The taxi rate to LaGuardia is at the regular metered rate (plus tolls), and the same metered rate applies to Newark, with the addition of a $15 surcharge.
- There is express bus service every 20 minutes to and from LaGuardia and JFK. Buses stop at a variety of hotels and major transportation centers such as Penn Station, the Port Authority, and Grand Central. For more info, go to www.ny airportservice.com or stop by the Transportation Desk in the terminal after you arrive. From Newark, there is bus service to Penn Station every 30 minutes ($15) via Air-Train; check www.njtransit.com for details. A slower option is Olympia Airport Express, also $15. www.coachusa.com/olympia.
- If you want to avoid traffic altogether, you can fly from JFK or Newark to one of two Manhattan helipads in just 10 minutes on U.S. Helicopter. Deals start at $99 each way. www.fly ush.com.

GETTING AROUND

There's no need to rent a car for your visit to New York. Driving is a nightmare, and parking is ridiculously expensive (and nearly impossible in some neighborhoods). It's much easier to get around using public transportation, taxis, and your own two feet. If you're going to visit Aunt Erma on Long Island or you have some other need to travel beyond the five boroughs, call one of the major car-rental companies, such as **National** (© 800/227-7368; www.nationalcar.com), **Hertz** (© 800/654-3131; www.hertz.com), or **Avis** (© 800/230-4898; www.avis.com), all of which have airport and Manhattan locations.

By Subway

You can ask for a free subway map at the token booth of any subway station, or use the black-and-white map on p. 5. To

For More Bus & Subway Info

For transit information, visit **www.mta.info** or call the Metropolitan Transportation Authority's **New York City Transit Travel Information Center** (© 718/330-1234). Extensive automated information is available 24 hours a day, and live agents are on hand to answer questions and provide directions daily from 6am to 10pm.

You can get bus and subway maps at most information centers. A particularly helpful MTA desk is located at the Times Square Information Center, at 1560 Broadway, between 46th and 47th streets, where you can also buy MetroCards. Maps are usually available in subway stations (ask at the token booth), but rarely on buses.

use the subway (and bus), buy a **MetroCard,** a magnetic card that is swiped at the turnstile as you enter a station. On a Pay-per-Ride MetroCard, an additional 15% is added to the card with the purchase or addition of $7 more. Initial Pay-per-Ride minimum purchase is $4. Even better, there's a $25 card that provides 7 days' worth of unlimited travel, and a 14-day card for $47. There is also a 1-day unlimited-ride Fun Pass for $7.50. If you're over 65 and have a Medicare card, you're eligible for a 50% discount on any MetroCard. Go to www.mta.info for details. *One of the best bargains in town:* Note that when you swipe your MetroCard at the subway, you get a free bus transfer if needed.

By Bus

Buses are easy to use and may feel safer to you than the subway; unfortunately, they are much slower. If you want to get someplace in a hurry, do what all locals do: Walk.

When you take the bus, you can get a free transfer that's good for travel within 2 hours. Bus routes are clearly marked on signposts, but ask the driver to confirm that you're headed the right way. Buses cost the same as the subway ($2 per ride).

By Taxi

If you just can't do the walk, flag a taxi. If the middle light on the top of the cab is lit, the car is available; if the outer lights on the top of the cab are lit, it is off-duty. Get into the taxi and shut the door before you give your destination. This avoids the hassle of the driver telling you he doesn't want to go where you want to go.

A fare hike may be in the works, but at press time, the flag drops at $2.50 once you get into the cab, and then the meter starts up from there; taxi drivers expect a 15% tip.

By Car Service

While limos are standard fare in New York, you can also get a sedan to drive you around for less than a limousine. And frankly, who really needs a limo? Just be sure you book through a legit car service.

Car services can be booked by the hour, by the job, or for a standard run—such as going to the airport. Rates do not include tolls (this is most applicable to airport runs) or tips. A 15% tip may be automatically added onto your bill.

You may want to try **Dial 7 Car Service,** my regular. From Manhattan, it charges a flat $48 to JFK or Newark and $33 to LaGuardia, not including tips and tolls. Its phone number is easy to memorize (© 212/777-7777), or go to www.dial7.com. If you're traveling with a dog, say so when you book.

DIRECTIONS

You're hot to trot, but please, study up on your New York neighborhoods before you pounce (see the map on p. 1).

Most of Manhattan is laid out on a grid system. Avenues run north and south, while streets run east and west. Fifth

Avenue divides the East and West sides, so building numbers start at 1 heading east or west from Fifth.

In many places in the world, "downtown" is a specific place. Not in Manhattan, however. Here, all directions are given in reference to where you are standing and where you are going: Uptown is north and downtown is south.

If you're looking for a specific address on a numbered street (not an avenue), the even numbers are usually on the south side of the street and the odd numbers are on the north side of the street.

If you are at all concerned about where a shop or address may be, call ahead for directions. Ask for the nearest cross streets to know exactly where in the grid of Manhattan you will be going. There are a few parts of Manhattan that do not work on a grid, but you can spot these on a map.

INFORMATION SOURCES

I love this one: It's called **It's Easy** (© **866/ITS-EASY** [487-3279]; www.itseasypassport.com). It arranges travel needs, including passports, visas, passport photos, and more. You pay; they do the hard work. It's Easy is located at 360 Lexington Ave., in the American Airlines Center, with another branch at JFK Airport Hotel Desk, Terminal 4.

Other quite helpful sources include the visitor centers in some department stores. The welcome desk at **Saks Fifth Avenue** is almost like a concierge service—it has free copies of local guide magazines like *Where* and *In New York,* which are advertisement-driven but still useful. The visitor center at **Bloomingdale's** offers personal shopping assistance, coat and package check, hotel package delivery service (minimum purchase $250), theater tickets, and reservations for car services, tours, and restaurants. These centers frequently offer a promotional gift (like a store-logo tote bag) if you bring your receipts in after a day's shopping. The minimum for the gift at Bloomies is $100, but this can vary from store to store.

SAFETY

··

According to current crime statistics, New York is safer than any other big American city. While that's quite encouraging for all of us, it's still important to take precautions. Visitors in particular should be vigilant, as swindlers and criminals are expert at spotting newcomers who appear vulnerable.

Panhandlers are seldom dangerous and can simply be ignored (more aggressive pleas can be answered with a firm "Sorry"). If a stranger walks up to you on the street with a long sob story ("I live in the suburbs and was just attacked and don't have the money to get home"), it's likely to be a scam, so don't feel any moral compulsion to help.

Be wary of an individual who "accidentally" falls in front of you or causes some other commotion, as he or she may be working with someone else who will take your wallet when you try to help. *And remember:* You *will* lose if you place a bet on a sidewalk card game or shell game.

ONLINE & PRINT GUIDES TO NEW YORK

··

If you're tempted to buy a lot of guidebooks about New York—don't. *Frommer's New York City* is a great tool to help you navigate the city. It includes hotel and restaurant reviews, details on attractions, walking tours, and nightlife listings. The free package from **NYC & Company** (www.nyc.com) is a good starting point as well. Then you might want to think about purchasing a *Zagat* dining map or guide.

In your search for basic and up-to-date information, check out the monthly magazine *Where,* which is distributed free at hotels and at the welcome desk at Saks. Besides listing the expected tourist information, *Where* announces the big fashion shows, designer house shows, antiques sales, public sales, and auctions.

Site-Seeing: The Big Apple on the Web

The official site of **NYC & Company** (formerly known as the New York Convention & Visitors Bureau), **www.nyc.com**, is an excellent resource offering tons of information on the city.

New York Today (www.nytoday.com) is the online arts, leisure, and entertainment arm of the venerable *New York Times*. You'll find comprehensive listings, including museum schedules and sports events, plus the newspaper's definitive restaurant reviews.

Citysearch (www.newyork.citysearch.com) is a hipper general-information site, with reviews and listings for restaurants, shops, hotels, attractions, and nightlife.

About.com maintains a useful New York page at **www.go nyc.about.com**, hosted by an insightful and opinionated local expert.

Each of the city's high-profile weekly magazines also maintains a useful site, including *New York* (www.nymag.com), *Time Out New York* (www.timeoutny.com), the *Village Voice* (www.villagevoice.com), and the *New Yorker* (www.new yorker.com).

Want a guide to area sample sales? Try the *S&B Report* (www.lazarshopping.com), described on p. 305, or www. dailycandy.com. There's also a weekly column of sales and bargains in *New York* (www.nymag.com) and *Time Out New York* (www.timeoutny.com).

SECRET SOURCES

I've been using two very interesting websites, which are member-only deals. You have to be invited to join, but they are free to join. In both cases, friends just gave me the links. Urban Daddy (**www.urbandaddy.com**) gives insider dish on a variety of cities; sometimes their NYC stuff is a yawn, but when they told me how to get into the private Tom Ford and Calvin Klein sales by downloading passes from their site, I was hooked. The site **www.gilt.com** is another member-only site and offers auctions and sales on designer goods. My problem is that very often I've never heard of the brand they are touting.

SHOPPING HOURS

As the town that never sleeps, New York prides itself on having some retail services available on a 24-hour basis. Not at Bloomingdale's, mind you, but there are some stores open whenever you may need them.

Regular retail hours are roughly 10am to 5:30 or 6pm, Monday through Saturday. Thursday is the late night, with stores usually open until 9pm. But irregular is often the rule, so you should call ahead to make sure. Here are some guidelines:

- Stores in business areas, such as Wall Street, tend to open rather early in the morning to serve locals on their way to work. Stores often open at 7:30 or 8am on weekdays and are frequently closed on Saturday and Sunday.
- Power chains with enough money and staff often keep their stores open more nights of the week or later every night of the week. **Barneys** is open until 8pm 5 nights a week.
- Midtown stores that sell business apparel usually open at 9am. But stores that open at 9am may close at 5 or 5:30pm.
- Monday and Thursday are traditional late nights for department stores, which stay open until 9pm. But if a store has only 1 late night per week, then it's Thursday night.
- Bookstores seem to have their own rules about hours, especially now that certain ones have become the substitute for the village green. Some are even open until midnight.
- During Christmas season, anything goes.
- In summer, fancy stores—such as Madison Avenue boutiques—close at noon on Saturday or don't even open at all.

- Most stores close earlier on Saturday evening than during the workweek, be it at 5 or 5:30pm, maybe 6pm. Few stay open until 9pm on Saturday. There are exceptions; this is a general rule for traditional retail.

Sunday Shopping

I can't go so far as to say everything is open, but Sunday is a huge day for retail in Manhattan. Certain neighborhoods have a big social-retail-dining scene, like SoHo and the Upper West Side. Locals go out for brunch and then go shopping.

Not only are all major department stores and chains open on Sunday, but the hours they keep also seem to be extending. While regular Sunday hours seem to be from noon to 5pm, the opening times are creeping earlier and earlier. Many stores open at 11am now, and a few even open at 10am.

Religious Hours

Please note that stores owned and operated by observant Jewish people may have special hours; they will close at 2pm on Friday and remain closed throughout Saturday. They then reopen first thing on Sunday morning. This is true of many businesses on the Lower East Side as well as individual stores here and there.

Holiday Hours

If it's a shopping holiday (like Christmas), look for extended hours. If it's summer, look for retracted hours. Do note that more and more stores need cash and will do whatever it takes to keep the electricity on, so store hours are becoming more flexible (and extended).

Funky Hours

Now that so many funky neighborhoods have become "in," a whole new set of operating hours is coming into style. Most stores in downtown areas (SoHo, Nolita) open at 11am and stay open until 8pm, and often much later during the summer. They may open at 10am on Saturday, and again, they may not.

BEHIND CLOSED DOORS: PRIVATE SALES

There is enormous business being done privately in Manhattan. People with taste, a little money, and a few friends are pursuing their personal interests and selling from their collections on a private basis. They usually sell out of their homes, which is why their numbers and addresses are kept quiet.

While there are a few clothing and accessories people who operate this way, the bulk of the business is in antiques and collectibles—especially items picked up at markets around the world and brought in on an individual basis. If you have an area of interest, ask dealers if they can recommend any private resources who might help out. You'll need an appointment and usually the name of your connection before you can get the address.

BAD BUYS OF NEW YORK

There are people who will tell you that anything you buy in New York that costs full retail is a bad buy, but I'm not one of them. I think the things to avoid are the things you can buy at home at much cheaper rates, such as dry-cleaning services, some makeup, vitamins, and pantyhose.

Computers, electronics, and cameras may be available for less in your hometown if you live in a major U.S. city. I've done some rather extensive electronics research and have discovered the basic operating ploy for the Midtown Fifth Avenue and even Sixth Avenue electronics stores that claim to offer such incredible deals: Typically, they base their prices on what those goods sell for in Europe and Japan and in the world's most expensive duty-free stores. That way, the prices seem like bargains to international visitors. These Midtown stores survive because the people who frequent them often live out of town and may never come back to New York again to complain—or because people don't know that they can do much better. Don't get taken.

PERSONAL/SPECIAL SHOPPERS

Large New York stores offer many free services to help busy people with their shopping. Every department store has a service that will pull together everything you want to look at and then have it ready for you to peruse on an appointment basis at your convenience.

A special shopper will work the entire store with you, helping to coordinate your outfits or put together table settings for a dinner party. Or a special shopper will pick clothes *for* you and then invite you into the store to try them on. They can even bring them to your home if you don't like to go to stores or if you have time constraints.

Store translators are generally available if you would prefer to work in a language other than English. Make an appointment and specify what language you will be speaking.

You should not pay extra for the services of a shopper, since they are employees of the department store. Special shoppers will not use outside resources for your buying, and they won't tell you where to get bargains or discounts. They may give you fashion tips and point you toward a good buy, but their job is to sell the store's merchandise. Note that this service is not just for women—many men also use special shoppers.

CHARGE & SEND

If you are on a mad shopping spree, your concierge can call a messenger to pick up your packages at the stores and deliver them to the hotel on the same day (for a fee, of course).

Most department stores have shopping services that will deliver to your hotel for you, with a minimum purchase.

Department stores will also usually mail-order any item you see advertised in the newspaper. Many of the fancy boutiques offer shop-by-phone and online options as well.

Stores will happily send a package to any address for you—but they'll probably bill you a flat fee for the packing, wrapping, and mailing. Insurance probably is not included. Technically, mail costs should be charged by weight and distance—but many stores guess at the weight and charge you a flat fee for the whole works.

Businesses traditionally ship their merchandise via **UPS,** which takes several days depending on your delivery zone, or **FedEx,** which offers next- or second-day delivery. Every now and then, a store will throw in free shipping for you.

Tip: The old send-it-to-avoid-New-York-sales-tax trick doesn't always work anymore. New York now has a rule that requires shoppers to pay sales tax for anything purchased here—whether you ship it or not. However, shipping your merchandise home does mean that at least you won't have to worry about airline overweight fees, or about thieves who may break into luggage that must stay unlocked.

If you want to go with the U.S. Postal Service, it offers **Express Mail,** which promises next- or second-day delivery. There's also **Priority Mail,** which is good for small packages. You can use these services yourself through any post office.

NEW YORK SALES TAX

This one is tricky, as it has changed several times in the past few years. Forget everything you knew or thought; here's the skinny.

Most items are taxed at a relatively high 8.375%. Ever since 2005, however, the city sales tax of 4% is waived on clothing or footwear purchases under $110, meaning you pay only the state's 4.375% sales tax.

New York has two tax-free weeks a year—usually one in January and one in June—when the sales tax is waived.

Note that some people shop in New Jersey or Pennsylvania specifically to avoid New York sales taxes, as taxes there can be lower or nonexistent. Sometimes you can also avoid sales tax through postal tricks (see above), but New York has recently cracked down on shipping purchases out of state in order to get a tax break—you're supposed to pay the tax at the point of purchase.

There are no refunds on tax (VAT) for international visitors.

Chapter Three

....

SHOPPING TIPS FOR INTERNATIONAL VISITORS

THROUGH MY EYES

....

There are wonderful things to buy in Europe and Asia, and I do indeed write an entire series of books about those items; but no one makes or merchandises low-cost merchandise like the United States. The cost of living—and living well—in Europe has gone through the roof. Even with the euro as strong as it is right now, shopping with dollars becomes a real treat.

In fact, international visitors may want to consider all of New York on sale. For shoppers from Europe and Asia, it's like we're having an across-the-board, one-third-off sale—the dollar has fallen that far in the past 5 years.

There may be financial problems all over the world, but there's always a bargain in New York. Step this way—*venez par ici.*

American Retail

American retailers sell at every point along the price spectrum in order to get their products to people of all socioeconomic backgrounds. Sometimes the exact same merchandise is sold in different packaging or with different labels at different prices. The U.S. retail scene also offers a wide number of sales, promotional events, and outlet stores (see chapter 11).

Come Sale with Me

National governments usually control European sales, and although European sales are very nice, they do not compare with American ones, where the intent is to clear out all the merchandise before the store has to give it away. Visitors from abroad will be amazed by the promotional events that bring superlow prices in the U.S. You should seriously consider flying to New York for the summer or after-Christmas sales.

Welcome to Deal City

Yes *(sí, oui, ja, da)*, if you are visiting from another country, there are plenty of tips throughout this guide; believe me, this isn't the only chapter to read. Of course, I want you to read the whole book, but be sure to see the chapter on bargains (chapter 11) and the information on factory outlets (such as **Woodbury Common;** p. 298) to learn some tricks of the retail trade so that you go home with a smile on your face and an extra piece of luggage!

The airlines' rules are changing regarding checking excess baggage from the U.S. to your home destination. In some cases, you'll be charged by the unit, sometimes by the size and/or the weight. In all cases, the fees are skyrocketing, so check with your airlines before showing up at the airport with several big bags to check. If your purchases go big time, consider having them sent from the store or by shipping service before you get on the plane.

So if the shopping is going well, it may be worth expanding your horizons. The bad news: You may have to pay duty on your purchases when you return to the E.U.

Cash on Demand

If you don't have any U.S. dollars in your wallet, don't fret. They are expensive if you buy them at a *cambio* in Europe or

Canada, so wait until you get to the airport at your U.S. port of entry and use your bank card there. ATMs are located just outside the Customs areas at JFK and Newark. Then go to a shop and buy a newspaper or a candy bar and get change in $1 bills. *Remember:* The $1 bill is your key to tipping in the U.S.

When you use a foreign ATM, expect a charge from your European-based bank as well as a $1.50 charge on the U.S. end.

If you plan to ride the bus or the subway, you will need a MetroCard, which can be purchased from a kiosk in any subway station. Both cash and credit cards are accepted.

ARRIVING IN NEW YORK

Most international travelers come to the Big Apple via **John F. Kennedy International Airport (JFK)**, in Queens; or **Newark Liberty International Airport (EWR)**, in New Jersey. **LaGuardia Airport (LGA)** frequently gets arrivals from Canada.

Of these three airports, JFK has the most international traffic and therefore is the most congested and most likely to be confusing; Newark is a lot newer and, I think, easier to use. JFK has also become infamous for its scams on travelers who do not know enough about New York to know they are being cheated. While police have cracked down on these scams in order to protect international visitors, you sometimes don't know you're in trouble until it's too late. Therefore, a few tips:

Luggage Carts

In international terminals, they're free. Otherwise, pay for them with a credit card.

Skycaps

If you page a skycap to help you with your luggage, there is no predetermined fee, as there is in many European airports or train stations. You tip at your own discretion. The norm is $1 per bag.

Getting a Taxi at the Airport

Ignore all drivers who approach you and offer you a ride; this includes well-dressed limo drivers or people with "honest" faces. Use only a yellow licensed cab. When you get into your taxi, take out a pen and paper and copy down your taxi driver's name and shield number, and the name of the cab company. Make sure he or she sees you doing this little ritual. The New York City Taxi and Limousine Commission states that a driver's license will be revoked if he or she is caught overcharging a passenger by more than $10.

There is a fixed price for taxis to the city from JFK: $45. This fee does not include the tip or bridge and tunnel tolls. The fare to and from Newark is the metered rate, plus $15 surcharge. The fare to LaGuardia from the city goes by the meter.

Other Ground Transportation

There is public transportation from each airport into Manhattan and to the suburbs. Go to the Ground Transportation desk, located across from the baggage carousels or in the lobby outside of U.S. Customs, after arrival. You have your choice of bus, subway, or private transport to take you into the city and suburbs of the Tri-State area (New York, New Jersey, and Connecticut).

SIZING UP AMERICAN SIZES

For a conversion chart of U.S., Continental, and British clothing and shoe sizes, see the inside back cover of this book.

Also note that towels and bed linens in the U.S. rarely match their Continental or British counterparts, but may work with some successful juggling or recalculating.

It helps to bring a tape measure with you that has metric

measurements on one side and the U.S. measuring system on the other. My friend Ruth, who lives in London, says an American queen-size sheet fits two British twin beds pushed together.

Meanwhile, when it comes to clothing styles, you should know that a European cut is different from an American one; that Far Eastern sizes are often scaled to the petite; and that size charts are a beginning, but nothing to bet on—always try clothes on and go by fit, not by label.

There are various names for sizes and types of cuts in the U.S. For example, size charts usually refer to women's sizes in even numbers—sizes 4, 6, 8, 10, and so on. They don't tell you that in America we also have junior sizes, which are sizes 3, 5, 7, 9, 11, and so on. Misses sizes are usually a tad shorter, rounder, and roomier in the bust, and should not be confused with petite sizes, which usually have a P next to the size number and are proportionately smaller all over.

Large sizes for women come with a variety of names, from "queen size" to "women's size" to "plus size" to simply 1X, 2X, 3X. In addition to sizes that are written as S (small), M (medium), and L (large), there are usually also XL for extra-large and sometimes XXL for extra-extra-large. See p. 225 for special-size resources.

Men's sizes are found up to about size 44, or maybe 46, in regular stores; after that you need a store for "big and tall" men (p. 224).

FRAGRANCE DIFFERENCES

Fragrances in the United States, even when labeled MADE IN FRANCE, are made with denatured alcohol rather than potato alcohol, which is the base for European perfumes. This type of alcohol may wear differently on your skin, even if the scent in the bottle smells the same. Huh?

It all has to do with the U.S. Food and Drug Administration (FDA) and what it will allow onto American shores. For this same reason, many shades of cosmetics are different in the United States than in other parts of the world. They may or may not bear the same color name, number, or designation.

ELECTRONIC DIFFERENCES

Despite the number of stores that sell low-cost DVDs and videos—to say nothing of street vendors who offer up illegal copies of the same—there are several things to watch out for: the difference in voltage and in current, as well as in DVD zones and even TV types. Most newer-model European TVs play NICAM and NTSC. Do not buy videos unless you know for sure that your TV plays NTSC or you are willing to invest in a new set. See "Gadget Lowdown" (p. 54) for more information.

CLOTHING COLOR DIFFERENCES

Global marketing has brought brand names from their countries of origin to stores all over the world, and colorations are geared for specific markets—European colors for Gap are often darker than U.S. colors. Don't be surprised if you find styles or color groups in the States that are not available in Europe.

Colors in fashion will usually match if they're from same-season collections, but colors may not match if the goods were made, or dyed, in different parts of the world.

As I mentioned before, shades of makeup can have the same code numbers throughout the world yet still be different colors in different parts of the world. In fact, many cosmetics colors don't match up at all!

If you're not flexible, don't buy in the U.S.

PRICES IN NEW YORK

Most international visitors to New York are so dazzled by the price tags at regular retail that they fail to understand the concept of bargain shopping—to realize that there are places where you can get the same, or similar, merchandise for less money.

The first step toward getting a bargain is to create a list of target acquisitions and their prices and availability at home. List the regular retail prices and then check out convenient bargain resources, alternative retail (such as resale shops), and factory outlets.

Value-Added Tax (VAT) & Sales Tax

European shoppers may at first be shocked that the ticketed price on an item in the United States is not the final price, so an advance warning: Once you go to the cash register, *taxes are added on.*

Unfortunately, the U.S. does not presently have a value-added tax (VAT) or an export-tax program. We may get one, but we haven't got it now. International visitors are required to pay the state sales tax and cannot get a refund on this money when they leave the country. Sorry, I know that doesn't sound very fair, but that's the way it works.

Sales tax varies from state to state. Some states have no tax on clothes, no tax on clothing items up to a certain amount, or no tax at all. New York happens to have one of the highest sales taxes anywhere in the United States, currently at 8.375%. However, the city sales tax of 4% is waived on clothing or footwear purchases under $110, meaning you pay only the state's 4.375% sales tax on those items.

MONEY CHANGING

The single best way to exchange money is simply to withdraw it from a wall—ATMs are conveniently located throughout the city. It's a good idea to call your bank before you leave home and advise them of your travels; foreign transactions sometimes trigger a false theft warning.

Another good bet is to buy traveler's checks in U.S. dollars before you leave home. Although there is usually a fee for doing this, it allows you to freeze your rate of exchange at the time of purchase.

Some stores and businesses will accept Canadian currency at an automatic (and possibly unfair) discount rate; few stores will accept other foreign currency.

While you can change funds at airports and most banks, several services in Midtown specialize in money exchange and international traveler's checks. Most are open 7 days a week. These include **American Express,** with multiple locations, including 822 Lexington Ave. (at 63rd St.) and **Chequepoint,** at 22 Central Park S. (between Fifth and Sixth aves.).

If you travel to the United States frequently and stockpile cash, you may want to keep track of what you paid for your money. With currency fluctuations, you may find it smarter to sit on your cash and convert new funds, or to rely mostly on credit cards for a better rate of exchange.

INTERNATIONAL MAILING & SHIPPING

If you've bought more than you can carry home, you may want to send some packages overseas. The small-package airmail rate is the least expensive and has minimal paperwork. Once you get into big or heavy packages, however, it does get more expensive, especially if you send by airmail. Even surface mail (which is by sea) gets pricey if the item is large or heavy.

For surface mail to Europe or Asia, figure 6 to 8 weeks before your package will arrive; for airmail, about 1 week. Various courier services carry overnight mail around the world, although with time changes and the international date line, the service is rarely overnight. It will take 2 to 4 days, depending on the destination. (Too bad you can't fax yourself a sweater!) The

U.S. Postal Service does have 3-day international airmail that is similar to courier service but is less expensive.

The biggest problems with shipping are not American prices or laws, but laws on the receiving end—many people cannot afford the duty on the gifts that you send them. You could always ship your old, dirty, travel-worn belongings home and pack your new purchases in your luggage.

Note: With the airlines' newly imposed excess baggage fees, it may be less expensive to ship a package home.

POSTCARDS

Postcards are sold just about everywhere; the best prices are on those sold in minibulk from touristy electronics shops in Midtown. Your hotel should have free postcards, featuring the hotel, of course. Postage for an international postcard or letter up to ½ oz. is 90¢.

E-MAIL

Most hotels have dataports in each room, or they have separate business centers where you can send and retrieve e-mail. You may need to bring your own cables or rent them from your hotel, so call in advance to find out what the options are.

Internet cafes are dotted around the city. Try **CyberCafe Times Square** at 250 W. 49th St., open Monday to Friday 8am to 11pm, Saturday to Sunday 11am to 11pm.

You can also access free Internet at New York's public libraries. The mid-Manhattan location is at 455 Fifth Ave. (at 40th St.), with other locations at 20 W. 53rd St. and 40 Lincoln Center Plaza.

SALE SEASONS

Sales are held much more frequently in the United States than in Europe. Because Americans think that a good sale is part of the American way, retailers look for any occasion to host a blowout or a promotion that will make shoppers think they are saving money. The events can be seasonal, pegged to holidays, or once-a-year events.

Yes, there are big January and July sales in New York as in every other city in the world, but there are also sales you may have never heard of, such as these:

Thanksgiving: The Christmas season officially begins with this American holiday, which is celebrated on the fourth Thursday in November. The following day, Friday, is usually the single biggest day in retail for the year. Sometimes stores begin their pre-Christmas sales on this date.

Pre-Christmas: Recently created to goose Christmas shoppers with the warning that the store has less merchandise than usual, these sales prod you to buy before it sells out.

Post-Christmas: Various stores have their own patterns for post-holiday sales—some stores begin their sales at 8:30am the day after Christmas, while some stores wait until after January 1. It's rare for a store to wait until Epiphany, because it's rare to find an American who knows when (or what) Epiphany is.

Whites: Usually in January, this is a sale of bed linens, rarely white these days since colors and patterns replaced traditional whites in the 1960s.

January Clearance: While most department stores have their end-of-season sales right after Christmas or New Year's, most of the European boutiques in New York have their clearance sales toward the end of January, starting around the 20th. These events, even at stores as exclusive as Hermès, are often advertised in the *New York Times*.

Valentine's Day: February 14 is Valentine's Day, a big day for lovers to express their feelings with traditional gifts such as flowers, chocolates, or fancy undies. These types of items, along with fragrances, jewelry, and anything with a heart-shaped motif, are heavily promoted.

Presidents' Day: Promotional sales are usually on for this entire holiday weekend in late February. This is a good time to pick up winter clothes, furs, and ski equipment.

Memorial Day: Stores hold promotional events for summer merchandise during the long weekend at the end of May.

Fourth of July: Bathing suits and some summer apparel go on sale before the Fourth of July weekend. Fourth of July weekend sees blowout sales events, summer clearance sales, various specials offered for a day or two, and special-event sales. Outlet stores in the New York area often do big sales at this time.

Midsummer Clearance: From late July throughout August, there are major summer sales on European brands. Sales on American brands usually begin right before Fourth of July weekend.

Back-to-School: During the last 2 weeks in August, there are promotional sales for school supplies, furnishings, and clothing.

Columbus Day: Coats and early fall clothing are sold at these sales in early October.

Election Day: These sales in November are a good time to buy coats and fall merchandise that you can still wear this season.

HOTEL PROMOTIONS

American hotels are far bigger on promotional deals than European hotels, so there may be freebies and extras that you are not used to asking for or getting. Most frequently, these promotions are for weekends, but there are hotels that offer upgrades at check-in, discounted parking, breakfast, or even a free T-shirt. It never hurts to ask.

PRIX-FIXE MEALS & RESTAURANT PROMOTIONS

Almost every famous restaurant in New York has a fixed-price lunch or dinner. The fixed price usually does not include wine and rarely includes tip. Pre-theater fixed-price meals offer perhaps the best deals you can find. However, you must eat dinner before 7pm, which many visitors consider uncivilized. Even the most famous restaurants in Manhattan offer these promotions, including the Four Seasons, where you'll be offered a three-course dinner including coffee for $75.

During New York's Restaurant Week, held twice a year, in late June/early July and late January/early February (see www.nycvisit.com for details), all kinds of swanky restaurants offer three-course meals at a special price—in 2008, it was $24 for lunch and $35 for dinner.

TIPPING

When in doubt, give a dollar. The basic tip in America for **small services** (luggage porters and so on) is the $1 bill.

It is rare for an American restaurant to automatically add in a service charge or tip unless you are part of a party of eight or more diners. At **restaurants,** tip between 15% and 20% of the total bill *before* the tax was added. In **taxis,** give the driver a percentage of the total meter cost, usually 15%. At **beauty salons** and **spas,** tip 15% to 20%.

Please pay attention to the fine print regarding tipping, especially in hotels. It is very common for a hotel to add the tip for room service and to then leave a second blank space labeled "gratuity" so that those people who are not paying attention will add in another 10% to 15%. Be careful!

BOOZE NEWS

This is a tricky category, so you may want to stay sober enough to take notes. Liquor in Manhattan, especially when sold from fancy liquor stores near the city's finest hotels, is outrageously expensive. Outrageously. I mean, liquor can cost 50% more than it should. Compared to these inflated prices, duty-free liquor is a bargain. But wait! If you can get to a part of America or even Manhattan where real people live (instead of superstars), liquor prices in regular stores are lower than in the duty-free shops.

GADGET LOWDOWN

Many a European visitor has come to the United States and planned his or her free time around electronics shopping, since electronics and small business machines cost about 30% less in the U.S. than in Europe.

Since there are many pitfalls awaiting you, I have lots of guidance. Electronics are not as easy to buy as you think they are. Proceed with care. I personally went through hell in order to fulfill an order for a personal computer for my friend Richard. It took approximately 20 hours of my time to research the buy, several transatlantic phone calls back and forth to make sure Richard understood the findings, and then a week of bated breath while we waited for a computer guru in Nice to figure out if the parts would work. Throughout the research and the agony, I kept screaming at Richard: "No amount of savings is worth going through this!" Think about it.

AMERICAN BRANDS

As a general rule, international brands cost less in the country of origin than they do when exported. Therefore, a trip to the U.S. is the time to stock up on brands like Levi's, Gap, Coach, OshKosh, Estée Lauder, Donna Karan, Calvin Klein, and so on.

European shoppers should consider buying European brands only if the items are on sale or are being sold at a factory outlet or discount source.

DUTY CALLS

All airlines have duty-free shopping onboard, and frequently publish a beautiful color brochure in the seatback in front of you with the other magazines. In many cases, the airline duty-free price is lower than the airport duty-free price. The best way to be sure is to look at the brochure (take it along with you) and price what you want on outbound travel. When you leave the United States, price the item in the airport duty-free shop. Then look it up in your brochure to decide whether you want to buy on the plane.

Speaking of airport duty-free stores, various terminals at JFK have different shops—some are downright sorry-looking while others are more gorgeous than in any U.S. mall. Many of them publish a price guide. If you have a lot of time before a flight, you might want to wander.

Note: "Duty-free" stores in Manhattan offer no serious bargains. You'll do better at discount sources.

Chapter Four

....

EATING & SLEEPING IN NEW YORK

MORE TO EAT THAN APPLES

....

I've based the restaurant selections in this chapter on my personal needs as a shopper and visitor, with the assumption that good meals and never-to-be-forgotten dining experiences are among the things you are shopping for while you're in New York. The restaurant information below will also help you get a great meal at a great price.

Chapters 5, 6, and 7 contain additional dining suggestions, which are related to specific New York neighborhoods.

Hotel Dining Deals

One of the most important lessons I've learned as a traveler is that hotels are always looking for lunch business in their dining rooms, even when their dining rooms are famous. As a result, you can often get some of the best lunch deals around at the top hotels in town. Several of the city's snazziest places, including the **Plaza Athenee,** have fixed-price luncheon menus that allow you to enjoy three courses for a flat price that varies from about $30 to $40 per person. At many other places in town, you'd have to pay that same amount and get less food, less service, less atmosphere, and less quality.

Pre-Theater Deals

Broadway curtains usually rise at 7:30 or 8pm, and most restaurants in Midtown offer pre-theater dinner specials that allow you to get a fabulous meal at a fabulous price—if you eat early enough. You don't have to show your theater tickets at the door to prove that you're going to the theater; you just have to come to terms with eating dinner at 6pm. A three-course pre-theater meal at a good restaurant usually comes in at around $32 to $35 per person, which is considerably less than it would cost if eaten a la carte after 8pm.

Big-Time Chefs

I recently ate at Café Boulud, one of Daniel Boulud's restaurants, and noted a three-course lunch menu for $24, a special due to New York's **Restaurant Week,** held twice each year (see www.nycvisit.com for details). Granted, after iced tea, wine, and tip, the total comes to more than $24 per person, but this is still an extraordinary value.

There are all sorts of dining deals like this; some are offered in slow seasons, others are offered year-round, and still others are available only during promotional periods. Ask around and check the website above to find out what dining deals are on during your stay in New York.

Also, following a trend that started in Europe, many big-name, big-time, big-price chefs have opened smaller cafes or bistros that offer great food at affordable prices—a real New York experience.

The listings below are arranged by chef.

DANIEL BOULUD

A French chef more famous in the U.S. than in France, Boulud has some of the best tables in the city. Check it all out at www.danielnyc.com.

CAFÉ BOULUD
20 E. 76th St., between Fifth and Madison aves. (Subway: 6 to 77th St.).

This is not the most low-key of Boulud's eateries, but it's still less expensive than the star chef's fanciest restaurant. Café Boulud is located in a fabulous shopping neighborhood. Reservations are taken (and recommended) up to 1 month in advance. ✆ 212/772-2600.

DB BISTRO MODERNE
55 W. 44th St., between Fifth and Sixth aves. (Subway: B, D, F, or V to 42nd St./Bryant Park).

A casual spot near the Theater District, DB Bistro is the home of the famous DB burger—stuffed with foie gras or truffles and sold for the whopping price of about $35. To be honest, my burger sort of crumbled in my hands and was more of a concept than a heavenly meal. Takeout lunches are available. Book up to 1 month in advance by phone or on www.opentable. com. ✆ 212/391-2400.

ALAIN DUCASSE

M. Ducasse is back in New York with a dinner-only restaurant. Now here's the shopper's tip: Despite the fact that the most-starred chef in the world has expensive restaurants dotted around the world, there is a $110 set-price five-course degustation menu or you can eat at the small bar and nibble on small plates, at $12. Of course, the restaurant is known for its wine cellar and that's where it can get expensive.

ADOUR
St. Regis Hotel, 2 East 55th St., at Fifth Ave. (Subway: E or V to Fifth Ave./53rd St.).

✆ 212/710-2277. www.adour-stregis.com.

THOMAS KELLER

Keller came to fame with the French Laundry, in Napa Valley, and is often considered the reigning American chef in the galaxy of big names that dot the U.S.

PER SE
Time Warner Center, 10 Columbus Circle (Subway: A, B, C, D, or 1 to 59th St./Columbus Circle).

Per Se is per expensive and not as elaborate as the French Laundry. It offers a five-course lunch on Fridays, Saturdays, and Sundays for $175. Book by phone or on www.opentable.com 2 months in advance. © 212/823-9335. www.perseny.com.

GRAY KUNZ

The chef from the very tony Lespinasse (which has been recreated as Ducasse's new restaurant) has now opened a restaurant in the Time Warner Center.

CAFE GRAY
Time Warner Center, 10 Columbus Circle (Subway: A, B, C, D, or 1 to 59th St./Columbus Circle).

The lighting is terrifyingly bright, the decor is overbearing, the service is not great, but the food is terrific. Prices aren't bad considering the location and the pedigree of the chef; dinner for two with a glass of wine for each, plus tip, ran $225. Open for dinner daily, lunch Monday through Saturday. © 212/823-6338. www.cafegray.com.

JEAN-GEORGES VONGERICHTEN

This is the French chef with the Alsatian name so difficult for Americans to pronounce that he is most often called Jean-Georges, which is also the name of his fanciest restaurant. Go to www.jean-georges.com for all the details. All tables can be reserved by phone or on www.opentable.com.

JEAN-GEORGES
1 Central Park West, between 60th and 61st sts. (Subway: A, B, C, D, or 1 to 59th St./Columbus Circle).

This could be the best lunch in town. Choose two plates from the extensive seasonal menu for $28, and add dessert (yes, you really must) for only $8 more. We shared four choices four ways and all were winners. © 212/299-3900.

NOUGATINE
Same address as Jean-Georges.

The cafe portion of Jean-Georges's most famous eatery serves breakfast, lunch, and dinner, and is not as expensive as the main dining room. © 212/299-3900.

PERRY STREET
176 Perry St., near West St. (Subway: 1 to Christopher St.).

If you're a Jean-Georges groupie like I am, then you're ready to move on to his latest, which is near the Meatpacking District but not in the midst of the shopping world. You have to go out of your way not only to get here, but also to grab a table, as the place is small. If you're looking for a better location while out on a spree—and if you can stand the crush and the hipsters—then Spice Market is still the best bet. © 212/352-1900.

SPICE MARKET
403 W. 13th St., at Ninth Ave. (Subway: A, C, E, or L to 14th St./Eighth Ave.).

This restaurant, which Vongerichten created with chef Gray Kunz (see above), is similar to Market, Vongerichten's restaurant in Paris. The food is great—an even broader version of the cuisine at Vong. The crowd is trendy beyond belief. © 212/675-2322.

VONG

200 E. 54th St., between Third and Second aves. (Subway: 6 to 51st St.; or E or V to Lexington Ave./53rd St.).

This is one of Jean-Georges's first restaurants, serving French-influenced Thai cuisine. It's a great choice for a somewhat spicy meal in an exotic atmosphere. Come here for the food rather than the people-watching. ✆ **212/486-9592.**

In-Store Dining

All of the major department stores have a place for you to eat, and some of them actually have several places to eat, offering a variety of dining experiences. Such is modern retail.

Cafes have become really important to smaller shops; you'll find one or two in the basement or on the mezzanine of just about every name brand in New York, from **DKNY** to the **NBA Store.** Most of these cafes have a gimmick: There are bagels and health-food snacks at DKNY on Madison Avenue, and so on. **ABC Carpet & Home** has four restaurant choices, including a branch of **Le Pain Quotidien** (say "Kwoh-tee-*dyen*"), a Belgian chain known for the quality of its bread. Some stores have gone the extra step and offer fine dining: **Nicole Farhi**'s downtown outpost, **202,** doubles as an eatery as well.

BARNEYS NEW YORK

660 Madison Ave., at 61st St. (Subway: 4, 5, 6, N, R, or W to 59th St./Lexington Ave.).

Fred's, the stylish cafe in the uptown Barneys store, has a sort of moderne Milan feel. This is very much the place to be seen having a nosh. In fact, I'm not a big fan because it's simply too too, my dear. But you should do it at least once in your life. Without the kids, please. ✆ **212/833-2200.** www.barneys.com.

BERGDORF GOODMAN

754 Fifth Ave., between 57th and 58th sts. (Subway: F to 57th St.).

The Café on 5 is on, duh, the fifth floor; there's also a cafe in the basement in the new beauty portion of the store. I sometimes go across the street to Bergdorf Men to eat at Café 745, a tiny cafe with great salads and no tourists. ✆ **212/753-7300.** www.bergdorfgoodman.com.

BLOOMINGDALE'S
1000 Third Ave., at 59th St. (Subway: 4, 5, 6, N, R, or W to 59th St./Lexington Ave.).

Several choices for several different eating styles: Le Train Bleu (a sit-down restaurant that resembles the inside of the famous French train from the Belle Epoque), 40 Carrots (health food), and B Café (light lunches and great ice cream). ✆ **212/ 705-2000.** www.bloomingdales.com.

MACY'S
151 W. 34th St., at Broadway (Subway: B, D, F, N, Q, R, V, or W to 34th St./Herald Sq.).

There are dining choices on every floor, offering a variety of ethnic eats, old faves, and even a Starbucks. The Cellar in the basement is like the Harrods food halls in London, while the Cucina marketplace is a relatively classy and healthy fast-food option. ✆ **212/695-4400.** www.macys.com.

SAKS FIFTH AVENUE
611 Fifth Ave., at 50th St. (Subway: E or V to Fifth Ave./53rd St.).

Cafe SFA is one of my favorite places for lunch in New York. It's elegant without being stuffy, serves great raisin-and-walnut bread, offers a good choice of light fare for those who want only a salad or such, and boasts moderate prices. ✆ **212/753-4000.** www.saksfifthavenue.com.

Snack & Shop

When I am having an intense shopping day, I do not want a 2-hour lunch, nor do I want to spend what is the equivalent of a pair of shoes for my lunch. I want quick, I want cheap, I want convenient, and I want good (though charming and chic are nice bonuses).

BURGER HEAVEN
9 E. 53rd St., near Fifth Ave. (Subway: E or V to Fifth Ave./53rd St.); multiple other locations.

There's an entire menu with a variety of choices, but I dream of the Roquefort burger. There are a handful of locations; my regular is right off Fifth Avenue on East 53rd Street, a great shopping location. © 212/752-0340. www.burgerheaven.com.

OLLIE'S NOODLE SHOP
200 W. 44th St., near Seventh Ave. (Subway: 1, 2, 3, 7, N, Q, R, or W to Times Sq./42nd St.); 1991 Broadway, between 67th and 68th sts. (Subway: 1 to 66th St./Lincoln Center); 2315 Broadway, at 84th St. (Subway: 1 to 86th St.).

This is a low-priced noodle shop that actually has a full Chinese menu as well as dim sum and then some. I like the one on Broadway and 84th Street for a break while shopping in that area, but the business has grown and opened up all over town, even in the Theater District, where Ollie's makes an attractive pre- or post-theater possibility. © 212/921-5988 for West 44th Street location.

Teatime

Although tea is a British tradition, it's especially welcome in New York, where you can easily get exhausted by a hard day on your feet. Tea is also a great option when you are going out to the theater and not having dinner until 11pm—it will curb your appetite before the play without making you full. There are only a few specialty teahouses in New York, but all of the major hotels, including **The Peninsula** (700 Fifth Ave., at 55th St.; © 212/956-2888), do a big business in tea.

The **Carlyle Hotel** (35 E. 76th St., between Madison and Fifth aves; © 212/744-1600) hosts the *Madeline Tea Party* every weekday afternoon in the Hotel's Bemelmans Bar, named after the Madeline books' late author, Ludwig Bemelmans. The high tea service includes sandwiches, scones, cookies, and tea for $40 per person. (Suri Cruise loves it.)

As we go to press, the refurbished Palm Court in **The Plaza Hotel** (Fifth Ave., at Central Park South; © 212/759-3000) has just reopened with Didier Virot as its chef. The new menu will blend classical and moderne French. Since rooms begin at $1,000 a night, you might think tea is all you can afford, and they do a humdinger here with caviar and lobster for $100 per person. If you really just want old-fashioned teatime, that can be arranged at $60 per person. Note there is a dress code, even for tea.

SoHo So Great

You'll have no problem getting something to eat in SoHo: There are grocers, kiosks, fast-food joints, takeout places, and cutting-edge chic restaurants.

BALTHAZAR
80 Spring St., between Broadway and Crosby St. (Subway: R or W to Prince St., or 6 to Spring St.).

Right near the most commercial area of SoHo shopping, Balthazar is a Paris-style bistro with a great crowd and affordable prices. Naturally, you can get a good steak and fries here. It also has a takeout department and a bread shop. Reservations can be hard to get, although lunch is much easier to do than dinner. You can also go for morning café au lait. © 212/965-1785. www.balthazarny.com.

BAROLO
398 West Broadway, between Spring and Broome sts.
(Subway: C or E to Spring St.).

Before Balthazar, this was my regular place. Barolo is great for pasta, and there's a garden for alfresco dining. I do it for a late lunch—I get to beat the crowds and can usually escape calling ahead if I come at 1:30pm or later. ✆ **212/226-1102.**
www.nybarolo.com.

BISTRO LES AMIS
180 Spring St., at the corner of Thompson. (Subway: C or E to Spring St.).

We had a great lunch at this tiny gem in SoHo. Menu selections include salads, pastas, and a perfect croque-monsieur. ✆ **212/226-8645.** www.bistrolesamis.com.

SLEEPING IN NEW YORK

There seems to be two completely different schools of thought when it comes to booking hotels. Some people say, "Hey, I'm only sleeping there," and want the least expensive room they can get in a safe neighborhood. Not me. I usually want my hotel to be part of my whole travel experience. I travel to make my life something it isn't when I'm at home, so I want service and location and pretty flowers and sheets made of very crisp, real linen.

Since the kinds of hotels I like are generally very expensive, I am constantly looking for deals—or at least little extras that make luxury a smart choice. I've devoted less space to the totally glam hotels and more to the specialty hotels below, as I have been very freaked out by the high cost of accommodations.

While it's easy to spend upwards of $600 to $800 for a luxury hotel room, it's also easy to book a perfectly respectable room in a three-star hotel for under $300. Various websites including www.hotels.com, www.expedia.com, and www.travelocity.com offer promotional hotel rates in locations convenient for shoppers throughout New York. You can also score a good deal on www.priceline.com, but you won't know where you're staying until the reservation is confirmed. What you will know is that you've found a four-star hotel at a two- to three-star price.

Know that the price of the same room can vary depending on the site. After you obtain a few quotes from online services, call the hotel directly and see what it can offer. Admit to being confused, and then ask for the best deal, with extra amenities thrown in, please (upgrades, breakfasts, and so on).

If you don't want to stay in a hotel, or crave the comforts of more space and your own kitchen, consider renting an apartment. **Craig's List** (www.newyork.craigslist.org) is a good resource for local short-term rentals, and Suzy and I loved our apartment in Chelsea, rented through **Herrick Suites** (p. 73).

Parking Concepts

If you have a car with you, pick your hotel with parking needs in mind. I don't want to sound discouraging, but some hotels charge up to $50 a day for parking! This is unusually high, but the norm is about $25 per day.

New York Hotel Deals

You may want to keep in mind a few standing promotions for which you might qualify:

AAA & AARP RATES   Members of the American Automobile Association and AARP will often find member discounted rates online, usually on the hotel website. If you're reserving by phone, ask if you're entitled to one of these deals.

CONVENTION RATES   Professionals visiting New York for a convention should be aware of special rates offered by certain hotels that cater to conventions or to visitors coming for market weeks. Even Garment District buyers coming to work the market qualify.

CORPORATE RATES   Most hotels offer corporate discounts, often a 20% discount off rack rates. Since the rack rate can be outrageously high, though, this still may not be the best rate the hotel has available; ask and compare. At some chains, you can fill out a form to become a corporate member. Leading Hotels of the World (www.lhw.com) has such a policy and offers a fine corporate price break for all of its properties.

NEW HOTEL RATES   When a new luxury hotel opens, there are often get-acquainted deals.

THEATER PACKAGES   Many hotels, especially the ones in the Theater District, offer packages that include theater tickets. This can mean either that the hotel's concierge will get theater tickets for you, which you will then pay for, or that the price of the tickets is included in the package. Make sure this is all clear when you book.

WEEKEND RATES   Because there are so many business travelers visiting the Big Apple during the week, hotel prices are steep—and climbing every year. However, when those guys go home, weekend rates make a city stay attractively affordable. The rates vary with the time of year and with availability, but so do the choices.

Weekend visitors should check the Sunday Travel section of the *New York Times* for various weekend rates and promotions—note that some are per room and some are per person. Ask which days are considered weekend days, since some hotels include Sunday as part of the weekend while others do not. Usually a weekend is only Friday and Saturday nights.

Seasonal Discounts

Room rates can vary dramatically—by hundreds of dollars in some cases—depending on the time of year. Winter, January through March, is best for bargains, with summer (especially July–Aug) second best. Fall is the busiest and most expensive

Hotel Tax Alert

While New York's occupancy tax has been lowered, it's still high—13.5%—and can add a shocking amount to your total bill. If price is a consideration, you might want to ask a few questions before you book, such as what the total rate will be including city tax, hotel tax, and any other extras that might not be included. Don't be shocked when you check out; be prepared before you check in.

season after Christmas, but November tends to be quiet and rather affordable, as long as you're not booking a parade-route hotel on Thanksgiving weekend. All bets are off at Christmastime—expect to pay top dollar for everything.

Luxury Shopping Hotels

Luxury hotels are New York's middle name; if you're coming to New York to be part of the scene, then you'll want to stay in one, if only for a night or two. Between the **St. Regis** (2 E. 55th St., near Fifth Ave.; © 212/753-4500), the **Peninsula New York** (700 Fifth Ave., at 55th St.; © 212/956-2888), the **Sherry-Netherland** (781 Fifth Ave., near 59th St.; © 212/355-2800), and the hotels listed below, you can have all the luxury you crave and still be a few feet from a fine shopping district. The **Mandarin Oriental** (80 Columbus Circle, at 60th St.; © 212/805-8800) has teamed up with Bergdorf Goodman to offer a Super Chic Shopping Package. Many luxury hotels are members of Leading Hotels of the World and can be booked by calling © 800/223-6800. The **Four Seasons** is so stunning you will be absorbed into Manhattan culture for a mere $800 a night. Thankfully, you're down the street from the off-pricer **Daffy's**. Four Seasons has tea and lobby bar service (good for gawking at other guests) as well as a famous kitchen. Rooms are huge and bathrooms are plush—in the style of this brand. For this edition we tested only one new hotel; see below.

THE PLAZA ATHENEE HOTEL

37 E. 64th St., between Madison and Park aves. (Subway: 4, 5, 6, N, R, or W to 59th St./Lexington Ave.).

This European-style boutique hotel is perfect for shoppers; in fact, it's just about perfect for anyone. There is little similarity to the Paris branch of the hotel but much to swoon for. The rooms are large and luxurious with marble bathrooms, separate foyers, and dressing areas; some are outfitted with minikitchens, as well. The location is shopping heaven. The chef is well-known.

The Plaza Athenee is one of the few five-stars that has good Web promotions. Look for shopping deals with Saks and Bloomingdale's and 3 nights for the price of 2 during the winter months. © **212/734-9100.** www.plaza-athenee.com.

Four-Star Shopping Hotels

I've never found a four-star hotel in New York that compares with the city's luxury five-star hotels. And I'm not just talking about fancy rooms or better bars of soap: A five-star luxury hotel functions in a seamless manner that a four-star hotel simply can't quite get down pat. It may not seriously offend you and the price difference may be worth the inconvenience, but never make the mistake of considering a four-star property a close cousin to a five-star property. Four-star properties are for those who don't mind the difference and like saving the cash.

THE ALEX

205 E. 45th St. (Subway: 4, 5, 6, 7, or S to Grand Central/ 42nd St.).

Since I am a regular to **Leading Hotels of the World,** I rushed to test this new hotel and, my heavens, what a surprise. First of all, this is a totally new location to me and one that is very convenient to shopping right out the door and nearby shopping in Midtown.

The hotel is in the moderne style, very sophisticated—small lobby with attentive staff. Most of the rooms are two-bedroom suites, which makes the hotel perfect for families or groups of friends shopping together. We had two bedrooms, Frette linens, a kitchenette and living area with a desk and free Wi-Fi, and yummy Frédéric Fekkai bathroom amenities. Not only are they dog-friendly but they gave Toffee a gift. Rates begin at $399. © 212/867-5100. www.thealexhotel.com.

THE BENJAMIN
125 E. 50th St., near Lexington Ave. (Subway: 6 to 51st St., or E or V to Lexington Ave./53rd St.).

The Benjamin is an Executive Suite hotel designed to lure the business crowd, and their dogs. Each room has a complete office center featuring in-room fax/copier/printer, high-speed Internet, and two-line phones. The suites have small kitchens (you can preorder groceries), and a 10-pillow menu is available for all accommodations.

The Benjamin's Dream Dog program offers your pooch a choice of three doggie beds, a plush bathrobe, a doggie DVD, *Dog-On Television* (to entertain him when alone in the room), gourmet room service, spa treatments, and a consultation with a pet psychic. Rates begin at around $350 a night, but you can often get a promotional deal online. © 212/715-2500. www.the benjamin.com.

HOTEL WALES
1295 Madison Ave., near 92nd St. (Subway: 6 to 96th St.).

For those interested in proximity to Museum Mile, the enclave of Upper Madison Avenue shopping in Carnegie Hill, or the idea of a secret hotel at a good price, this is a find. It was once a residential hotel, but renovations have made it chic. The hotel's restaurants include Sarabeth's, a cult favorite for home-style cooking, and Joanna's Italian Restaurant, a longtime Upper East Side favorite. Pets are welcome. Room rates are around $225 with online promotions. © 866/WALES-HOTEL or 212/876-6000. www.waleshotel.com.

MILLENNIUM BROADWAY
145 W. 44th St. (Subway: 1, 2, 3, 7, N, Q, R, S, or W to Times Square/42nd St.).

Do not confuse this hotel with the Millenium Hilton; see below. Note that they spell *Millennium* differently.

This hotel is a member of the British chain Millennium & Copthorne and is a huge tower between Fifth Avenue, the Theater District, and Times Square. It's also one of my best finds, and I have been staying here for years, especially when they do their $199 promotion—that's per room not per person. Note that right out the door, on West 44th Street, is a string of great eats. © 212/768-4400. www.millenniumhotels.com.

SURREY HOTEL
20 E. 76th St., between Madison and Fifth aves. (Subway: 6 to 77th St.).

I found this hotel by accident while I was shopping on Madison Avenue; you certainly can't beat the location or the fact that Café Boulud is in the lobby.

This was once an apartment building and is now part of the Affinia group. The lobby is simple, but moderately swank. The rooms may remind you of furnished apartments—the basics are there and they're fine, but the decor is nothing special. But then again, you're here for the location, the price, and the wow of it all. Daily, monthly, promotional, and weekend rates are all available. A one-bedroom suite begins at $339. © 212/288-3700. www.affinia.com.

THE WARWICK
65 W. 54th St., between Fifth and Sixth aves. (Subway: E or V to Fifth Ave./53rd St.).

This is the kind of find that every smart shopper wants to know about, mostly because the rates are about half that of a five-star hotel and the rooms are large. The Warwick is an old, very famous New York hotel that went downhill for a while and therefore may have fallen off your list. However, the place has been completely refurbished. Know that it has a tiny lobby, but *grrrreat* rooms with rates around $325 per night. © 212/247-2700. www.warwickhotels.com.

Downtown/SoHo

MILLENIUM HILTON
55 Church St. (Subway: E to World Trade Center).

The good news is that this hotel is across the street from Century 21, it's great for visiting downtown and Ground Zero, and it has been totally redone and recently reopened. The bad news is that the hotel is well-known and can be mobbed, especially on weekends. With Hilton promotions, this is still a worthwhile choice for smart shoppers. © 212/693-2001. www.hilton.com.

60 THOMPSON
60 Thompson St., between Broome and Spring sts.
(Subway: C or E to Spring St.).

This is a small luxury hotel in such an incredibly fabulous Village/SoHo shopping area that you may never leave downtown. © 877/431-0400 or 212/431-0400. www.60thompson.com.

SOHO GRAND HOTEL
310 West Broadway, between Grand and Canal sts.
(Subway: A, C, or E to Canal St.).

Located conveniently on the edge of SoHo, the Soho Grand is swank and moderne—in keeping with the cutting-edge nature of this neighborhood. Rooms are stark, small, and very chic, with Dean & DeLuca goodies stocked in the minibars. Rates begin at $325 per night. © 212/965-3000. www.sohogrand.com.

Apartment Living

Considering that you could buy a fab handbag for the price of a night in a luxury hotel, you may want to consider booking an apartment. A good option for families or girlfriends traveling together, an apartment will give you more space plus the luxury of having a kitchen. Many apartments are available for short stays (2–3 nights), but you'll find the most value by renting for a week or more. Try www.newyork.craigslist.org or my new best find: **Herrick Suites**; see below.

HERRICK SUITES
Various locations throughout Manhattan.

Herrick has about 20 apartments dotted around the city, mostly in lower Manhattan addresses, all in luxury buildings of the sort you'd kill to live in.

We tested a one-bedroom in Chelsea, with a winter special rate of $250 a night! This same apartment costs $415 a night in season or $2,760 a week. I inspected a duplex in the east teens that was worthy of a magazine spread. There are apartments in Chelsea, Greenwich Village, the Financial District, South Street Seaport, and so on. Check out the offerings and the prices through Yellin Hotels (www.yellinhotels.com) or go to www.herrickguestsuites.com.

Chapter Five

················

UPTOWN SHOPPING NEIGHBORHOODS: WEST

DIRECTIONALLY SPEAKING

··

There is no other city in the world that I know of where what you call the various parts of town depends on where you're standing. There is no precise center of New York called "downtown." Although it generally refers to anything below 14th Street, "downtown" also means down from where you are standing—unless you are in the river below the bottom of the island, and then it's all uptown.

Since this is all so arbitrary, I've created a few random map boundaries in these pages: I decree 34th Street the divider between uptown and downtown. Fifth Avenue has always been the divider between east and west. In this book, uptown neighborhoods for the East Side and West Side are in two different chapters, followed by a chapter on downtown.

Sometimes the best way to shop is to head for a general destination and then let your feet do the wandering. I have included a few lunch possibilities here as well, although there is another section on restaurants in chapter 4.

WEST 34TH STREET

··

The West 34th Street neighborhood stretches from Penn Station (between Seventh and Eighth aves.) to Fifth Avenue. The addition of **Kmart,** inside Penn Station, has extended the shopping district and given everyone a place for one-stop shopping. But the real energy comes from **Old Navy** and **H&M,** both across the street from Macy's. There's also a branch of **Daffy's** (one of New York's most famous off-pricers—although this is not my favorite location), a **Gap,** and a big **Banana Republic.** Right on the corner of 34th Street and Broadway is **Victoria's Secret.** Another off-pricer, **Conway,** has several stores dotted around here.

Remember that just because a lot of this strip has been revitalized, it's still not Fifth Avenue. In fact, shopping here is far from chic—it's practical. *Buyer Beware:* There are a number of street vendors in this area; many sell fake designer perfumes or presumed-to-be big-name perfumes bought in the Caribbean.

You can take the A, C, E, 1, 2, or 3 train to 34th Street/Penn Station; or the B, D, F, N, Q, R, V, or W to 34th Street/Herald Square.

KMART
1 Penn Plaza (W. 34th St., at Seventh Ave.).

Maybe Kmart isn't your idea of a find, but if you live in New York, this discount drugstore-and-more is a godsend. ✆ **212/760-1188.** www.kmart.com.

OLD NAVY
150 W. 34th St., between Broadway and Seventh Ave.

This is the Old Navy flagship in Manhattan, and all I can say is wow—it's retail entertainment at its finest. See p. 175 for more on the Old Navy brand. There's a 1950s-style diner downstairs in the Old Navy store. ✆ **212/594-0049.** www.oldnavy.com.

GARMENT DISTRICT

The Garment District is the name of a neighborhood on the west side of Manhattan where most, but not all, of the needle

Sample-Sale Venue

Parsons School of Design (as seen on *Project Runway*) is in this neighborhood, at 560 Seventh Ave. (at 40th St.). Frequent sample sales and shopping events are held in the school's auditorium. Call © **212/229-8959** for further information.

trades have their showrooms, offices, and, sometimes, cutting rooms. The main area, where you'll see the racks whizzing by with their dozens of brand-new fashions, is on Seventh Avenue around 40th Street.

Broadway bisects Sixth Avenue at 34th Street, so this part of Broadway, which is very close to Seventh Avenue, also houses much of the trade. Many buildings have two different entrances (and sometimes two different addresses): one on Broadway and one on Seventh Avenue.

Some people like to wander around the Garment District buildings on a Saturday to see what vibes (and bargains) they can pick up. The big Broadway buildings (1407 and 1411) are totally locked up, but the smaller buildings have an elevator operator on duty who will take you to a specific floor for an appointment. *A note to the crafty:* These elevator operators are savvy professionals; they can spot a tourist a mile away. Don't try to fool them. Simply ask if any of the showrooms does business on Saturday. Many sample sales are posted on the elevator or building doors in the lobby; the doormen know everything.

Note: The **Fur District** is adjacent to the Garment District, farther downtown. The streets around 30th Street and Seventh Avenue house small mom-and-pop furriers and suppliers, as well as a few skyscrapers packed with showrooms.

SAMPLE SALE WHOLESALERS
42 W. 36th St., between Fifth and Sixth aves.

This place is not a real sample sale, but rather a store that concentrates on Italian brands for the Italian-visitors market. The hours are a bit unusual: Tuesday through Friday from 10am to 6pm. *Web Tip:* Log on to the website to see what's available before you visit the store. © **888/DEAL-123** (332-5123). www.dutyfreeapparel.com.

TIMES SQUARE

I wish I could tell you that the new Times Square is a must-do neighborhood and a shopper's heaven. However, though the area has undergone an enormous cleanup and has been vastly improved, this is still not a retail paradise. You'll find chains such as the **World of Disney, Sephora,** and **Virgin Megastore,** as well as snazzy hotels and even the Condé Nast building—but mostly this is an area that is far from classy.

The **Times Square Alliance,** 1560 Broadway, near 47th Street (© **212/768-1560;** www.timessquarenyc.org), is a good one-stop source for information, MetroCards, maps, and so on.

You can take the 1, 2, 3, 7, N, Q, R, S, or W train to Times Square/42nd Street.

TKTS
Duffy Sq., Broadway, at 47th St.

I tell you about this with a heavy heart, as I hate to see you spend precious New York time standing in line. On the other hand, bargains are bargains, so here goes: This discount booth sells same-day, half-price theater tickets. Cash and traveler's checks only. The booth opens at 10am for matinee tickets, and 3pm for evening performances.

Best Bets: If you want to see a Broadway performance and don't really care which one, visit the booth late in the afternoon, up to an hour before curtain time; some tickets will still be available and you'll avoid the lines. www.tdf.org/tkts.

Toys "R" Us
1514 Broadway, at 45th St.

If you're interested in retail as theater, check out this amazing branch of the toy retailer. They ain't got one like this back home. © 646/366-8800. www.toysrus.com.

Eats

I am amused by the **McDonald's** on West 42nd with the Broadway-style marquee; I also think it's funny that **Red Lobster** came here from suburbia. Those going to the theater often prefer the side streets around Sixth Avenue, especially on West 44th and West 45th streets, where there are plenty of really nice restaurants, many of them in hotels. For you guys out there, the **ESPN Zone** (1472 Broadway, near 42nd St.) is incredible, with food, games, retail, free wireless Internet access, and large screens for watching sports.

THEATER DISTRICT

The Theater District is a subset of Times Square, located in the area from West 42nd to West 52nd streets, mostly west of Seventh Avenue. I mention it because there is a small amount of specialty retail here. Most Broadway productions have their own merchandise, sold in the lobby of the theater: This is "You've seen the play, now wear the T-shirt" kind of stuff. There are also the usual TTs (tourist traps) with souvenirs.

Take the 1, 2, 3, 7, N, Q, R, S, or W train to Times Square/42nd Street; or the 1, N, R, or W to 49th Street.

Colony Music
1619 Broadway, at 49th St.

Musical scores, sheet music, CDs, posters, and other print materials. You can go nuts here. Open late for after-theater browsing. *Best Bets:* You'll find a complete selection of original Broadway soundtrack DVDs, along with sheet music.

Many of these are otherwise hard to find, such as a DVD for Follies, $24. ✆ **212/265-2050.** www.colonymusic.com.

DRAMA BOOK SHOP
250 W. 40th St., between Seventh and Eighth aves.

This shop specializes in plays and theater-related publications. ✆ **212/944-0595.** www.dramabookshop.com.

MANNY'S MUSIC
156 W. 48th St., between Sixth and Seventh aves.

This is a musician's source for instruments and supplies such as strings. Not to be confused with shoe-guru Manolo Blahnik. *Web Tip:* The one-page website lists the address and phone number; there's no information about inventory and no online catalog. ✆ **212/819-0576.** www.mannysmusic.com.

ROCKEFELLER CENTER
....

On the west side of Fifth Avenue, Rockefeller Center is home to over 100 shops, including **Façonnable** (636 Fifth Ave., at 51st St.), **Anthropologie** (50 Rockefeller Center, at 50th St.), **Banana Republic** (626 Fifth Ave., at 50th St.), and **Anne Fontaine** (610 Fifth Ave., between 49th and 50th sts.). The promenade leading to the skating rink has chocolate shops, and a branch of **Brookstone.** Specialty bookstores in the area include **Librairie de France** (610 Fifth Ave., near 49th St.) and **Kinokuniya** (10 W. 49th St., at Fifth Ave.).

Take the B, D, F, or V train to Rockefeller Center.

WEST 57TH STREET
....

No visit to New York is complete without worshiping at the corners of Fifth Avenue and 57th Street—all four of them. Even if you don't buy anything, between the window-shopping and the crowd-staring, this is what you came for.

The block of 57th Street between Fifth and Sixth avenues has all sorts of retail. Italian hotshots such as **Bulgari** and **Laura Biagiotti** show no sign of being disappointed with the location, and there's also **Club Monaco** and the British stationery retailer **Smythson of Bond Street**—quite a creative mix of stores. One block south, check out **Suarez**'s new location (5 W. 56th St.). This is a leading resource for top-quality, designer-inspired handbags without the designer label or price tag. **Fortunoff's** has moved here too (3 W. 57th St.).

Take the F to 57th Street/Sixth Avenue, or the N, R, or W to Fifth Avenue/59th Street.

KATE'S PAPERIE
140 W. 57th St., between Sixth and Seventh aves.

See p. 114 for details on this fabulous paper store. © 212/459-0700. www.katespaperie.com.

OMO NORMA KAMALI
11 W. 56th St., between Fifth and Sixth aves.

This is cutting-edge chic for those who like unique clothes, from Indian saris to reflective Lycra sportswear. © 212/957-9797. www.normakamalicollection.com.

COLUMBUS CIRCLE

Oh me! Oh my! What a difference a decade makes. This neighborhood has been born again and is now the hottest place in town, home to many big-time chefs and a new high-rise. Welcome to the new **Time Warner Center,** with a Mandarin Oriental hotel and a large "retail complex," which is basically business-speak for "mall." If you have limited time in New York, it's a one-stop-shopping zone for luxury goods.

A shocking contrast to all that glitz is my regular branch of beauty-supply chain **Ricky's** (332 W. 57th St., near Eighth Ave.). See p. 241 for more info and locations.

Take the A, B, C, D, 1, or 9 train to 59th Street/Columbus Circle.

Eats

Pop into the Time Warner Center and explore the hotel (**Mandarin Oriental**), the new **Whole Foods** (with a sushi bar and sit-down area!), or the mall for eats.

UPPER WEST SIDE

Broadway has become home to numerous superstores, discounters, and lifestyle resources, while Columbus Avenue has lost its energy and seems to function more as a mall, with branches of chain stores. Amsterdam Avenue has a few funky stores, antiques dealers, and resale shops. I've come to like the area best for the food stores on Broadway.

Take the 1, 2, 3, B, or C train to 72nd Street; or the 1 to 79th Street; or the B or C to 81st Street/Museum of Natural History.

Broadway

Many of the old staples are clustered from the high 60s to the mid-80s. There's an **Ann Taylor** (2017 Broadway, near 69th St.). Choose from two **Gap** stores (1988 Broadway, at Lincoln Sq.; and 2373 Broadway, near 86th St.). Check out **The Body Shop** (2159 Broadway, near 76th St.), and don't forget **Urban Outfitters** (2081 Broadway, at 72nd St.) for teens and 'tweens. For off-price retail, pop into **Filene's Basement** (2222 Broadway, at 79th St.), though its other Manhattan locations are better. You'll see street vendors selling used books around West 72nd Street, or stop in **Barnes & Noble** (1972 Broadway, at 66th St.) for new ones. **Loehmann's** (2101 Broadway, between

73rd and 74th sts.) has opened a huge new store and **Sephora** (2164 Broadway, between 76th and 77th sts.) has moved to glitzy new digs.

You may want to book a spa treatment at the new **Blue-mercury Apothecary and Spa** (2305 Broadway, at 83rd St.).

This area has become very residential, so there are stores for real people who live here. The grocery store **Fairway** (2127 Broadway, at 74th St.) has redone itself and competes more than ever with **Zabar's** (2245 Broadway, near 80th St.). For home decor, choose from **Pottery Barn** (1965 Broadway, at 67th St.) and **Gracious Home** (1992 Broadway, at 67th St.).

Amsterdam Avenue

If you stroll along the whole avenue, you may think I've sent you to the wrong neighborhood. So aim high—head straight to the blocks in the 70s and 80s.

ALLAN & SUZI
416 Amsterdam Ave., at 80th St.

If you're looking for an eye-popping ensemble at a bargain price, look no further. Don't even stop to stare at the funky 8-inch platform shoes in the window; just dash right in and start trying on "gently worn" designer items. *Best Bets:* Vintage glitz! Think Pucci, Gucci, Prada. . . . With prices ranging from $10 to $8,000, there's something here for everyone's taste and budget. © 212/724-7445. www.allanandsuzi.net.

Columbus Avenue

Welcome to the mall. There's no other area in all of Manhattan with a greater concentration of stores that you'd find in any suburban shopping mall. Some unique retailing gems are still here, but you have to look past all the big chains to find them. Please note that many of the stores in this neighborhood do not open until 11am, and be warned that this area is super-crowded on weekends.

Betsey Johnson
248 Columbus Ave., near 72nd St.

Teen angel, are you with me? I've never met a teenage girl who didn't crave to be dressed by Betsey. So here you go, moms and daughters alike—have a look. The clothes are slightly on the cutting edge without being too crazy. *Web Tip:* Sale items are featured online, so log on, and then call to see if your choices are available in the shop. © **212/362-3364.** www.betsey johnson.com.

Danskin
159 Columbus Ave., at 67th St.

This place has a wide choice of gym and dance attire for women and girls. This store stocks a good selection of plus sizes. © **212/724-2992.** www.danskin.com.

Eileen Fisher
341 Columbus Ave., at 77th St.

One of the branch stores of my heroine; see p. 90 for more about her. © **212/362-3000.** www.eileenfisher.com.

Eats

Try the cafe upstairs at **Fairway** (2127 Broadway, at 74th St.). **Magnolia Bakery** (200 Columbus Ave., at 69th St.), the sweet shop that started the cupcake craze, has opened a new branch uptown. In addition to the famed cupcakes, breakfast pastries and other sweets have been added to the menu. One thing has not changed: the limit of 12 cupcakes per customer.

West Harlem

After Bill Clinton moved his office to West 125th Street, Harlem quickly became New York City's newest celebutante neighborhood. The area's rebirth has sent real estate prices soaring, and trendy boutiques have appeared in former mom-and-pop storefronts. Of the three different parts to Harlem (East,

Central, and West), this area—from West 125th to West 155th streets—is the hottest.

Pieces of Harlem (228 W. 135th St.) is the place to go for premium-label T-shirts and denim. For more formal wear, guys will want to check out Harlem's haberdasher, **B. Oyama Homme** (2339 Seventh Ave., between 136th and 137th sts.), for contemporary dress shirts and English-cut suits. **N** (114 W. 116th St., near Malcolm X Blvd.) is Harlem's largest designer boutique and it could easily be at home on Madison Avenue. You'll find high-end sportswear and party clothes, as well as tailored suits for men. **Atmos** (203 W. 125th St., at Adam Clayton Powell Jr. Blvd.), Tokyo's popular sneaker store transplant, offers custom shoes in partnership with Nike and Reebok, along with a wide variety of exclusive styles including the Nike X ATmos Free 5.0.

Subway: A, B, C, or D to 125th Street.

Eats

Sylvia's Restaurant (328 Lenox Ave., between 126th and 127th sts.) serves a Sunday Gospel brunch from 11am to 2pm, where Bill and friends come for the dietetic smothered chicken, slammin' meatloaf, and great music. © **212/996-2669**.

Chapter Six

······················

UPTOWN SHOPPING NEIGHBORHOODS: EAST

DIRECTIONS

Since this is the eastern portion of the uptown neighborhoods chapters of this guide, I have again used 34th Street as the dividing line between uptown and downtown.

EAST 42ND STREET

East 42nd Street is not much of a neighborhood, per se. But wait—there's action on two fronts here, maybe more. **Grand Central Terminal** (42nd St., between Vanderbilt and Lexington aves.) is gorgeous and filled with great stores (and an excellent market). The eastern portion of shopping on East 42nd Street, and the subsequent opportunities on Third Avenue up toward 50th Street, will mostly make you feel like you're in a mall. It's convenient for those using Grand Central; it has nothing that you need to go out of your way to find.

Take the 4, 5, 6, 7, or S train to Grand Central/42nd Street.

SEAN JOHN
475 Fifth Ave., at 41st St.

This is the first store in Sean "Diddy" Combs's retail empire. The clothes are urban casual and great for young men with high style and fashion attitude. They also come in a very wide range of sizes. *Web Tip:* Don't waste time cruising the website. Collections are not shown and you can't order online. © 212/220-2633. www.seanjohn.com.

MIDTOWN FIFTH AVENUE

What locals refer to as Midtown is what visitors consider the main shopping guts of the city. It's also one of the main business areas—between 57th Street and 34th Street. Main Street USA in this case is Fifth Avenue, which is a legend in its own time.

To get in the spirit, begin your tour at Fifth Avenue and 58th Street. Walk down Fifth all the way to 34th Street, noting the changes in the crowds, the types of stores, and the very feel of the air. It's fancy uptown and gets less so as you walk downtown. The specialty department stores are **Bergdorf Goodman** (two stores on Fifth Ave., near 58th St.) and **Takashimaya** (693 Fifth Ave., at 54th St.), a drop-dead elegant place. **Blanc de Chine** (637 Fifth Ave., at 53rd St.) offers three floors of chic Euro-Asian clothing for women and men.

I'm not certain which is more a tribute to human spirit and imagination, the **Disney Store** (711 Fifth Ave., at 55th St.) or **Gianni Versace** (647 Fifth Ave., between 51st and 52nd sts.). The **NBA Store** (666 Fifth Ave., at 52nd St.) is in a class by itself. Even if you don't buy anything, go in and stare—this is what sizzle is all about. There are plenty of affordable places now: Get a look at **Mexx** (650 Fifth Ave., at 52nd St.), a Dutch brand that's slightly more upmarket than H&M.

My favorite subway line is the F train, which will get you to Rockefeller Center, or you can take the E train to Fifth Avenue/53rd Street, exactly where you want to be.

BLANC DE CHINE
637 Fifth Ave., at 53rd St.

This is one of the best stores in the world. The Asian-style clothing is made from the finest silks and woolens in subtle earth tones. Women's sizes run small and top out at U.S. 12, but the men's clothing, especially jackets and trouser suits, will fit most ladies. It's very expensive, but worth every dollar. I paid $900 for a trouser suit, but I live in it.

Best Bets: A fab new collection called Bleu de Chine, featuring leisurewear for active lifestyles (priced $200–$1,000), is showcased on the third floor of the shop. *Web Tip:* The website has great graphics with clear photos of the collections; but no prices are given and you can't order online. ✆ 212/308-8688. www.blancdechine.com.

H&M
640 Fifth Ave., at 51st St.

H&M is the signal to the world that Fifth Avenue has changed. This Swedish chain sells clothes for men, women, and kids; it can knock off the latest trends from the catwalks faster than you can say, "What's new, pussycat?"

Shop early in the day to avoid the crowds and long fitting-room lines. Inventory moves at lightning speed; by late afternoon, the displays are messy and the choices few. ✆ 212/489-0390. www.hm.com.

NBA STORE
666 Fifth Ave., at 52nd St.

From the sublime to the ridiculous, perhaps, but this store is unlike anything in the world—a new generation of retail entertainment that owes its inspiration to Niketown (but has more bells and whistles). To say nothing of WNBA Barbie!

Insider's Secret: You can book a birthday party in this store. *Web Tip:* Click on your favorite team to see what's available in logo merchandise. ✆ 212/515-6221. http://store.nba.com.

TAKASHIMAYA
693 Fifth Ave., near 54th St.

If you have time to see only one store in Manhattan, speed through Takashimaya. The store is a museum of good taste; it all looks incredibly expensive, but some of it is actually affordable. Takashimaya artfully blends Asian inspiration with country French and sophisticated Continental looks to provide one smooth international arena of finesse and magic. The florist is Christian Tortu, the toast of Paris. © **212/350-0100.** www.takashimaya-ny.com.

Eats

I'm always at **Burger Heaven** (p. 63), but you can also pop into the cafe at **Saks Fifth Avenue** or choose from any number of eats at **Rockefeller Center.** (There's a **Dean & DeLuca** gourmet grocery at Rock Center with tables upstairs.) If you're with the kids, try the cafe at the **NBA Store.** For the best quickie snack, stop by **Garrett Popcorn Shops** at 560 Fifth Ave., at 46th Street, and indulge in the caramel/cheese corn mix.

MIDDLE MADISON AVENUE

I call Midtown Madison Avenue (from 57th St. to 42nd St.) "Middle Mad." The lower end of the stretch, in the 40s, is geared toward haberdashery. If you're looking for the older version of **Brooks Brothers** (346 Madison Ave., at 44th St.), you'll still find it, along with **Jos. A. Bank** (366 Madison Ave., at 46th St.), **Paul Stuart** (350 Madison Ave., at 45th St.), and **Thomas Pink** (520 Madison Ave., at 53rd St.).

The stretch beginning around 54th Street is filled with big chains. There's the flagship **J. Crew** (347 Madison Ave., near 44th St.), and there's an okay branch of the off-pricer **Daffy's** (335 Madison Ave., at 44th St.) as well. Don't forget **Talbots** (525 Madison Ave.) and **Talbots Mens** (527 Madison Ave.), both between 53rd and 54th streets, and **H2O Plus** (511 Madison Ave., at 52nd St.). This is very real shopping without being overly glam—it's just all here.

You can use the E or V stop at Fifth Avenue/53rd Street. If you're beginning lower on Madison and then plan to walk uptown (a good idea), take the 4, 5, 6, 7, or S train to Grand Central/42nd Street.

AMERICAN GIRL PLACE
609 Fifth Ave., at 49th St.

If you have a young daughter, you know about this amazing series of dolls and the marketing concept that goes behind them. See p. 203. © 877/247-5223. www.americangirlplace.com.

BELGIAN SHOES
110 E. 55th St., between Park and Lexington aves.

There is no place more "in" and "New York" than this shoe store, which has its own look and is, therefore, an icon of style—flat shoes in zillions of colors and styles, with a distinctive cut and shape. This store keeps banker's hours, closing early at 4:30pm. © 212/755-7372. www.belgianshoes.com.

CROUCH & FITZGERALD/THE SHERPA SHOP
400 Madison Ave., near 48th St.

A staple for fine leather goods for as long as I can recall, this store has been sold and downsized but still has plenty of great merchandise, including briefcases and carryalls for business-women and travelers. The house-brand luggage is crafted from canvas and belting leather—handsome, practical, and well-made.

The in-store **Sherpa Shop** sells doggy totes and travel gear. *Best Bets:* Toffee travels the world in his Sherpa tote; it's the best pet carrier on the planet. Most styles are $75 to $100. © 212/755-5888. www.crouchandfitzgerald.com.

DAFFY'S
335 Madison Ave., at 44th St.

This branch isn't the largest Daffy's, but you'll make do here, just as I do. Sometimes you find the big names; sometimes you don't. © **212/557-4422.** www.daffys.com.

EILEEN FISHER
521 Madison Ave., near 53rd St.

Positioned as a way-of-life dress style, Fisher's clothes are moderately priced yet high in fashion, chic, and comfort. Colors are the selling point: They are always new, with an almost European palette. There are other stores around town; shop them all. The outlet in Woodbury Common (p. 298) is worth the schlep. © **212/759-9888.** www.eileenfisher.com.

Eats

Try **Burger Heaven,** on Madison Avenue between 54th and 55th streets (p. 63).

PARK AVENUE

For the most part, Park Avenue is not a street with too much retail. Instead, it has tulips. However, there are some nuggets right in the heart of town, in the mid-50s. **T. Anthony** (445 Park Ave., at 56th St.) sells distinctive and chic canvas and leather luggage. And **Syms** (400 Park Ave., at 54th St.) is an off-pricer with men's, women's, and kids' clothing—lotsa Italian designer stuff.

Take the N, R, or W train to Fifth Avenue/59th Street, or the 4, 5, or 6 train to 59th Street/Lexington Avenue.

EAST 57TH STREET

This is what you've come for: 57th Street is both a state of mind and a neighborhood. It's a high-ticket address for residential and retail, especially where it bisects Fifth Avenue. It's also the new home of casual chic designers, like those represented by the **LVMH** group. Everyone from **Dior** to **Chanel** is here.

The luxe shopping area begins at Park Avenue and ends between Fifth and Sixth avenues. In these blocks, you'll find a few galleries and antiques shops (many are upstairs), elite European boutiques, and America's own retail landmark, **Tiffany & Co.**

Hop an F train to 57th Street/Sixth Avenue, or an N, R, or W train to Fifth Avenue/59th Street.

CUSTOM DESIGN BY MIMI
116 E. 57th St., at Seventh Ave.

Mimi Sason, who ran Joe's Fabric Warehouse on the Lower East Side for 14 years, has opened a new store filled with textiles of all kinds, including silk, cotton, linen, wool, mohair, and cut velvet. She sells these decorator fabrics at designer discounts or better. ***Best Bets:*** The bargain tables; prices begin as low as $20 a yard and most are under $95. © 212/355-0533.

SONY STYLE
550 Madison Ave., at 56th St.

The Sony Style flagship is home of the Sony Wonder Technology Lab, a virtual-reality amusement park/museum, kind of like a Nike store that doesn't have any shoes. You can explore all sorts of technology here.

Buyer Beware: Prices at Sony Style are full retail, so you may want to visit, play, take notes, and then purchase from a discounter or big-box retailer. © 212/833-8800. www.sony style.com.

Eats

My secret spot is the cafe in **Bergdorf Goodman Men,** 745 Fifth Ave., at 58th Street (p. 61). There's also a **Burger Heaven** at 536 Madison Ave., at 55th Street (p. 63).

UPPER MADISON AVENUE (57TH ST. & BEYOND)

The average visitor to Manhattan perceives Madison Avenue as a dream shopping stretch that begins at 57th Street and works its way uptown. The stroll from 57th into the 90s is a must-do, even if you're just window-shopping. The little whimsical stores are long gone, but the series of fancy "drugstores" here are enormous fun. The street offers all price points, so don't assume it's too expensive for you. High-end European designers are located in the 60s to mid-70s, with local names and specialty boutiques lining Madison in the 80s and 90s.

If you haven't yet caught up with **Eileen Fisher** (p. 90 for my rave), there's a branch at 1039 Madison Ave., at 79th Street. **Adrien Linford** (p. 266) is a great little gift shop at 1339 Madison Ave., at 94th Street. Interior designer **Charlotte Moss** (20 E. 63rd St., at Madison Ave.) has converted a landmarked 1930s town house into five floors of beautiful (and expensive) merchandise, including antiques, linens, tabletop, fragrance, and gift items.

Newcomer **Samantha Thavasa** (965 Madison Ave., at 76th St.) carries handbags designed by local celebutantes including Tinsley Mortimer and Nicky Hilton, and **Ann Ahn** (961 Madison Ave., between 75th and 76th sts.) is *the* place to shop for Euro-Asian classic investment clothing. **Sigerson Morrison**'s new shop (987 Madison Ave., at 77th St.) is a best bet for ballet flats, designer party shoes, and handbags.

A residential area of grace and refinement, Carnegie Hill, in the low 90s, has a good selection of children's shops clustered on Madison Avenue (I call this area "Upper Mad"). Some are branches of European stores, like **Jacadi** (1296 Madison Ave., at 92nd St., and 787 Madison Ave., between 66th and 67th sts.) and **Bonpoint** (1269 Madison Ave., at 91st St.). Others are original retailers, like **Magic Windows** (1186 Madison Ave., at 87th St.) and **Marie-Chantal** (1992 Madison, between 87th and 88th sts.).

Mixed in with the specialty stores and the chains are several resale shops (p. 307). Most of them have upstairs addresses, so don't be afraid to climb a flight of stairs.

I walk from the F stop at 57th Street/Sixth Avenue, but you can also take a bus uptown and pop off at any point on Madison Avenue. Or take the 4, 5, or 6 train to 86th Street/Lexington Avenue, or the 6 train to 96th Street/Lexington Avenue.

CLYDE'S
926 Madison Ave., near 74th St.

Clyde's is one of the fanciest drugstores you'll ever see. It's also neater and more sophisticated than the competition. Check out the "What's Hot" counter at Clyde's, where you'll find new products featured in leading beauty magazines such as *Elle* and *Bazaar.* Spend $100 and get a free Clyde's tote bag.

Best Bets: The store carries a number of hard-to-find beauty lines from Europe, as well as many American brands that you may have never seen before. The Clyde's line of bath products is well priced, beginning at $15. © 212/744-5050. www.clydes onmadison.com.

GHURKA
683 Madison Ave., between 61st and 62nd sts.

The new Ghurka flagship sells a fabulous line of canvas and leather items made in a very specific look, which I call "Ralph Lauren Fisherman Meets Isak Dinesen on Safari." They're outrageously expensive, very statusy, and quite chic. There's an outlet at Woodbury Common (p. 298). © 212/826-8300. www.ghurka.com.

RALPH LAUREN
867 Madison Ave., at 72nd St.; and 888 Madison Ave., at 72nd St.

You absolutely must visit these stores, if only to get a look-see. The Rhinelander Mansion, at 867 Madison Ave., is one of the most beautiful stores you will ever see in your life. And then there's the store across the street that specializes in active sporting gear. Both could be tourist sights—if they sold tickets for admission, I would certainly pay up. See p. 258 for more on Lauren's home style. ✆ 212/606-2100. www.polo.com.

ZITOMER
969 Madison Ave., near 76th St.

Zitomer began as a pharmacy but is really a tiny department store, with even a pet boutique selling fancy dog toys. Every nook and cranny is filled with beauty, health, and luxury items. It also carries a wide range of costume jewelry, hair accessories, and a cashmere shawl or two in season; I saw real (not fake) Judith Leiber handbags when I was here last. See p. 246 for more. *Web Tip:* If you can't make it to the store, you can order just about everything online. ✆ 212/737-5560. www. zitomer.com.

Eats

I like **Café Boulud** (p. 58), but I also like a diner called **Three Guys** (960 Madison Ave., near 75th St.), which serves breakfast all day long. If you're walking all the way up Madison, shopping as you go, there are two other branches of this diner: 1232 Madison Ave., near 88th Street; and 1381 Madison Ave., near 96th Street. **Sarabeth's** (in the Hotel Wales, 1295 Madison Ave., at 92nd St.) serves decadent breakfast dishes through the lunch hour.

BLOOMINGDALE'S COUNTRY

Bloomingdale's may be the promised land of retail, but there is plenty of nearby shopping as well. There are good stores on Lexington Avenue leading up to Bloomingdale's from East 57th Street, and on Third Avenue heading uptown. To explore the neighborhood fully, start at Bloomingdale's and then branch out.

On the Lex side, you'll find mostly teen-oriented stores. **Diesel** (770 Lexington Ave., at 60th St.) is the flagship for the Italian brand of jeans and other trendsetting clothing.

On Third Avenue, you get more upmarket chains, such as **Club Monaco** (1111 Third Ave., near 65th St.), along with **Dylan's Candy Bar** (1011 Third Ave., near 60th St.), a fancy penny-candy store with sweets and lovely gift baskets. At 70th Street, don't miss **Gracious Home,** which stocks everything you'd ever want for renovating your home (p. 263).

Farther away, but worth a hike if you're furnishing a home, is superstore **Bed Bath & Beyond** (410 E. 61st St., under the 59th St. Bridge).

There's a nice big subway station right under Bloomies; you can reach it by taking the 4, 5, 6, N, R, or W train to 59th Street/Lexington Avenue. If you're going a bit farther uptown, take the 6 train to 68th Street/Hunter College. Stay away from this whole area on weekends if you can.

AVEDA
1122 Third Ave., near 65th St.

This is one of a handful of Aveda shops in the city; the hair and beauty products are sensational and are of such high quality that you won't mind the correspondingly high prices. Although the products are sold all over the world, it's a very New York kind of line and makes a great gift or souvenir. © **212/744-3113.** www.aveda.com.

THE CONRAN SHOP
407 E. 59th St., at First Ave., under 59th St. Bridge.

The Conran Shop specializes in Terence Conran's brand of home style and wit. See p. 262 for more. © **212/755-9079.** www. conran.com.

KATE'S PAPERIE
1282 Third Ave., near 74th St.

Another branch of the fancy paper-and-crafts store. See p. 114 for details. *Best Bets:* The gift wrap section for hand-made decorative papers and exquisite ribbons. Most ribbons retail for $4 to $12 per roll, but you'll save 20% when you buy 12 or more rolls. ✆ **212/396-3670.** www.katespaperie.com.

SCOOPNYC
1275 Third Ave., near 73rd St.

A trendy chain-let of Manhattan boutiques filled with lines like James Jeans, Marc by Marc Jacobs, and Theory for Scoop (created just for these stores). *Best Bets:* The ScoopNYC Personal Shopping service is one of the best in the city. ✆ **212/535-5577.** www.scoopnyc.com.

SEPHORA
1149 Third Ave., at 67th St.

Beauty supermarket Sephora is the purveyor of many brands you may have never heard of. It sells the Bourjois line, made in the same factories as Chanel cosmetics. ✆ **212/452-3336.** www.sephora.com.

Eats

Gino (780 Lexington Ave., at 61st St.; ✆ **212/758-4466**) is the locals' Italian restaurant of choice. (Cash only! No reservations!) If you want something quicker, there are eats right inside **Bloomies** as well.

UPPER LEX
....

Lexington Avenue in the 60s, 70s, and into the 90s has reinvented itself as a mostly design and home style neighborhood with a wonderful in-the-'hood feeling and a mile of style. This area beginning at 60th Street is now the anti–Madison Avenue where shoppers bask in the glow of an intimate shopping scene and a truly friendly vibe.

Check out the boutiques for furniture, style, clothes, and jewelry such as **Jackie Rogers, CK Bradley, Peiper & Leojer,** and, up there around 90th street, **Edit**—clothing for women too busy to make it downtown to Bergdorf's.

Take the 6 train to 68th Street/Hunter College or the F train to Lexington Avenue/63rd Street.

AMADEO
958 Lexington Ave., at 70th St.

Tiny jewel box jewelry store of creative and fun jewelry all based on themes with cameos, but these are not your grandmother's cameos. © **212/737-4101.** www.cameos.com.

FRENCH SOLE
985 Lexington Ave., at 72nd St.

One of the few French Sole (sometimes written FS) stores in the U.S., this one has a slew of the famous ballet flats that the it girls all clamor for. Sales are spectacular. *Best Bets:* The new suede ballet flat comes with a triple cord bow knot, telling the world you have the newest style, about $250. © **888/639-7247.** www.frenchsoleshoes.com.

WILLIAM WAYNE
850 Lexington Ave., at 64th St.

This gift and home style shop is a wonderland for shopping, touching, and getting tabletop ideas. It sells hostess gifts, garden and patio accessories, and wonders from around the world, chosen with a careful eye toward sophistication and chic. *Web Tip:* Their excellent website also tracks your personal information (only what you provide) and purchases so they can get to know you and make shopping suggestions. © **212/737-8934;** also at 40 University Place, at 9th Street, © **212/533-4711.** www.william-wayne.com.

EATS

There's a French-style bistro called **Orsay** on 1057 Lexington Ave., at 75th Street, and also the **Payard Patisserie** (1032 Lexington Ave., near 74th St.). For those with a social memory, there's **Swifty's** (1007 Lexington Ave., near 72nd St.)—on the site of the old Mortimer's, which died even before Babe Paley did.

Chapter Seven

....

DOWNTOWN SHOPPING NEIGHBORHOODS, INCLUDING BROOKLYN

DOWNTOWN IS A STATE OF MIND

Downtown is more than a state of mind in Manhattan—it's a place and it's an attitude; it's a complete way of life. Downtown has become so uptown that limos pull into districts that once gave people the creepy-crawlies, and the Meatpacking District is the epitome of trendy. Union Square? It's never been so hip to be that square.

Meanwhile, a lot more than a tree is growing across the bridge in Brooklyn. Several areas are blooming in full force and attracting many young people who can't afford to live in Manhattan. And Carroll Gardens, which sounds like an address from Monopoly, has developed a hot retail strip on Smith Street (p. 131).

Note that the expression "downtown" also refers to the Wall Street and Ground Zero areas. You'll feel a few somber moments when you pass the Site, but that's part of what New York is about—a phoenix rises from heartbreak and ashes. If you haven't visited the area in a couple of years, you won't recognize the neighborhood. Wall Street is emerging as a luxe leader in all areas—residential, restaurants, and retail.

LOWER FIFTH AVENUE

Lower Fifth was the start of something big years ago; now it continues to evolve and is definitely worth a visit since the neighborhood puts you within walking distance of **Union Square,** one of the hottest parts of town these days. You'll find branches of **M.A.C.** (1 E. 22nd St., at Fifth Ave.) cosmetics and **Eileen Fisher** (166 Fifth Ave., between 21st and 22nd sts.), along with **Waterworks** (7 E. 20th St., between Fifth Ave. and Park Ave. S.), which recently added a bath and skin-care department. **Paul Smith** (108 Fifth Ave., at 16th St.) is a best bet for hip menswear. While you're here, you can hit the **Greenmarket,** the over-the-top emporium **ABC Carpet & Home,** all the discounters and big-box stores on Sixth Avenue, and the streets of SoHo and the Village.

If you take Broadway farther downtown from Union Square, you'll hit **Forbidden Planet** (840 Broadway, at 13th St.), for comics galore; and the **Strand Book Store** (828 Broadway, at 12th St.), for discounted new and well-priced used books. By the time you get to East 12th Street, you will be in an antiques neighborhood (p. 282). At East 9th Street, you'll hit an array of stores so hip and hot that they attract busloads of Japanese tourists. Head east on 9th to get to the heart of this area.

Fifth Avenue buses stop at the Flatiron Building before continuing downtown on Fifth. If you want to really see the whole area, pop off the subway at either 23rd Street/Sixth Avenue (take the F or V) or 23rd Street/Broadway (take the R or W). Or you can take any train to Union Square and work your way west and uptown.

ABC CARPET & HOME
888 Broadway, at 19th St.

Be still, my heart. If I were making a movie of New York's best stores, this would be the star. Years ago, it was just a carpet store. But then it expanded into bed linens, and now it has everything you could possibly need (or want) for your home—and with its focus on selection over price, you may find yourself wanting a lot more than you can reasonably buy.

This store's look changes more frequently than I do—the Zen period seems to be over, and some of the old boho swagger has been restored. The addition of the **Silk Trading Co.** doesn't change the whole gestalt, but it does add another reason to visit. See p. 279 for details.

Best Bets: ABC Carpet is the largest retailer of floor coverings in the world, and you'll find rugs from every corner of the world in every size and price range. Their sales are legendary; expect to find carpet prices slashed up to 70%. © 212/473-3000. www.abchome.com.

Anthropologie
85 Fifth Ave., at 16th St.

Anthropologie, the brainchild of the man who created Urban Outfitters, sells clothes, home furnishings, gift items, and even some pet accessories. It's a very warehouse-cum-touch-this-and-that-store, with a look that's rich hippie chic; prices are not bad. I love this place—it's certainly one of my favorite stores in New York. There are two other branches—one in SoHo, and a new flagship at Rockefeller Center—but this one is the cherry on the whipped cream of this shopping district. © 212/627-5885. www.anthropologie.com.

Club Monaco
160 Fifth Ave., at 21st St.

This is the flagship of a Canadian chain, now owned by Ralph Lauren. It's great for trendy fashion at affordable prices. *Web Tip:* This is a quick website with great graphics showing what's in store and about to arrive. © 212/352-0936. www.clubmonaco.com.

Fishs Eddy
889 Broadway, at 19th St.

Did someone say dishes? I am bonkers for dishes. And thus for Fishs. Fishs Eddy's original concept was to resell restaurant supply and hotel has-beens, but the store has become so popular that it now casts old molds and sets its own trends. Prices vary from what-a-deal to stratospheric for almost-ready-for-the-big-time collectibles. Dinner plates from a fine London hotel go for about $50 a pop—not cheap. But you'll have a ball as you explore this small, crammed museum of old dishes and hotel services.

Web Tip: If you can't make it to the store, visit the website for easy ordering and great selection. Almost everything in the store is listed on the website. © **212/420-9020.** www.fishs eddy.com.

GREENMARKET
Broadway, between 14th and 17th sts.

I don't care if you're a visitor or a local—you do too need a greenmarket. This one has a very special New York feel about it, especially in fall, when the whole city celebrates the change from the dog days of summer to the crisp autumn. The best apples I've ever eaten in my life came from this market. Vendors sell all kinds of fruits and veggies, cheeses, wines and ciders, and even flowers. It is simply heaven . . . although I'm not sure if heaven is this crowded on a Saturday. While the market is held Monday, Wednesday, Friday, and Saturday year-round, it is a tad sparse in the winter months. Saturday is always the busiest day. © **212/788-7476.** www.cenyc.org.

JO MALONE
949 Broadway, near 23rd St.

The stores selling the products of Jo Malone, British cult heroine in the world of scent and beauty, are owned by Lauder, hence the New York locations. The prices are outrageously high, but the product is unique. See p. 248 for more. © **212/673-2220.** www.jomalone.com.

Hip to Be Square

The era of Union Square being seedy is over—the glory days have arrived. The 14th Street side of the square is home to a whole slew of stores that will make bargain and organic shoppers (that's the same thing, right?) quite pleased with themselves. **Whole Foods** (40 E. 14th St., near University Place) and **Trader Joe's** (142 E. 14th St., between Park and Third aves.), plus the **Greenmarket** (14th St., at Union Sq. E.), reinforce the area's status as a food festival.

Near Whole Foods are **Forever 21** (49 E. 14th St.), the poor teen's H&M; **DSW** (40 E. 14th St.); and **Filene's Basement** (Union Sq. at 14th St.), all near University Place. And don't miss the big-box action—**Petco** (860 Broadway, at 17th St.), **Virgin Megastore** (52 E. 14th St., at Broadway), and so on—on the streets directly surrounding Union Square.

PAUL SMITH
108 Fifth Ave., at 16th St.

Smith is a London designer known for his inventive touches. His traditional-looking clothes have a tiny twist, such as the use of unusual colors or fabrics. He makes both men's and women's wear, much of it very hip. Prices are high to match the quality, but the store does have regular sales. *Web Tip:* The website is updated daily. You'll often find sale items online not available in the store. ✆ **212/627-9770.** www.paulsmith.co.uk.

Eats

There are several cafes inside **ABC Carpet & Home.** Don't miss the **Greenmarket** at Union Square—and if you like it funky, go to the coffee shop called **Coffee Shop** (29 Union Sq. W., at 16th St.), a Brazilian spot that's a scene to be seen.

MEATPACKING DISTRICT

Don't look now, but the Meatpacking District is now known as MePa by some people. There goes the neighborhood.

I think this is one of my favorite parts of the new New York, not because everyone says it is *the* spot, but because it still feels, uh, raw. Yes, there are wholesale butchers and sights to unsettle you. It is very, very real down here, especially on 14th Street itself, right around Ninth and Tenth avenues. But like many other places, it's becoming more and more gentrified every day.

Blame it all on **Jeffrey New York** (449 W. 14th St., near Tenth Ave.), an alternate version of Barneys in what was once the middle of nowhere. For more on Jeffrey, see p. 166.

Even before Jeffrey arrived, there were signs of the times here: clubs, galleries, restaurants, and uptowners slumming it with a smugness that bordered on glee. Several name designers have moved into the area, such as **Stella McCartney** (429 W. 14th St.) and **Alexander McQueen** (417 W. 14th St.). **La Perla** (425 W. 14th St.), **Tracy Reese** (641 Hudson, at Horatio St.), and **Trina Turk** (67 Gansevoort St., between Greenwich and Washington sts.) are newcomers, and don't miss **Christian Louboutin** (59 Horatio St., between Greenwich and Hudson sts.). **Diane von Furstenberg**'s boutique is located on the ground floor of her new DVF studio (874 Washington St., at 14th St.). Los Angeles's **Poleci** (32 Gansevoort St., between Hudson and Greenwich sts.) has also arrived on the scene, and **Yohji Yamamoto** has added a second location at 1 Gansevoort St., near Eighth Avenue. Try to book into **Sally Hershberger Downtown** (425 W. 14th St.; © 212/206-8700) if you want to be as blond as Meg Ryan.

As for how to get here, I don't want to sound like a wimp, or someone who doesn't do public transportation, but I usually take a taxi to Jeffrey and then explore on foot from there. I do this because the area is extremely spread out and even the subway stations don't get you that close. Do note, however, that you *can* take the A, C, E, or L to 14th Street/Eighth

Avenue, or the crosstown bus on 14th Street. Free transfers on buses, you know!

Eats

There's always a hot new restaurant to try in this district, but **Pastis** (9 Ninth Ave., at W. 12th St.; ☎ **212/929-4844**) is an icon where you can worship trendiness and take in the whole scene.

CHELSEA

The dimensions of Chelsea, one of the city's hot neighborhoods, are changing enormously: Chelsea is now considered the area from the West 20s all the way down to West 14th Street, and from Seventh Avenue to Eleventh Avenue.

Formerly a mostly residential area, Chelsea began to make news when many art galleries from SoHo relocated to this district. Then **Comme des Garçons** became the first must-see clothing boutique—and you must see it: part gallery, part boutique, part museum of modern art.

Now almost all of the SoHo art galleries have moved to Chelsea. In fact, Chelsea has expanded so much that it endangered the best flea market in New York: The Annex was forced to move to Hell's Kitchen because the parking lot it called home was sold to developers.

Note that Chelsea is huge, and the distances between the avenues are so far that you cannot stroll and shop as easily as you can in SoHo and Nolita. By subway, take the 1 to 23rd Street/Seventh Avenue or the C or E to 23rd Street/Eighth Avenue; be prepared to walk.

BARNEYS CO-OP
236 W. 18th St., between Seventh and Eighth aves.

Barneys' answer to Jeffrey on West 14th Street is this store, housed in part of the company's old warehouse, and meant to be young, hip, and attractive to the kids of the regular Barneys shoppers. © 212/593-7800. www.barneys.com.

BARNEYS WAREHOUSE SALE
255 W. 17th St., between Seventh and Eighth aves.

Twice a year, Barneys still hosts its famous warehouse sale at this facility near the Co-Op store. The sale is quite an event, and people really do line up. Hours vary, so call the hot line for dates and times and plan to arrive when the doors open for the best selection. The hours of the sale are announced in ads in publications like the *New York Times* and *Time Out New York;* note that they do differ as the sale progresses. *Best Bets:* Prices change daily, so markdowns can be 50% to 80% off on clothing for men, women, and children, as well as gifts. © 212/450-8400.

CHELSEA MARKET
75 Ninth Ave., at 15th St.

This monster building, once a factory for the National Biscuit Company, serves as a cutie-pie-renovation-turned-retail space. It mostly sells food, though occasionally there are design sample sales here. (Honest.) Great for one-stop shopping or snacking, this place is truly visually exciting. *Web Tip:* Check the website for special events such as art shows, concerts, and tango lessons. www.chelseamarket.com.

COMME DES GARÇONS
520 W. 22nd St., near Tenth Ave.

It's worth cab fare to head directly to this address; don't miss it if you love avant-garde retail, architecture, creativity, and chutzpah. © 212/604-9200.

SHOOZ
128 Seventh Ave., between 17th and 18th sts.

This shoe stop carries cult labels including Naot and Robert Zur; comfort shoes are a specialty. *Best Bets:* You'll find a great selection of wellies, priced under $100. © **212/727-7446.**

Eats

For lunch, try **Cafeteria** (119 Seventh Ave., at 18th St.; © **212/414-1717**)—I love the crowd and the food, especially the lemon soufflé pancakes.

LADIES' MILE

Ladies' Mile is in the district some people call Chelsea. Around the time of the Civil War, when department stores were just beginning to catch on and ladies were allowed to go shopping without chaperones, the great names in New York retail stood in a row along Sixth Avenue and stretched from 14th Street to 23rd Street. Remember that the world of Manhattan was built from the bottom up, and 14th Street was sort of the edge of civilization at that time; so it would have been an exciting area to be in.

Although some of the retailers who had stores here have stayed in business, most of them moved uptown as trade moved uptown. As a result of this exodus, most of the buildings stood empty and abandoned. For almost 100 years, Ladies' Mile was a wasteland of gorgeous, empty, hulking cast-iron beauties. Then, *voilà*, they were rediscovered! Most have now been saved and are occupied by famous retailers and big-box stores.

Most of the tenants here are value-oriented, making this a serious shopping destination. The area is continuing to develop, not just on Ladies' Mile itself, but also on the side streets. And more big-box retailers from the suburbs are moving in—don't miss **Home Depot** (40 W. 23rd St., between Fifth and Sixth aves.), even if only to gawk at the building.

Stores right on Sixth Avenue at 18th Street include everything from **Old Navy** to **Filene's Basement** plus **T.J. Maxx, The**

Container Store, and **Bed Bath & Beyond. Burlington Coat Factory** is on Sixth between 22nd and 23rd streets. West 18th Street is home to **West Elm** (112 W. 18th St., at Sixth Ave.), and don't miss off-pricer **Loehmann's** (101 Seventh Ave., between 16th and 17th sts.).

There's a new **Pottery Barn Bed & Bath** (100–104 Seventh Ave., between 16th and 17th sts.), and teens flock to **Urban Outfitters** (526 Sixth Ave., at 14th St.).

I usually arrive by subway (take the 1 to 18th St., or the F or V to 14th St.) and depart via the Sixth Avenue bus, which heads uptown. *Note:* Weekends are usually a zoo in these parts. However, most of the stores stay open until 9pm Monday through Saturday.

BARNES & NOBLE
675 Sixth Ave., at 22nd St.

While there are several B&N superstores in Manhattan, this one is special because it helps round out the personality of the neighborhood and makes a great pit stop. © **212/727-1227.** www.bn.com.

THE CONTAINER STORE
629 Sixth Ave., at 19th St.

The Container Store is known for its chic storage devices and organizational goods. If you're furnishing a home, trying to better organize your life, or looking for household souvenirs to take back to Europe, this is the place to start. *Web Tip:* Check the website for in-store events and special promotions. © **212/366-4200.** www.containerstore.com.

HOUSING WORKS THRIFT SHOP
143 W. 17th St., between Sixth and Seventh aves.

Of the thrift shops, Housing Works is my favorite—partly because of the store's uptown clients. Most of the place is devoted to home style, but you'll also find some clothes. *Web Tip:* Check out their online auction; you can bid on designer clothing, jewelry, and accessories. © **212/366-0820.** www. housingworks.org/thrifts.

Eats

For lunch, there's **Cafeteria** (p. 107), which always gets my vote and my stomach. Snacks can be found at the cafe inside **Bed Bath & Beyond.**

EAST VILLAGE

For my purposes, the area I refer to as the East Village extends east of Broadway from 14th Street down to Houston Street. This is where independent designers and artists take advantage of the relatively low rents to open wonderful storefront shops and galleries.

Shopping in the East Village is not for the faint of heart. You'll have to push past bikers in leather, a crush of NYU students, and panhandlers who compete for sidewalk space with street vendors. It's not overly cute, but it is funky.

If you're out with teenagers, a trip down St. Marks Place (E. 8th St.) will immediately establish you as the coolest grownup around and give you a taste of the East Village.

Begin your tour at St. Marks and Third Avenue, the corner of the busiest block in the East Village, and walk east. An eclectic mix of stores and restaurants is crammed into this short block. You'll find CD and record shops, bookstores, and boutiques advertising "Rock Star Clothing." Check out **St. Mark's Comics** (11 St. Marks Place) for a huge selection of comic books and T-shirts. If skin-tight leather pants are your teen's style— or yours—don't miss **Trash and Vaudeville** (4 St. Marks Place) for the best in punk gear.

As you cross Second Avenue and continue east, the crush of shops gives way to hipper-than-thou cafes and cutting-edge boutiques. Stroll East 9th Street between Third Avenue and Avenue A to see the newest trends in everything from home furnishings to lingerie.

And, yes, I have trolled the **Kmart** (770 Broadway, at 9th St.) here, waiting to be impressed. I like the branch at Penn Station, but this one doesn't seem as good. But you didn't come to this part of town for Kmart, now did you?

The easiest way to take in the whole area is to hop the 6 train to Astor Place, get out, and prowl. *Note:* Most of these stores open late in the morning (around 11am)—this is not an area for early birds.

EILEEN FISHER
314 E. 9th St., between First and Second aves.

If you shop nowhere else on East 9th Street, a visit to this store is worth the trip. *Best Bets:* This shop has samples, markdowns, and odd rejects along with the regular merchandise. Bargain prices begin at $20 per item. ✆ **212/529-5715.** www.eileen fisher.com.

GABAY'S OUTLET
225 First Ave., between 13th and 14th sts.

Check out this shop for overstock from department stores like Bergdorf Goodman. ✆ **212/254-3180.**

JOHN DERIAN
6 E. 2nd St., between Second Ave. and Bowery.

See p. 268 for details. ✆ **212/677-3917.** www.johnderian.com.

KIEHL'S
109 Third Ave., at 13th St.

It's hard to call Kiehl's a find since it's been around for well over 100 years, its products are sold in many uptown department stores, and it has a cult following that includes just about everyone in New York. But if you're from out of town, you might not know that the original Kiehl's store—home to all sorts of beauty lotions and potions—is right here, and has been since 1851. See p. 245 for more. ✆ **212/677-3171.** www.kiehls.com.

BOWERY

You can consider the Bowery a subdivision of the East Village if you want and, yes, there are fewer bums and more, uh, beach bums. **Blue & Cream,** a Hampton's store and way of life for the spiritually uplifted, has opened in Manhattan (1 E. 1st St., at Bowery; ✆ 212/533-3088; www.blueandcream.com). Note that this location is not that far from **John Derian**'s atelier, he of the decoupaged plates and the grandfather of this still up-and-coming district. See p. 268 for more on Derian.

SOHO

SoHo stands for "South of Houston" (say "*House*-ton"). Today, it has become more of a destination than ever, partly because real estate prices have risen and partly because European visitors and retailers are comfortable here. So the stakes have risen and the area is all but deluxe . . . and boring, over-saturated as it is with every big name and brand in the world and lacking in the true charm that turned us on in the old days. Plain-old funky doesn't cut it here anymore. Expensive funky is the trend, and mainstream funky is following quickly.

But wait! There are still a few people with a sense of humor. **Todd Oldham by La-Z-Boy** (73 Wooster St., near Spring St.), for one, brings a breath of fresh air to SoHo.

There are plenty of names that must be wincing at the arrival of La-Z-Boy to these refined blocks: **Ted Baker** (107 Grand St., at Mercer St.), **Chanel** (139 Spring St., at Wooster St.), **Louis Vuitton** (116 Greene St., between Prince and Spring sts.), and **Ralph Lauren** (379 West Broadway, near Broome St.), to name a few. You'll also find your chicer-than-thou types, such as **Marc Jacobs** (163 Mercer St., between Houston and Prince sts.) and **Yohji Yamamoto** (103 Grand St., at Mercer St.).

Meanwhile, merchants keep opening stores. Boho French arrival **Cotelac** (92–94 Greene St., between Prince and Spring sts.) and **TSE** (120 Wooster St., between Spring and Prince sts.) just opened fab boutiques, and don't miss the **Apple Store** (103 Prince St., between Mercer and Greene sts.), with its Genius Bar set up in an old post office; **Taschen** (107 Greene St., between Prince and Spring sts.), the German bookstore with cool architecture and well-priced tomes on pop culture and the arts; **Sur La Table** (75 Spring St., at Crosby St.), the Seattle-based kitchen-and-tabletop store; and a branch of **Daffy's** (462 Broadway, at Grand St.)—which proves that the neighborhood has room for everything, even a good off-pricer. For affordable basics, stop by **Madewell** (532 Broadway, between Prince and Spring sts.), a slightly edgier sister to J. Crew.

Before those of you in the know start thinking SoHo is going to the dogs, or isn't worth your time because you hate designer labels, shuffle over to Lafayette Street, where much of the new excitement in SoHo is coming from. Lots of little home-furnishings boutiques are opening up here in the cheaper real estate to the east, and SoHo excels in the home-decor market (see chapter 10).

Don't let the scant number of listings below throw you: I could do a whole book on SoHo alone, since just about every store of note has a branch in these environs, many of them flagships or showcases. But to simplify things, for example, I have not listed **Eileen Fisher** (395 West Broadway, between Spring and Broome sts.) below since there are many pages of this book devoted to her work. (See p. 110 for more on Fisher.)

You should devote at least a whole day to SoHo, and you should consider your visit an event, a time to celebrate retail at its best. When referring to addresses in this or any guide, keep in mind that stores in SoHo open and close at such a rapid pace that you'll probably do better just wandering and enjoying.

Note: Stores tend to open at 11am or later in these parts. *Warning:* I recently came down here on a Sunday afternoon and left screaming—it was a zoo.

Take the C or E to Spring Street/Sixth Avenue, the 6 to Spring Street/Lafayette Street, or the R or W to Prince Street/Broadway.

AMORE PACIFIC
114 Spring St., between Mercer and Greene sts.

This looks like a spa, but it also sells beauty and skin-care products from Korea—sublime, expensive, and worth every penny. The cult brand is sold uptown at Bergdorf's. See p. 251 for more. ✆ **212/966-0400.** www.amorepacific.com.

ANTHROPOLOGIE
375 West Broadway, between Broome and Spring sts.

See p. 101 for details on this store; I mention it here because I've rarely met an Anthropologie store I could resist. *Web Tip:* Anthropologie has a huge online catalog and will ship to 34 countries worldwide. ✆ **212/343-7070.** www.anthropologie.com.

CATHERINE MALANDRINO
468 Broome St., between Greene and Mercer sts.

Catherine is the new best friend (of the moment) of every fashion editor in town. Clothing here is very Gallic, whimsical, and *charmant. Web Tip:* Sizes run very, very small; order one to two sizes larger than you would normally wear. ✆ **212/925-6765.** www.catherinemalandrino.com.

CB2
451 Broadway, between Grand and Canal sts.

Hipper spinoff of home style maven Crate & Barrel. *Best Bets:* Great furnishings for a first apartment; love the orange plastic clothespin chopsticks, $3.95. ✆ **212/219-1454.** www.cb2.com.

HOTEL VENUS
382 West Broadway, between Spring and Broome sts.

Silly you, it's not a hotel at all! Patricia Field has long been one of the most famous names in downtown fashion (you know her as the woman who pulled all the clothes for *Sex and the City*). Her SoHo shop sells affordable funky styles—think color and disco. © 212/966-4066. www.patriciafield.com.

KATE'S PAPERIE
561 Broadway, between Prince and Spring sts.

This SoHo shop sums up all that SoHo was ever meant to be. Kate's sells assorted handmade and art papers by the sheet, notebooks, stationery, artsy-fartsy this and that, rubber stamps, and even papier-mâché. It's sheer heaven. Not cheap, but great fun and very sophisticated. *Best Bets:* The gift wrap and ribbon selection; see p. 22. © 212/941-9816. www.katespaperie.com.

KIRNA ZABÊTE
96 Greene St., between Prince and Spring sts.

This hot boutique space has fashionistas drooling over its Euro designer names, many of them difficult to find in the U.S. The downstairs features lotions, potions, and aromatherapy notions. The upstairs is full-service, with everything from clothes to shoes to accessories. Kirna Zabête is famous for cool pieces that have style but also whimsy, from either a famous designer such as Balenciaga or a not-so-well-known member of the Antwerp group. © 212/941-9656. www.kirnazabete.com.

LAFCO/SANTA MARIA NOVELLA
285 Lafayette St., near Houston St.

If you can't get to the centuries-old *farmacia* in Firenze for Santa Maria Novella beauty products, then a trip to SoHo is in order. This store also offers Italian design for the home in a wow setting—ranging from furniture to tabletop objects. It's a good stop for gifts, if you're willing to pay $11 and up for a bar of soap. © 212/925-0001. www.lafcony.com.

MORGANE LE FAY
67 Wooster St., between Broome and Spring sts.

I saw the dreamiest chiffon dresses in the world here, including some in white that would make magnificent wedding gowns. Some things that I loved were $180 and others were $630. Ouch. Still, the shop is pure heaven—everything you want a stylish, secret, SoHo source to be. There's also a Madison Avenue location. ✆ **212/219-7672.** www.morganelefay.com.

MUJI
455 Broadway, between Grand and Howard sts.

This Tokyo-based megastore specializes in sleek housewares that design purists adore for their simple aesthetics. The line was formerly carried exclusively by MoMA shops in the U.S. ✆ **212/334-2002.** www.muji.com.

PRADA
575 Broadway, near Prince St.

Yeah, yeah, I know, I said I wasn't gonna list the obvious. This flagship store is anything but normal, though, and a must-see by anyone interested in architecture, interior design, retail theory, or moments of thunderstruck wonder. It was designed by Rem Koolhaas. ✆ **212/334-8888.** www.prada.com.

PYLONES
69 Spring St., near Crosby St.

This French chain of novelty/gift shops sells whimsical, offbeat, and odd pieces that will make you smile. ***Best Bets:*** Great source for unusual pet-inspired items. Who doesn't need a doggie door stop ($12), or paper clips in the shape of dog bones ($10)? ✆ **212/431-3244.** www.pylones-usa.com.

TEMPERLEY
453–455 Broome St., 2nd floor, at Mercer St.

Alice Temperly's romantic '70s-inspired dresses and separates are worth the climb to this airy loft boutique. In addition, you'll find accessories including handbags and bed linens. Prices are slashed up to 60% during sales. ⓒ **212/219-2929**. www. temperlylondon.com.

YASO
62 Grand St., between West Broadway and Wooster St.

Yaso specializes in one-size, flowing dresses and charming hats, and it also boasts a new line of home goods. The dresses cost close to $200 and are usually made of luxurious fabrics. ⓒ **212/941-8506**.

Eats

Mercer Kitchen (Mercer Hotel, 99 Prince St., at Mercer St.; ⓒ **212/966-5454**) is part of the Jean-Georges group and offers great fresh-made pizza. It boasts a lively brunch scene on Sunday. www.jean-georges.com. See p. 64 for more ideas.

CANAL STREET/CHINATOWN

While you're in SoHo, you might want to wander south on Broadway until you reach Canal Street, at the edge of Chinatown, where all the fake designer goods in the world are sold.

I don't actually suggest that you buy any of this junk, unless you're looking for joke gifts; but friends from Europe love it here and teenagers seem to think that these items ("name brand" handbags, watches, sunglasses, and more) are musthaves. Trust me, very little down here will fool anyone. This is seedy fun for those who enjoy down-market atmosphere and want to buy fake merchandise. Not for blue bloods.

But wait, before I toss you out on your fake Chanel earrings, let's talk about the Chinese department store **Pearl River Mart** (477 Broadway, between Grand and Broome sts.). I've seen better in San Francisco and much better in Hong Kong. Nonetheless, it is so popular that it now has added a third floor to expand its Home Department. **New Kan Man** (200 Canal St., at Mulberry St.) is good for exotic teas, and at **Lin Sister**

Herb Shop (4 Bowery St., at Doyers St.) diagnosticians will custom blend herbs to treat what ails you.

If you don't walk here from SoHo, take the A, C, E, J, M, N, Q, R, W, Z, 1, or 6 train to Canal Street.

Eats

Chow down on six dumplings that come with a free egg roll—pick any of the zillions of Chinese restaurants in the area. For a break, stop at **Vivi Bubble Tea** (49 Bayard St., between Bowery and Mott sts.) and treat yourself to a Taiwanese tapioca pearl drink made with fresh fruit.

NOLITA

Although the name of this area is derived from the term "North of Little Italy," the area is also adjacent to SoHo. My guess is that the two will soon merge.

The defining feature of the whole neighborhood is that store owners in this part of town make real personal statements with their spaces, much as if their boutiques were art galleries. Here, the owner is the star of the show—and often the sole employee. If you're thinking low prices, forget it. If you're thinking cutting-edge chic, you've come to the right place.

To get here, take the 6 to Spring Street/Lafayette Street. The best streets in the area are Elizabeth and Mott in the blocks from Houston to Prince.

CALYPSO
280 Mott St., between Houston and Prince sts.

Christiane Celle has been so successful with her boho-hippie-chic fashions that she has also opened up stores uptown. In addition, she owns the nearby Calypso Bijoux (252 Mott St.) and several shops in SoHo, including Calypso Kids and Home (407 Broom St.), Calypso Enfant & Bebe (426 Broome St.), and Calypso Home (199 Lafayette St.; p. 257). © **212/965-0990**. www.calypso-celle.com.

CATH KIDSTON
201 Mulberry St., between Kenmare and Spring sts.

Cath Kidston, the British textile designer with several shops in London, has finally come to the U.S. Her work is an update of 1930s kitsch. *Best Bets:* This is a great source for oilcloth fabric in bright prints with polka dots, flowers, and tablecloth plaids, priced at $40 per meter. © **212/343-0223**. www.cath kidston.co.uk.

SIGERSON MORRISON
28 Prince St., at Mott St.

You'll find one of the city's best selections of ballet flats and other designer women's shoes in this shop. Then head around the corner to their annex (242 Mott St.) for handbags. © **212/ 219-3893**. www.sigersonmorrison.com.

UNIS
226 Elizabeth St., at Prince St.

Eunice Lee keeps her clothing line basic; there are several jacket styles including one military coat and a few trousers in neutral colors. The laid-back everyday looks are within reach of most wallets. *Web Tip:* The website is not worth your time; the photos are artsy-fartsy and don't show any details of the clothing. © **212/431-5533**. www.unisnewyork.com.

ZERO MARIA CORNEJO
225 Mott St., between Prince and Spring sts.

Maria Cornejo, icon to the stylish street fashion crowd, calls her work "conceptual fashion." (Conceptual fashion means that if you're over 30, you're too old.) Worship here and tell people you've been—you can't talk the talk without visiting this store. © **212/925-3825**. www.mariacornejo.com.

This is a hot area of town for savvy shoppers— ... SoHo and far more original. Nolita borders on Houston Street, so you have to cross over Houston to get to NoHo (shorthand for "North of Houston").

Lafayette Street runs through both NoHo and SoHo, so don't get confused. By train, take the 6 to Bleecker Street.

BOND 07
7 Bond St., between Broadway and Lafayette St.

This is one of the shrines to alternative retail, fashion, and tight pants. It helped make the street what it is today. © **212/677-8487**. www.selimaoptique.com.

SoHo Style Near NoHo: Aaron & Jenny Do Lafayette Street

Triple Five Soul (290 Lafayette St., between Houston and Prince sts.) is one of the coolest clothing lines in stores today. The T-shirts, jeans, sport coats, messenger bags, jackets, and hoodies always push the boundaries of design in a unique and interesting direction. The SoHo store has a huge selection and a few healthy discounts. Strongly recommended.

The creators of one of New York's finest underground magazines also own the **Vice Store** (252 Lafayette St., between Prince and Spring sts.). The free magazine, best known for its hilarious "Do's and Don'ts" section, is always on the cutting edge of new trends in the city, be they in fashion or music, and this SoHo store is just the same. Loud indie rock blares as you look through racks of ridiculously priced denim and sneakers. The sale rack at the front of the store can be pretty reasonable—it was home to the cheapest Evisu Genes I've ever seen (which were still ridiculously expensive).

DARYL K
1 Bond St., between Lafayette St. and Bowery.

The grandma of downtown, and the first tenant to really make Bond Street worth the trip, Daryl K is known to dress celebs and rock stars. Daryl K also wholesales and is sold in a few hip SoHo boutiques. *Web Tip:* I found great prices online; the dress I ordered was marked down from $325 to $105. © **212/ 529-8790.** www.darylk.com.

TRIBECA

This one stands for the "Triangle Below Canal Street." TriBeCa is a funkier version of SoHo, with less retail and a much less commercial feel. TriBeCa is just a stone's throw from the West Village, so you have no excuse not to visit this neighborhood!

To get here, take the 1 to Franklin Street/Varick Street.

BAKER TRIBECA
129 Hudson St., at Beach St.

Baker Furniture is as mainstream and highbrow as it gets—so this outpost really signals the arrival of a neighborhood that will become a powerful force in the spending of downtown dollars. Although the line is known for traditional looks, it includes contemporary pieces and 1930s-inspired designs from Barbara Barry. © **212/343-2956.** www.bakerfurniture.com.

ISSEY MIYAKE
119 Hudson St., near N. Moore St.

The shop carries the designer's Issey Miyake, Fete, Pleats Please, HaaT, and me Issey Miyake/Cauliflower collections. This you-gotta-see-it space was designed in conjunction with Frank Gehry. © **212/226-0100.** www.isseymiyake.com.

Eats

Frankly, I don't usually find enough serious shopping in TriBeCa to end up eating a meal here, but there are quite a few well-known restaurants in the area, including Japanese hot spot **Nobu** (105 Hudson St., at Franklin St.; ✆ 212/219-0500); David Bouley's **Danube** (30 Hudson St., near Duane St.; ✆ 212/791-3771); **Tribeca Grill** (375 W. Greenwich, at Franklin St.; ✆ 212/941-3900), owned by Robert DeNiro; and the bistro **Odeon** (145 West Broadway, at Thomas St.; ✆ 212/233-0507), which helped start the area on its rise to trendiness.

WEST VILLAGE

Also known as Greenwich Village, or even the Village, this is the area west of Fifth Avenue, from 14th Street to Houston Street, which actually comprises several neighborhoods woven into a warren of little Colonial streets.

There's teen heaven on West 8th Street (very touristy); there's a gay and lesbian area around Christopher and West 4th streets; and there's the funky antiques-store-heavy part of town, mostly on Bleecker Street (my main drag), which boasts a nice variety of design, antiques, clothing, gift, and aromatherapy shops. You'll see a few name brands, such as bath-and-beauty people **Fresh** (388 Bleecker St., near Perry St.), along with the antiques shop that many knew as Pierre Deux—now called **Les Pierre Antiques** (369 Bleecker St., between Charles and Perry sts.) since both of the Pierres have passed on. You'll find designers **Ralph Lauren** (380 and 381 Bleecker St., between Charles and Perry sts.), **James Perse** (361 Bleecker St., between Charles and Perry sts.), **Cynthia Rowley** (376 Bleecker St., between Charles and Perry sts.), **Marc Jacobs** (three shops at 382 and 385 Bleecker St., both at Perry St.; and 298 W. 4th St., at Bank St.), and **Lulu Guinness** (384 Bleecker St., between Perry and W. 11th sts.). Coach has opened its first **Coach Legacy** boutique (372 Bleecker St., at Perry St.). Check out the

Personal West Village Bliss

A stroll up Bleecker Street is a lesson in NYC chic. Start your shopping spree at the intersection of Christopher and Bleecker streets, beginning with **Satya Jewelry** for ornate Indian-inspired pendants (330 Bleecker St.). **Blush** (333 Bleecker St.), a little boutique directly across the street, is also worth a visit. Continue along Bleecker Street, which is lined with designer stores: **Juicy Couture** (368 Bleecker St.), **Cynthia Rowley** (376 Bleecker St.), and **Lulu Guinness** (394 Bleecker St.) are just a few. I like **Intermix** (365 Bleecker St.) and **Olive and Bette's** (384 Bleecker St.) for young, trendy, and bright clothes.

Head back to West 10th Street to get to my favorite neighborhood store: **Housing Works** (245 W. 10th St.). This branch of the NYC thrift shop chain happens to have a fantastic selection of high-end clothing; I purchased a pair of Citizens of Humanity jeans for $25, and a (new!) Kenneth Cole skirt for a mere $20.

Other worthwhile stores in the neighborhood are **Brooklyn Industries** (500 Hudson St., at Christopher St.), the ultimate entry into Brooklyn hipsterdom; **[hus]: a scandinavian store** (11 Christopher St.), for all things Scandinavian; and **Diana Broussard** (22 Christopher St.), for elegant, sleek shoes. Wander around the quiet streets of the West Village, and you're bound to stumble on some fantastic find.

—by Jennifer Polland

"big willy" boxers at **Lord Willy's** (102 Christopher St., at Bleecker St.) and don't miss **Condomania** (351 Bleecker St., between Charles and W. 10th sts.) for condoms, party favors, and cheap laughs. At **Ludivine** (172 W. 4th St., near Jones St.), you can design a custom handbag, which will be ready within a week.

The Far West Village, from Perry to Horatio and Hudson to West, is still slightly shabby, but with the quirky charm comes creative retail and unique finds. **Castor & Pollux** (238 W. 10th St., between Hudson and Bleecker sts.) caters to the sophisticates who wear designs from Philip Lim, Mint, and Sonia Rykiel.

To get here, take the 1 train to Christopher Street.

Eats

Cornelia Street Café (29 Cornelia St., between Bleecker and W. 4th sts.; © 212/989-9319) is open all day and evening for meals, snacks, and people-watching, and offers a full schedule of music, theater, poetry readings, and other entertainment. **Extra Virgin** (259 W. 4th St., between Perry and Charles sts.; © 212/691-9359) serves good Mediterranean fare and great specialty cocktails. For dessert, try the famed cupcakes at **Magnolia Bakery** (401 Bleecker St., at W. 11th St.; © 212/462-2572). Prepare to wait in a line that stretches down the street and around the corner.

SOUTH STREET SEAPORT

I count this as a neighborhood, even though it consists of only a couple malls and a strip of stores. Built around the old Fulton Fish Market, South Street Seaport is wedged against the water on the east side of Lower Manhattan. Many of the shops are branches of chains, such as **J. Crew, Sharper Image, Brookstone,** and **Abercrombie & Fitch.** There's also a branch of the **Metropolitan Museum of Art Store.** The Wall Streeters are particularly dense during lunchtime; visitors take over on weekends. The maritime museum here is interesting, especially for kids.

To get here, take the 2, 3, 4, or 5 train to Fulton Street.

WALL STREET

In case you haven't noticed, Lower Manhattan is booming. It's bouncing back with lush parkland, new restaurants, and the city's hottest real estate. This isn't your father's Wall Street—forget the three-piece suits and Statue of Liberty gawkers—luxury shopping has arrived! **Tiffany & Co** (37 Wall St., between Nassau and William sts.) has created a contemporary emporium that's a departure from other Tiffany stores; your favorite baubles are displayed in glass cases stretching from floor to ceiling. There's a large **Borders** (100 Broadway, at Pearl St.), and don't miss the new **Hermès** boutique (15 Broad St., near Wall St.). **Century 21** (22 Cortlandt St., between Church St. and Broadway), the city's best off-pricer, continues to be worth the schlep.

Take the R or W to Cortlandt Street.

LOWER EAST SIDE

There's no question that the Lower East Side is changing, that it's no longer the discount area it once was . . . but the next SoHo? Not yet. It's quickly becoming an area dense with vintage clothes and young designers who can't yet afford the high rents in neighboring SoHo, Nolita, and the West Village.

Take the J, M, or Z train to Essex Street/Delancey Street, or the F or V to Second Avenue or Delancey Street.

A. W. KAUFMAN
73 Orchard St., between Broome and Grand sts.

If you are hooked on fancy-schmancy American, Japanese, or European underwear, you just might find it significantly discounted here. Harking back to the old-fashioned way: You don't touch the merchandise and you can't try it on. You know what you want, you ask for it, you pay for it. Cash is good. ✆ **212/226-1629.** www.awkaufman.com.

FINE & KLEIN
119 Orchard St., between Rivington and Delancey sts.

While Fine & Klein is one of the most famous stores in the area, and generations of women have been coming here to buy handbags for, well, generations, I find this place singularly boring, and the crowds of people make me crazy. However, there are many name brands and good buys. *Insider's Secret:* The staff here will be rude to you for free. *Best Bets:* There's a huge stock of a line called Sharif, which is one of my favorites (it's also sold at Neiman Marcus). Normally in the $300 to $500 range, you might find them priced at around $200 at F&K. ✆ 212/674-6720.

TG-170
170 Ludlow St., between Houston and Stanton sts.

The hottest rage for the trendies, this shop showcases up-and-coming clothing and bag designers. Some think it's great, but I am too old for this. ✆ 212/995-8660. www.tg170.com.

BROOKLYN

In having checked out the Brooklyn shopping scene over the years, I can tell you that there are some lovely areas and the shopping is getting better all the time. But the shopping is for locals. I do not think a tourist visiting Manhattan for a short stay, or even an international visitor wanting to learn all about the U.S., would gain too much from a day spent in Brooklyn.

Don't get me wrong, I understand that many of the young people who live in downtown Manhattan would rather go to Brooklyn for a shopping adventure than uptown Manhattan. Brooklyn has everything from a good-size **Target** to its own **Century 21.** There are also certain 'hoods that call out for attention.

If you think of Brooklyn as simply a place to shop big-box stores or visit for a day, you could be wrong. Slowly, hotels are coming into the area, but get this, they offer prices as steep as on the other side of the East River. Hummmph.

NYC Geography 101

Manhattan is one of five boroughs that make up New York, New York. The largest of the five is Brooklyn, located directly east of the island of Manhattan and, get this, on the far side of the East River. I bet you could have guessed that one. The tip, or north shore, of Brooklyn is lateral with Midtown, the main arteries taking traffic to Brooklyn are lateral to the Financial Districts downtown, and then the borough continues to dip south, running across the bay from Staten Island. Because Brooklyn is so large and so spread out, you need to know what part you want to visit. Various 'hoods are developing at different rates and in different manners than other parts. Note that the area code for this distant shore is 718.

Getting Around

As already mentioned, Brooklyn is large and densely packed. To get around: (1) know the neighborhood you want to visit, and (2) find the appropriate subway with the understanding that few areas interconnect. Even if you have a car, you won't find this easy going.

101 Ethnic Brooklyn

Traditionally speaking, boroughs other than Manhattan have the ethnic neighborhoods and the foods and shopping that accompany melting-pot cultures. A large part of Brooklyn is now inhabited by Jewish immigrants from all over the world; the Caribbean neighborhoods are shrinking. Market buildings, which traditionally have housed vendors who sell the produce and foodstuffs from back home, are being forced out in the name of real estate growth. It's a new world, Goldie.

Vintage Brooklyn

Shoppers who want to buy used, gently worn, and vintage clothing flock to Brooklyn, which they say beats Manhattan in terms

---

Eats

SEA (114 N. 6th St., between Wythe Ave. and Berry St.; ℂ **718/384-8850**) serves Thai fusion in a fairy-tale garden setting, accompanied by the ambient music of some of Brooklyn's premier DJs.

---

of price and selection. Vintage stores dot all neighborhoods, particularly those where young folks live.

Billyburg

Aaron and Jenny lived in France after graduating from college. When they returned to the U.S., Aaron moved to Williamsburg. He (and every other 20-something just out of school) was among those getting in on the ground floor of a neighborhood in the middle of gentrification. This neighborhood has become so hip that it even has its own nickname. Today Williamsburg is often written as Billyburg.

Don't get confused about where the prime shopping is: East Williamsburg (which is basically Bushwick) has not had the makeover that Williamsburg proper has, and is not very fabulous. In Williamsburg proper, the south side is still slightly seedy; the north side is the hipster hangout and home to chic boutiques. In summer, you'll see outdoor merchants selling their wares along Bedford Avenue as if the street were one giant yard sale.

To get here, take the L train to Bedford Avenue, the first stop in Brooklyn. Exit the subway toward Bedford (not Driggs), and you will be between North 7th and North 8th streets. Bedford Avenue is where it's all happening right now . . . with some action moving to the side streets.

Atlantic Avenue

Atlantic Avenue is actually the center of commerce and a variety of types of retail in the heart of downtown-ish Brooklyn.

Many of the antiques shops that could no longer pay the rent in Manhattan have moved to one part of Atlantic Avenue. The street is incredibly long and houses many, many antiques stores of varying quality and price range. From Manhattan, take the F train to Bergen Street. Walk back along Smith Street and turn right onto Atlantic after 3 blocks. On weekends, there's a flea market–like affair set up by dealers for locals. The greatest concentration of antiques shops starts at Hoyt Street and continues along Atlantic Avenue for about 10 blocks.

But that's only the beginning of the energy. There's an entire mall (**Atlantic Terminal Mall**) with the usual mall suspects in stores and a very wide mix of shoppers. You'll also find a **Target** store here, and a handful of other off-pricers such as **Daffy's, DSW,** and **Marshalls.**

The Terminal Mall is in two sections and is connected to a slew of subway lines: 2, 3, 4, 5, B, D, M, N, and R. Watch this space for more on the Atlantic Yard Stadium.

Aaron & Jenny's Williamsburg

BEACON'S CLOSET
88 N. 11th St., near Wythe Ave., Brooklyn

This is Williamsburg's finest store for vintage clothing and music, with the best selection and the most reasonable prices. The converted warehouse is across the street from the Brooklyn Brewery (home to one of the smoothest pale ales in North America). It's divided into huge men's and women's sections; three racks of T-shirts are organized by color and usually sell for under $10. The used-music selection is also top-notch. There's another location in Park Slope. © **718/486-0816.** www.beaconscloset.com.

BROOKLYN INDUSTRIES
162 Bedford Ave., at N. 8th St., Brooklyn

BI has some of the biggest indie brands, along with its own in-house designer who creates T-shirts, hoodies, and hats. There are great '70s-looking underwear and pants for the ladies, plus a nice sale section with "Ten-Buck-Tees." This is also the place to buy the ubiquitous shirts and hoodies with BROOKLYN sewn across them. © **718/486-6464.** www. brooklynindustries.com.

SALVATION ARMY/GRANDMA'S (BEST) KEPT SECRET
176 Bedford Ave., at N. 7th St., Brooklyn

The Salvation Army on Bedford Avenue used to be called "Grandma's Kept Secret" until the owners realized their odd word omission and awkwardly added a carat (^) and the word "best" in small letters to their awning. Perhaps an effort to amend their original assertion of a hidden grandma, or of a grandma as a kept woman? Regardless, this store is home to the absolutely cheapest collection of vintage clothes you will find in the whole 'burg, plus a sizable array of cheap furniture. Good finds are usually hidden . . . just like Grandma once was . . . we think. © **718/388-9249.** www.salvation armyusa.org.

WILLIAMSBURG MINI MALL
218 Bedford Ave., at N. 5th St., Brooklyn

This is a conglomerate of cool known locally as the Mini Mall. Aside from shopping for books, electronics, and clothes, patrons can check their e-mail, take a yoga class, or sip some java at the fun sidewalk cafe. One standout is the **Mini Mini Market** (not a typo, folks; let's just call it the MMM), one of the kitschiest clothing shops for blocks. Most of its stock is girl-geared, but it also has a modest selection of men's attire, plus fabulous hats and bags, some sneakers, beauty products, and throwback toys. Two other notables inside the mall are the local wine shop and the local cheese shop, both owned by some of the friendliest people in the 'burg.

Brooklyn Flea

Brooklyn has long been an alternative neighborhood for antiquing—now it's got its own flea market, held at Fort Greene on Sundays, spring and fall. This flea market is more like a festival market with crafts vendors, food vendors, and the usual junk and salvage. It is located in the schoolyard of Bishop Laughlin Memorial High School, 176 Lafayette Ave. (between Clermont and Vanderbilt aves.). For Brooklyn activities go to www.brownstoner.com.

Fort Greene

BAM (Brooklyn Academy of Music) is the most famous resident of this district, but the new stuff is mostly eats. The residential areas are either brownstones or prewar buildings with solid architecture. To see the scene, check out DeKalb Avenue between Fort Greene Park and Pratt Institute (the famous art and design school). Then head over to Fulton Street, starting close to BAM and the various streets that fork away and even lead to Atlantic Avenue (see above).

DUMBO

This is another of New York's famous acronyms, standing for "Down Under the Manhattan Bridge Overpass." This part of Brooklyn is now less seedy, and the low rents have attracted all sorts of galleries and eats.

About 10 years ago, the concept got hot and many retailers found a place here; many of them have since left. **West Elm** (75 Front St., at Main St.), the catalog firm, has moved in and stayed. Chocolatier **Jacques Torres** has taken a bite of the 'hood, too (66 Water St.; ✆ 718/875-9772).

What's become really thrilling about the area is the large number of artist ateliers and galleries that have opened recently. The developer Two Trees Management is leasing space for low, low everyday prices, and the area is filling quickly. Watch these cobblestones.

To get here, take the F train to York Street.

Smith Street

Take the subway to Bergen Street to check out the new world of retail on Smith Street (from Atlantic Ave. to Carroll St.), which has several small stores that are branches of big-name retailers (**Lucky Brand Jeans, American Apparel**) and several cutie-pie boutiques (**Flight 001,** which also has stores in Manhattan). This area is being called BoCoCa because of its location near Boerum Hill, Cobble Hill, and Carroll Gardens. Smith Street is also known for its restaurants.

Chapter Eight

....

NEW YORK RESOURCES A TO Z

ACCESSORIES

....

Oh, boy. I could write a whole book just on the accessories available in New York. We'll start with a few orders of business:

- All department stores have accessories departments; most boutiques also sell them. Designer boutiques make their cash flow on fragrance and accessories, since few people can afford the clothes. Can't spring for the dress? Never mind, just buy the scarf.
- For our purposes, accessories include jewelry and fake jewelry. But also see the "Jewelry" section, later in this chapter.
- Shoes and bags have their own sections, too, later in this chapter.
- There has been a recent trend of jewelry stores selling their own lines of handbags—Bulgari, Tiffany, and Cartier are all on the bandwagon.
- The stuff sold on the streets not only is fake, but also may finance terrorists. You never know.

ADD

461 West Broadway, between Houston and Prince sts.
(Subway: C or E to Spring St.).

A tiny store packed to the gills with frills that you'll want to touch and try on and own. There are dozens of different brands here, most of which I'd never heard of. ℭ **212/539-1439.**

BOHKEE

1077 Third Ave., at 63rd St. (Subway: 4, 5, 6, N, R, or W to 59th St./Lexington Ave.).

This is New York correspondent Paul Baumrind's find—he says the one-of-a-kind evening bags are seriously impressive. ℭ **212/319-0707.**

LAILA ROWE

1031 Third Ave., at 61st St. (Subway: 4, 5, 6, N, R, or W to 59th St./Lexington Ave.); 424 West Broadway, between Prince and Spring sts. (Subway: C or E to Spring St.); multiple other locations.

Laila Rowe is packed with accessories for the chic, with an ethnic fashion twist and low, low prices. This is not teeny-bopper land: Per the recent trends, there's plenty of wood, fake jade, and rhinestone brooches. This is the stuff that looks like it was featured in fashion magazines, only with dime store price tags. There are over a dozen branches dotted around Manhattan. *Web Tip:* New arrivals are listed on the website daily; if you can't find it in the store, it's probably available online. ℭ **212/949-2276.** www.lailarowe.com.

LESPORTSAC

1065 Madison Ave., between 80th and 81st sts. (Subway: 4, 5, or 6 to 86th St.).

We're talking about carryalls, totes, and handbags, all great for travel. The range sold in the Madison Avenue shop is always ahead of what they get at discount shops and off-pricers, and ther chic. You can't beat the prices. There's 176 Spring St., near West Broadway. © **212/** *r*.lesportsac.com.

MARIKO

998 Madison Ave., between 77th and 78th sts. (Subway: 6 to 77th St.).

Fashion alert! This is one of my best secret finds. I bought the best earrings of my life here. Many swoon for the copies of the most prestigious names in jewelry—yep, copies. Fancy copies. There are 18-karat gold earrings, too, in the $850 price range, darling. In addition to the jewels, they sell Mycra Pac raincoats, the best lightweight travel coats in the world.

Best Bets: The designer look-alike earrings for just over $100 will fool anyone. Prices on fakes are not low, but the work is sublime and—dare I say it—somewhat funky. In other words, not reproductions of your average big names—instead, copies of Vedura, Elizabeth Gage, and the like. Very sophisticated. © **212/472-1176.**

RALPH LAUREN EYEWEAR

811 Madison Ave., near 68th St. (Subway: 6 to 68th St./Hunter College).

To further prove that Ralph has conquered the world, note his free-standing eyewear store. Opticians are available to fill your prescription, but no exams are given. © **212/988-4620.** www.polo.com.

RENE

786 Madison Ave., between 66th and 67th sts. (Subway: 6 to 68th St.).

Like Mariko's stock, Rene's is very chic, though not as flashy. You'll see jewelry made with semiprecious stones: earrings in the most-under-$500 price range, as well as copies of famous collections for $100 to $250. You'll get good value for your money here. Note the handbags, very well made but not inexpensive. ✆ **212/249-3001.**

SERMONETA
609–611 Madison Ave., near 58th St. (Subway: 4, 5, 6, N, R, or W to 59th St./Lexington Ave.).

International travelers know the Sermoneta name from Italy; this is one of the best glove manufacturers in the world. *Best Bets:* I buy the cashmere-lined gloves for about $60. They're available in over 30 colors. ✆ **212/319-5946.**

VBH
940 Madison Ave., between 74th and 75th sts. (Subway: 6 to 77th St.).

This place looks like an art gallery or a branch of the San Francisco retail store Gump's—everything in the store is for sale, although the specialty is leather goods. It's all sleek and expensive and worthy of a movie set. *Web Tip:* Don't waste your time logging on; this website is one page with absolutely no information. ✆ **212/717-9800.** www.vbh-luxury.com.

ZITOMER
965 Madison Ave., near 75th St. (Subway: 6 to 77th St.).

Zitomer's next-door annex is filled with accessories of all kinds—even pet accessories. The look is sort of Euro-glitter. There is another member of the Zitomer family, **ZChemists,** at 40 W. 57th St. ✆ **212/737-5560.** www.zitomer.com.

ACTIVE SPORTSWEAR & SPORTS GEAR

I refuse to list every major active-sportswear chain in Manhattan. However, some specialty retailers are fit for a (sporty) king.

If you need to make a quick purchase, there are branches of the chain **Sports Authority** at 845 Third Ave. (near 51st St.)

and 636 Sixth Ave. (near 19th St.). Also note that the various athletic-shoe companies have snazzy shops, such as **Niketown,** 6 E. 57th St. (near Fifth Ave.).

ADIDAS
610 Broadway, at Houston St. (Subway: B, D, F, or V to Broadway/Lafayette St.).

This German athletic brand is back in style, and the store will knock your socks off (bring Peds). ✆ **212/529-0081.** www. adidas.com.

BILLABONG
1515 Broadway, between 44th and 45th sts. (Subway: 1, 2, 3, 7, N, Q, R, or W to Times Sq./42nd St.).

The first U.S. store for this Australian brand of surfer clothes; its skateboard division is also represented. *Web Tip:* This website is cluttered and interactive, but once you find the clothing and click on an item, a "Where to Buy" link will appear. No online orders. ✆ **212/840-0249.** www.billabong.com.

BURTON
106 Spring St., at Mercer St. (Subway: R or W to Prince St.).

Skiwear and snowboard gear for the with-it crowd. ✆ **212/966-8068.** www.burton.com.

CAPEZIO
1650 Broadway, at 51st St., 2nd floor (Subway 1 to 50th St.); Outlet, 1776 Broadway, at 57th St., 2nd floor. (Subway: 1, A, B, C, or D to 59th St./Columbus Circle).

No longer for dancers only, Capezio makes great gear for Pilates devotees. Don't miss the outlet for discounts. Store: ✆ **212/245-2130.** Outlet: ✆ **212/586-5140.**

EASTERN MOUNTAIN SPORTS
591 Broadway, at Houston St. (Subway: B, D, F, or V to Broadway/Lafayette St.; or R or W to Prince St.).

Part of a large chain of active outfitters, EMS has one of its largest stores on the edge of SoHo. You can get all your ski-wear, fishing gear, and hiking supplies at this one-stop sporting-goods mart. © **212/966-8730.** www.ems.com.

ORVIS
522 Fifth Ave., at 44th St. (Subway: B, D, F, or V to 42nd St./Bryant Park).

If L. L. Bean came to Manhattan, he would probably check into Orvis. Orvis is famous for its fishing supplies, but also sells gift items (such as fishy ties), dog accessories, and chic fishing clothes that are rather suitable for weekending in the country or for visiting Balmoral. *Best Bets:* Orvis has a good selection of Barbour wax cotton and waterproof jackets. Prices range from $100 to $500. © **212/827-0698.** www.orvis.com.

PARAGON SPORTS
867 Broadway, at 18th St. (Subway: 4, 5, 6, L, N, Q, R, or W to 14th St./Union Sq.).

This sporting-goods supermarket is near Union Square and part of the new Lower Broadway hoopla. It's the kind of store you whirl through with a shopping basket—it truly has everything you can imagine. © **212/255-8036.** www.paragonsports.com.

PATAGONIA
101 Wooster St., between Prince and Spring sts. (Subway: C or E to Spring St.; or R or W to Prince St.).

Though technical products for specific sports make up most of the inventory here, this status brand also sells stylish active clothing for men, women, and kids. There's another branch at 426 Columbus Ave., near 81st Street. *Best Bets:* Patagonia's fleece selection remains the best in the world. It offers fleece outerwear in various weights, with most items reasonably priced under $200. ✆ **212/343-1776.** www.patagonia.com.

BEAUTY & BEYOND

See chapter 9 for beauty resources.

BIG NAMES IN FASHION

Manhattan is packed with showcase shops that feature the creations of the world's top designers. For those who shop in these stores, the names, the faces, the looks, and the prices stay more or less the same. Therefore, I list only addresses for the sources in this section.

Please note that many of these designers have recently opened or are in the process of opening stores downtown. Also note that because of the amount of available real estate, the big names move around like mad and many stores that haven't moved have expanded or re-created themselves. (*Tip:* The quickest way to see a lot of brand names is always at a department store.)

American Big Names

Some of the big names listed below are described elsewhere in the book; others are such ubiquitous brands that no explanation is needed.

ANNA SUI
113 Greene St., between Prince and Spring sts. (Subway: R or W to Prince St.).
✆ **212/941-8406.** www.annasui.com.

CALVIN KLEIN
654 Madison Ave., at 60th St. (Subway: 4, 5, 6, N, R, or W to 59th St./Lexington Ave.).
© **212/292-9000.** www.calvinklein.com.

DIANE VON FURSTENBERG
874 Washington St., at 14th St. (Subway: A, C, E, or L to 14th St./Eighth Ave.).
© **646/486-4800.** www.dvf.com.

DKNY DONNA KARAN NEW YORK
655 Madison Ave., at 60th St. (Subway: 4, 5, 6, N, R, or W to 59th St./Lexington Ave.).
© **212/223-3569.** www.dkny.com.

420 West Broadway, near Spring St. (Subway: C or E to Spring St.; or R or W to Prince St.).
© **646/613-1100.** www.dkny.com.

DONNA KARAN
819 Madison Ave., near 68th St. (Subway: 6 to 68th St./ Hunter College).
© **212/861-1001.** www.donnakaran.com.

MARC JACOBS
163 Mercer St., between Houston and Prince sts. (Subway: R or W to Prince St.).
© **212/343-1490.** www.marcjacobs.com.

385 Bleecker St., near Perry St. (Subway: A, C, E, or L to 14th St./Eighth Ave.).
© **212/924-6126.** www.marcjacobs.com.

403 Bleecker St., at W. 11th St. (Subway: A, C, E, or L to 14th St./Eighth Ave.).
© **212/924-0026.** www.marcjacobs.com.

RALPH LAUREN
*867 Madison Ave., at 72nd St. (Subway: 6 to 68th St./
Hunter College).*
© **212/606-2100.** www.polo.com.

*888 Madison Ave., at 72nd St. (Subway: 6 to 68th St./
Hunter College).*
© **212/434-8000.** www.polo.com.

*380 Bleecker St., near Perry St. (Subway: A, C, E, or L to
14th St./Eighth Ave.).*
© **212/645-5513.** www.polo.com.

*381 Bleecker St., near Perry St. (Subway: A, C, E, or L to
14th St./Eighth Ave.).*
© **646/638-0684.** www.polo.com.

ST. JOHN
*665 Fifth Ave., at 53rd St. (Subway: E or V to Fifth Ave./
53rd St.).*
© **212/755-5252.** www.stjohnknits.com.

TORY BURCH
*257 Elizabeth St., between Houston and Prince sts.
(Subway: B, D, F, or V to Broadway/Lafayette St.).*
© **212/334-3000.** www.toryburch.com.

European & Japanese Big Names

You will probably recognize most of the names on this who's-who-of-international-fashion list.

AKRIS
*835 Madison Ave., near 69th St. (Subway: 6 to 68th
St./Hunter College).*
© **212/717-1170.** www.akris.ch.

ALEXANDER MCQUEEN
417 W. 14th St., near Ninth Ave. (Subway: A, C, E, or L to 14th St./Eighth Ave.).
© **212/645-1797.** www.alexandermcqueen.com.

ASPREY
853 Madison Ave., between 70th and 71st sts. (Subway: 6 to 68th St.).
© **212/688-1811.** www.asprey.com.

A/X ARMANI EXCHANGE
645 Fifth Ave., near 51st St. (Subway: E or V to Fifth Ave./53rd St.).
© **212/980-3037.** www.armaniexchange.com.

568 Broadway, at Prince St. (Subway: R or W to Prince St.).
© **212/431-6000.** www.armaniexchange.com.

129 Fifth Ave., at 20th St. (Subway: R or W to 23rd St.).
© **212/254-7230.** www.armaniexchange.com.

Time Warner Center, 10 Columbus Circle (Subway: A, B, C, D, or 1 to 59th St./Columbus Circle).
© **212/823-9321.** www.armaniexchange.com.

BALENCIAGA
542 W. 22nd St., between Tenth and Eleventh aves. (Subway: C or E to 23rd St.).
© **212/206-0872.** www.balenciaga.com.

BALLY
628 Madison Ave., at 59th St. (Subway: 4, 5, 6, N, R, or W to 59th St./Lexington Ave.).
© **212/751-9082.** www.bally.com.

BOTTEGA VENETA
699 Fifth Ave., between 54th and 55th sts. (Subway: E or V to Fifth Ave./53rd St.).
© **212/371-5511.** www.bottegaveneta.com.

BURBERRY
9 E. 57th St., between Fifth and Madison aves. (Subway: N, R, or W to Fifth Ave./59th St.).
© **212/407-7100.** www.burberry.com.

131 Spring St., near Greene St. (Subway: C or E to Spring St.; or R or W to Prince St.).
© **212/925-9300.** www.burberry.com.

CELINE
667 Madison Ave., near 61st St. (Subway: 4, 5, 6, N, R, or W to 59th St./Lexington Ave.).
© **212/486-9700.** www.celine.com.

CHANEL
15 E. 57th St., between Fifth and Madison aves. (Subway: N, R, or W to Fifth Ave./59th St.).
© **212/355-5050.** www.chanel.com.

139 Spring St., at Wooster St. (Subway: C or E to Spring St.; or R or W to Prince St.).
© **212/334-0055.** www.chanel.com.

737 Madison Ave., near 64th St. (Subway: 6 to 68th St./ Hunter College).
© **212/535-5505.** www.chanel.com.

CHLOE
850 Madison Ave., at 70th St. (Subway: 6 to 68th St./ Hunter College).
© **212/717-8220.** www.chloe.com.

CHRISTIAN DIOR
21 E. 57th St., between Fifth and Madison aves. (Subway: N, R, or W to Fifth Ave./59th St.).
© **212/931-2950.** www.dior.com.

CHRISTIAN LACROIX
36 E. 57th St., between Fifth and Madison aves. (Subway: N, R, or W to Fifth Ave./59th St.).
© **212/753-2569.** www.christian-lacroix.fr.

COMME DES GARÇONS
520 W. 22nd St., near Tenth Ave. (Subway: C or E to 23rd St.).
© **212/604-9200.**

D&G
434 West Broadway, between Prince and Spring sts. (Subway: C or E to Spring St.; or R or W to Prince St.).
© **212/965-8000.** www.dolcegabbana.it.

DOLCE & GABBANA
825 Madison Ave., near 69th St. (Subway: 6 to 68th St./Hunter College).
© **212/249-4100.** www.dolcegabbana.it.

EMANUEL UNGARO
792 Madison Ave., at 67th St. (Subway: 6 to 68th St./Hunter College).
© **212/249-4090.** www.ungaro.com.

EMILIO PUCCI
701 Fifth Ave., near 54th St. (Subway: E or V to Fifth Ave./53rd St.).
© **212/230-1135.** www.emiliopucci.com.

24 E. 64th St., between Madison and Fifth aves. (Subway: F to Lexington Ave./63rd St.).
© **212/752-4777.** www.emiliopucci.com.

EMPORIO ARMANI
601 Madison Ave., between 57th and 58th sts. (Subway: 4, 5, 6, N, R, or W to 59th St./Lexington Ave.).
© **212/317-0800.** www.emporioarmani.com.

410 West Broadway, at Spring St. (Subway: C or E to Spring St.; or R or W to Prince St.).
© **646/613-8099.** www.emporioarmani.com.

ERMENEGILDO ZEGNA
663 Fifth Ave., between 52nd and 53rd sts. (Subway: E or V to Fifth Ave./53rd St.).
© **212/421-4488.** www.zegna.com.

ESCADA
715 Fifth Ave., near 55th St. (Subway: N, R, or W to Fifth Ave./59th St.).
© **212/755-2200.** www.escada.com.

ETRO
720 Madison Ave., near 64th St. (Subway: 6 to 68th St./ Hunter College).
© **212/317-9096.** www.etro.com.

FENDI
677 Fifth Ave., near 53rd St. (Subway: E or V to Fifth Ave./ 53rd St.).
© **212/759-4646.** www.fendi.com.

GIORGIO ARMANI/ARMANI COUTURE
760 Madison Ave., at 65th St. (Subway: 6 to 68th St./ Hunter College).
© **212/988-9191.** www.giorgioarmani.com.

GUCCI
725 Fifth Ave., at 56th St. (Subway: E or V to Fifth Ave./ 53rd St.).
© **212/826-2600.** www.gucci.com.

840 Madison Ave., near 70th St. (Subway: 6 to 68th St./ Hunter College).
© **212/717-2619.** www.gucci.com.

HERMES
691 Madison Ave., at 62nd St. (Subway: N, R, or W to Fifth Ave./59th St.).
© **212/751-3181.** www.hermes.com.

15 Broad St., at Wall St. (Subway: 4 or 5 to Wall St.).
© **212/785-3030.** www.hermes.com.

ISSEY MIYAKE
802 Madison Ave., between 67th and 68th sts. (Subway: 6 to 68th St./Hunter College).
© **212/439-7822.** www.isseymiyake.com.

119 Hudson St., near N. Moore St. (Subway: 1 to Franklin St.).
© **212/226-0100.** www.isseymiyake.com.

JIL SANDER
1042 Madison Ave., between 79th and 80th sts. (Subway: 6 to 77th St.).
© **212/838-6100.** www.jilsander.com.

KRIZIA
769 Madison Ave., near 66th St. (Subway: 6 to 68th St./ Hunter College).
© **212/879-1211.** www.krizia.it.

LA PERLA
803 Madison Ave., between 67th and 68th sts. (Subway: 6 to 68th St./Hunter College).
© **212/570-0050.** www.laperla.com.

93 Greene St., near Prince St. (Subway: R or W to Prince St.).
© **212/219-0999.** www.laperla.com.

425 W. 14th St., near Ninth Ave. (Subway: A, C, E, or L to 14th St./Eighth Ave.).
© **212/242-6662.** www.laperla.com.

LOUIS FERAUD

717 Madison Ave., at 63rd St. (Subway: N, R, or W to Fifth Ave./59th St.).
© **212/980-1919.**

LOUIS VUITTON

1 E. 57th St., at Fifth Ave. (Subway: F to 57th St.).
© **212/758-8877.** www.louisvuitton.com.

116 Greene St., between Prince and Spring sts. (Subway: R or W to Prince St.).
© **212/274-9090.** www.louisvuitton.com.

MAX MARA

813 Madison Ave., at 68th St. (Subway: 6 to 68th St./Hunter College).
© **212/879-6100.**

450 West Broadway, at Prince St. (Subway: R or W to Prince St.).
© **212/674-1817.**

MISSONI

1009 Madison Ave., near 78th St. (Subway: 6 to 77th St.).
© **212/517-9339.** www.missoni.it.

NICOLE FARHI

10 E. 60th St., between Fifth and Madison aves. (Subway: N, R, or W to Fifth Ave./59th St.).
© **212/223-8811.** www.nicolefarhi.com.

NICOLE FARHI/202

75 Ninth Ave., near 16th St. (Subway: A, C, E, or L to 14th St./Eighth Ave.).
Combination eatery and clothing/home-decor shop. © **646/638-0115.** www.nicolefarhi.com.

PLEATS PLEASE ISSEY MIYAKE
128 Wooster St., at Prince St. (Subway: R or W to Prince St.).
© **212/226-3600.** www.pleatsplease.com.

PRADA
45 E. 57th St., between Park and Madison aves. (Subway: 4, 5, 6, N, R, or W to 59th St./Lexington Ave.).
© **212/308-2332.** www.prada.com.

724 Fifth Ave., near 56th St. (Subway: E or V to Fifth Ave./ 53rd St.).
© **212/664-0010.** www.prada.com.

841 Madison Ave., at 70th St. (Subway: 6 to 68th St./ Hunter College).
© **212/327-4200.** www.prada.com.

575 Broadway, near Prince St. (Subway: R or W to Prince St.).
© **212/334-8888.** www.prada.com.

ROBERTO CAVALLI
711 Madison Ave., at 63rd St. (Subway: 4, 5, 6, F, N, R, or W to 59th St.).
© **212/755-7722.** www.robertocavalli.com.

SALVATORE FERRAGAMO
655 Fifth Ave., at 52nd St. (Subway: E or V to Fifth Ave./ 53rd St.).
© **212/759-3822.** www.ferragamo.com.

SONIA RYKIEL
849 Madison Ave., near 70th St. (Subway: 6 to 68th St./ Hunter College).
© **212/396-3060.** www.soniarykiel.com.

STELLA McCARTNEY
429 W. 14th St., between Ninth and Tenth aves. (Subway: A, C, E, or L to 14th St./Eighth Ave.).
© 212/255-1556. www.stellamccartney.com.

3.1 PHILLIP LIM
115 Mercer St., between Spring and Prince sts. (Subway: N, R, or W to Prince St.).
© 212/334-1160. www.31philliplim.com.

VALENTINO
747 Madison Ave., at 65th St. (Subway: 6 to 68th St./ Hunter College).
© 212/772-6969. www.valentino.it.

YOHJI YAMAMOTO
103 Grand St., at Mercer St. (Subway: 6, A, C, E, J, M, N, Q, R, W, or Z to Canal St.).
© 212/966-9066. www.yohjiyamamoto.co.jp.

1 Gansevoort, at 13th St. (Subway: A, C, E, or L to 14th St./Eighth Ave.).
© 212/966-3615. www.yohjiyamamoto.co.jp.

Y-3 (YOHJI & ADIDAS)
317 W. 13th St., at Gansevoort St. (Subway: A, C, E, or L to 14th St./Eighth Ave.).
© 917/546-8677. www.adidas.com/y-3.

YVES SAINT LAURENT
3 E. 57th St., near Fifth Ave. (Subway: N, R, or W to Fifth Ave./59th St.).
© 212/980-2970. www.ysl.com.

855 Madison Ave., near 71st St. (Subway: 6 to 68th St./ Hunter College).
© 212/988-3821. www.ysl.com.

BOOKS

In addition to the choices below, there are the big chains: **Barnes & Noble,** with scads of locations including a popular outlet opposite Union Square, 33 E. 17th St. (© 212/253-0810; www.bn.com); and **Borders,** which has four stores in Manhattan including one in the Time Warner Center, 10 Columbus Circle (© **212/823-9775;** www.bordersstores.com).

ARCHIVIA BOOKS
993 Lexington Ave., between 71st and 72nd sts. (Subway: 6 to 68th St./Hunter College).

Shop this newly revamped shop for books on architecture, art, design, decorative arts, gardens, and interiors. © **212/570-9565.** www.archiviabooks.com.

BAUMAN RARE BOOKS
535 Madison Ave., between 54th and 55th sts. (Subway: 6 to 51st St.).

Titles include everything from Milton's *Paradise Lost* (1669) to a signed copy of Harper Lee's *To Kill a Mockingbird* (1960). ***Best Bets:*** Bauman's is one of the foremost resources for serious collectors willing to spend big money for pristine first editions. Prices can climb into the tens of thousands. © **212/751-0011.** www.baumanrarebooks.com.

BONNIE SLOTNICK COOKBOOKS
163 W. 10th St., between Waverly and Seventh Ave. (Subway: 1 to Christopher St.).

This place is heaven for anyone who loves cookbooks and food writing; thousands of books, both new and antiquarian, can be found on these shelves. © **212/989-8962.**

BOOKS OF WONDER
18 W. 18th St., between Fifth and Sixth aves. (Subway: 4, 5, 6, L, N, Q, R, or W to 14th St./Union Sq.).

You don't have to be a kid to fall in love with this charming bookstore, which served as the model for Meg Ryan's shop in *You've Got Mail.* © **212/989-3270.** www.booksofwonder.com.

DRAMA BOOK SHOP
250 W. 40th St., between Seventh and Eighth aves. (Subway: A, C, or E to 42nd St.).

Leading authority for books on all performing arts—not just the theater. *Web Tip:* Check the website for celebrity appearances and special events. © **212/944-0595.** www.drama bookshop.com.

RIZZOLI BOOKSTORE
31 W. 57th St., between Fifth and Sixth aves. (Subway: N, R, or W to Fifth Ave./59th St.).

This clubby Italian bookstore is the classiest—and most relaxing—spot in town to browse art and design books, plus quality fiction, gourmet cookbooks, and other upscale titles. © **212/759-2424.** www.rizzoliusa.com.

STRAND BOOK STORE
828 Broadway, at 12th St. (Subway: 4, 5, 6, L, N, Q, R, or W to 14th St./Union Sq.).

Something of a New York legend, the Strand is worth a visit for its staggering "18 miles of books" (revised from the previous 8 miles), as well as its extensive inventory of review copies and bargain titles at up to 85% off list price.

I am not overwhelmed easily (in a store, anyway) . . . but this place makes me dizzy. The narrow aisles mean you're always getting bumped; the books are only roughly alphabetized; and there's no air-conditioning. Nevertheless, it's a book lover's paradise.

Best Bets: It's unquestionably the city's best book deal—almost nothing is marked at list price—and the selection is phenomenal in all categories (there's even a rare-book department on the third floor). The website is also good, but you have to pay for shipping. © **212/473-1452.** www.strandbooks.com.

TASCHEN
107 Greene St., between Prince and Spring sts. (Subway: R or W to Prince St.).

I am always amazed by Taschen stores for their combination of incredible architecture, high style, and fabulous lifestyle books—which very often are not overly expensive. © **212/226-2212.** www.taschen.com.

BOUTIQUES

ANN AHN
961 Madison Ave., between 75th and 76th sts. (Subway: 6 to 77th St.).

This is the kind of small Madison Avenue boutique that you might pass without ever knowing that it is the "in" place for Upper East Side ladies who like the Euro-Asian-artsy-hippie-boho look—and are willing to pay $500 and up for classic trousers, jackets, and shrugs. Many one-of-a-kind pieces are classics in their own way, since they're so unique. The look here is something like that offered by the designer Eskandar, but more into fiber arts with an emphasis on texture.

Best Bets: One-stop shopping for accessories as well as clothes and coats. I bought the dress for my son's wedding here; it was $800, but I plan to wear it forever. © **212/288-6068.**

A.P.C.
131 Mercer St., between Prince and Spring sts. (Subway: N, R, or W to Prince St.).

French brand with just a few stores around the world, known for a lifestyle look of comfort and simple chic. Men's and women's clothing is sold in this store. This is where you go for killer jeans and a white shirt at fair prices. The only other U.S. store is in L.A. ✆ **212/966-0069.**

CALYPSO

815 Madison Ave., near 68th St. (Subway: 6 to 68th St./Hunter College).

Originally from the bijou island of St. Barth's, with a French accent *(bien sur)*, Calypso has consistently been able to take resort chic and turn it into an urban trend. Aside from clothes, there are some accessories and, of course, signature scents. The flagship is located in the old Versace space on Madison; there's also a branch at 935 Madison Ave. (near 74th St.), plus locations in trendy areas such as the Meatpacking District (654 Hudson St.), SoHo (424 Broome St.), and Nolita (280 Mott St.). See p. 257 for Calypso Home.

Web Tip: You'll find past season sale items online at unbelievable prices; I found a velvet dress marked down from $400 to $20, and it was available in most colors and sizes. ✆ **212/585-0310.** www.calypso-celle.com.

DARYL K

21 Bond St., between Lafayette St. and Bowery. (Subway: 6 to Bleecker St.).

Daryl Kerrigan was considered the It Girl of her time, yet without explanation she closed down her SoHo shop. Good news for those left naked in the dark: Sheeeee's baaaack. There are only about 25 styles created each season; cult followers stand in line to get them. Barneys Co-Op also sells the line if you can't get to this downtown boutique. ✆ **212/529-8790.** www.darylk.com.

DOSA •

107 Thompson St., between Prince and Spring sts. (Subway: C or E to Spring St.).

If you're into the rich hippie-dippy look with jewel-tone silks and cottons, fluid chic, and slightly ethnic droop, you may want to head directly here. ***Best Bets:*** This line is perfect for travel; the pieces are meant to be layered and most can be hand laundered. Prices range from $50 to over $200 per item. © **212/431-1733.**

OSKA

415 West Broadway, between Prince & Spring sts. (Subway: C, E, to Spring St.).

This German label is a line of separates in a mix-and-match-Armani-goes-Asian combo of muted colors and soft natural fabrics. There are tunics, pants, skirts, jackets, and outerwear, all perfect for imperfect bodies. ***Best Bets:*** Prices are slashed during the end-of-season sales: I paid $68 for a sweater and Sarah got trousers for $102. © **212/625-2772.** www.oska.de.

OTTE

121 Greenwich Ave., between Jane and 13th St. (Subway: A, C, E, or L to 14th St./Eighth Ave.); 132 N. 5th St., between Berry St. and Bedford Ave., Williamsburg, Brooklyn (Subway: L to Bedford Ave.).

You'll find an impressive group of both established and emerging independent designers in this well-stocked boutique. The West Village store specializes in urbane dressy looks, while the Brooklyn branch is a good source for designer jeans and more casual looks. West Village: © **212/229-9424.** Brooklyn: © **718/302-3007.**

PARACELSO

414 West Broadway, between Prince and Spring sts. (Subway: C or E to Spring St.).

Eco-Shopping

For guilt-free green shopping, stop by **Kaight**, 83 Orchard St., between Broome and Grand streets. The racks are filled with eco-friendly clothing made from recycled and/or organic materials, all sweatshop free. The clothing at **gominyc**, 443 E. 6th St., at Avenue A, is all made from environmentally responsible organic cotton, bamboo, and hemp, and the organic **Loomstate** label has joined forces with Barneys to offer 100% organic cotton jeans; a percentage of each sale goes to the global group One Percent for the Planet. For perfect-fitting jeans made from organic cotton, visit **R by 45rpm**, 169 Mercer St., between Houston and Prince streets. Donna Karan's **Urban Zen** (below) is another best bet.

Oh me, oh my, how to begin on this one? I have been shopping here for probably a decade and never told anyone because I was certain the store would close, but it's been here for 35 years—so here goes. The owner says she's from Milan but seems to be from a fashion planet. Her stock is a hodgepodge of Indian and vintage and Thai and chiffon. The store looks like a flea market but her ethnic designs and floppy clothes cannot be ignored. Average price for an item: $139. © 212/966-4232.

URBAN ZEN

705 Greenwich St., between 10th and Charles sts. (Subway: A, C, E, or L to 14th St./Eighth Ave.).

Initially launched as a 10-day well-being initiative by Donna Karan, Urban Zen was so successful it now has a permanent home in the West Village. The boutique promotes a healthy lifestyle by offering yoga literature, massage oils, and alternative healing videos along with Karan's Urban Zen clothing collection, made from sustainable recycled fabrics. The line includes comfy yoga pants, cashmere sweaters, cotton hoodies, and easy layering pieces. A portion of all sales goes to support Karan's initiative of the same name. *Web Tip:* The clothing line is featured on the website; but there are no prices listed, and you can't place online orders. ✆ **212/206-3999.** www.urbanzen.org.

Yaso
62 Grand St., near West Broadway (Subway: C or E to Spring St. or 1 to Canal St.).

I am particularly fond of luxurious droopy drape and ethnic chic, so I have been shopping here for well over a dozen years. This is a total-look kind of store, with some home furnishings and accessories along with clothing. ✆ **212/941-8506.**

BRIDAL

Many department stores have bridal departments, though many young women today prefer alternative retail—buying wholesale from the bridal suppliers in the Garment District, going to the Filene's Basement bridal sale (293), checking out the Vera Wang once-a-year sale (usually in Feb), and so on. See p. 18 for more information.

Adriennes
156 Orchard St., near Rivington St. (Subway: F or V to Second Ave.).

The bride is a little bit funky, a little bit rock 'n' roll—or perhaps she wants to work with a designer and have a lot of input in the creation. Dresses tend to be simple and elegant and priced under $5,000. *Web Tip:* Log on to the website for trunk show dates. ✆ **212/228-9618.** www.adriennesny.com.

Amsale
625 Madison Ave., at 58th St. (Subway: N, R, or W to Fifth Ave./59th St.).

Although she also does evening gowns and now has a list of very well-known celebrity clients, Ethiopian-born Amsale (say

"Am-*sah*-leh") Aberra is really just the gal behind the wedding dress—the sleek, elegant wedding dress that is devoid of froufrou excess. She calls herself a bridal designer; her gowns hang from the ceiling of her bridal boutique like fine art in a gallery.

Best Bets: As wedding confections go, the prices are reasonable—under $5,000 for the whole shebang. While well-known, Amsale remains a less obvious choice than Vera Wang yet serves the same clientele. *Web Tip:* The gowns are shown in large photos on the website with several views—front, side, and back—with close-up attention to detail. ✆ 212/583-1700. www.amsale.com.

B&J FABRICS
525 Seventh Ave., 2nd floor, at 38th St. (Subway: 1, 2, 3, 7, N, Q, R, or W to Times Sq./42nd St.).

See p. 169 for the listing for this store. The fabric for Carolyn Bessette Kennedy's wedding gown came from B&J. ✆ 212/354-8150. www.bandjfabrics.com.

KLEINFELD
110 W. 20th St., near Sixth Ave. (Subway: F or V to 23rd St.).

Many area brides make the trek here for the selection. Sometimes there are price breaks; other times the prize is a trunk show or a chance to work with a designer and to modify a design to suit. An appointment is required. *Web Tip:* Most gowns are shown online; however, prices are not listed. ✆ 646/633-4300. www.kleinfeldbridal.com.

MICHAEL'S
1041 Madison Ave., between 79th and 80th sts. (Subway: 6 to 77th St.).

This famous resale shop sells used wedding gowns in addition to a range of other clothing. See p. 309 for full listing. ✆ 212/737-7273. www.michaelsconsignment.com.

Insider's Secret: Vera Wang

If you can't afford couture Vera, remember that she does a low-cost line sold exclusively at **Kohl's** stores. There is no Kohl's in Manhattan; go to www.kohls.com for a store near you. There are no bridal creations in the Kohl's line.

REEM ACRA
14 E. 60th St., between Madison and Fifth aves. (Subway: N, R, or W to Fifth Ave./59th St.).

Wealthy bridezillas flock to this tony salon to buy gowns featuring intricate lace and embroidery. Very, very expensive. *Web Tip:* The collection is shown on the website; browse before booking an appointment. www.reemacra.com.

VERA WANG
991 Madison Ave., at 77th St. (Subway: 6 to 77th St.).

America's most famous name in fancy-schmancy wedding gowns. By appointment, m'dear. If you're planning way ahead, there's a warehouse sale in a downtown hotel once a year, usually in February (look in *New York* magazine for the exact date). A second location is scheduled to open on Mercer Street in Fall 2008; this shop will stock ready-to-wear. For bridesmaid attire, **Vera Wang Maids,** 980 Madison Ave., 3rd floor (© **212/628-9898**), has been created for the bridesmaids. *Web Tip:* All collections are featured on the website; no prices are given. © **212/628-3400**. www.verawang.com.

CASHMERE

Cashmere is difficult to buy at discount because there are so many tricks to the quality—you may pay a low price, but you'll get exactly what you paid for. You'll do better to pay more and get the best possible quality. If you take care of your cashmeres, they will last you a lifetime—or longer. I still wear a sweater of my mother's that is easily 50 years old.

Keep in mind that Italian cashmere is the best, followed by Scottish. Don't buy Chinese cashmere unless you like cheap thrills. Note that the big English brands usually sell Scottish cashmere.

The thought that anyone would walk into a cashmere store and pay regular retail is a joke to me. I'd buy during a sale period, of course! Or I'd use my regular discount sources, be they off-pricers or discounters. But pay full price? Eeeeek! When is the best time to buy cashmere, my dear? July, of course. That's when it's on sale and mere mortals get hot flashes when they think of it.

Big Names

A crop of cashmere specialty stores (mostly Italian) is located on Madison Avenue. In no way does the $99 cashmere special at Lord & Taylor compare to the cashmere that's sold in these stores. Some of these places sell more than cashmere—in fact, they have to, just to stay in business. I once bought my husband a bathing suit at Malo! Since the big-name makers sell different versions of basically the same thing, I merely list them below.

MALO
814 Madison Ave., at 68th St. (Subway: 6 to 68th St./ Hunter College).
© **212/396-4721.** www.malo.it.

MANRICO
922 Madison Ave., at 73rd St. (Subway: 6 to 77th St.).
© **212/794-4200.** www.manrico.com.

TSE
120 Wooster St., near Prince (Subway: N or R to Prince St.).

British designer Tess Giberson has taken TSE (say "Say") from traditional twin sets for ladies-who-lunch to a more fashion forward, yet wearable, line. The new boutique is as chic as the knits; cashmere curtains drape the fitting rooms. © 212/925-2520.

Discounters

You can expect to find off-price cashmere at any of the local off-price stores (p. 290) or area outlet malls (p. 296). The major department stores often have cashmere promotions or special sales as well. The store below offers promotional prices year-round.

BEST OF SCOTLAND
581 Fifth Ave., near 47th St., 6th floor (Subway: B, D, F, or V to Rockefeller Center).

The words "cashmere" and "discount" do not really go hand in hand. Prices are not low, and there is little here for less than $100; but if you like quality cashmere and those shawls with the little ruffles, this is your chance to buy at a slightly better price. *Best Bets:* If your preference (style, color, size . . .) isn't in stock, they will order it for you. © 212/644-0403. www.best ofscotlandnyc.com.

CHIC & SIMPLE

There is a trend in New York for women with money and style to avoid the big stores and concentrate on a single source or two that can supply simple yet perfect style and maximum service. The type of clothing that these women buy is classically chic—always refined, simple, elegant, and practical. Much of it is in the **Armani** style, but streamlined, and the palette is almost always monochromatic. These items are not inexpensive.

I've listed **Eileen Fisher** (p. 90) in this text about five million times; she offers the baggier and less expensive version of this look. If you're an Eileen Fisher fan, the outlet store in Wood-bury Common (p. 298) is worth the drive.

ANNE FONTAINE
687 Madison Ave., near 62nd St. (Subway: 4, 5, 6, N, R, or W to 59th St./Lexington Ave.).

This French chain now has several shops in Manhattan. Fontaine began by doing only white shirts and blouses, but now also sells black—everything from sporty to dressy. Other locations are at Rockefeller Center (610 Fifth Ave., near 49th St.) and in SoHo (93 Greene St., near Prince St.). *Web Tip:* The links move around the page, so you must click quickly to open the pages. ℭ **212/688-4362.** www.annefontaine.com.

BLANC DE CHINE
673 Fifth Ave., at 53rd St. (Subway: E or V to Fifth Ave./53rd St.).

Classic, tailored Chinese-inspired clothing for men and women. There are some home styles, too. Prices are up here: Expect to pay at least $700 for a blazer. (You'll never regret it.) Stores are popping up in all major shopping cities—try London and Beijing as well as hometown Hong Kong. The new Bleu de Chine collection is showcased on the newly opened third floor of the boutique. (See p. 86.) ℭ **212/355-1682.** www.blancde chine.com.

CP SHADES
60 Grand St., between West Broadway and Wooster St. (Subway: C or E to Spring St.).

I consider this line the poor gal's Eileen Fisher and a friend of anyone who likes the Armani palette of soft pastels. You'll find droopy, comfy clothes in tones that are nice but neutral. The look is a little too bohemian for normal workdays in Manhattan, but it's great for weekends or suburbia. *Best Bets:* The summer linens mix and layer beautifully and are machine washable. Prices range from $60 for a simple blouse to under $175 for a flouncy skirt. ✆ **212/226-4434.**

SHEN NEW YORK
959 Madison Ave., at 75th St. (Subway: 6 to 77th St.); 990 Lexington Ave., between 71st and 72nd sts. (Subway: 6 to 68th St./Hunter College).

This is the place for sublime, body-skimming, simple elegance in gorgeous fabrics. I saw a fluttery, lightly layered, froth-of-chiffon sleeveless top that was the whisper of everything I've always wanted to be. It was almost $200, but this is where you put your money when elegance is all you believe in. If I could afford it, I'd shop nowhere else. *Web Tip:* You really must visit one of the stores to see the collection. The Web photos don't do justice to the designs. ✆ **212/717-1185.** www.shennew york.com.

CRAFTS

Do-it-yourselfers, fire up your glue guns and check out these crafty resources.

BLICK ART MATERIALS
1–5 Bond St., between Broadway and Lafayette sts. (Subway: 6 to Bleecker St.).

The shop specializes in papier-mâché, beads, paints, and artists' brushes. ✆ **212/533-2444.**

BRUCE FRANK BEADS
215 W. 83rd St., between Broadway and Amsterdam Ave. (Subway: 1 to 86th St.).

All the makings are here for creative original jewelry; you just need to put it all together. Classes are offered as well. *Best Bets:* The selection of unusual and contemporary beads is the best in New York. Murano glass beads range in price from $5 to

$8, but are often discounted on the website. ✆ **212/595-3746.** www.brucefrankbeads.com.

FEMMEGEMS
280 Mulberry St., between Prince and E. Houston sts. (Subway: 6 to Bleecker St.).

This is a good resource for beads, baubles, and gear for fledgling jewelry designers. ✆ **212/625-1611.**

GOTTA KNIT
498 Sixth Ave., between 12th and 13th sts., 2nd floor (Subway: F or V to 14th St.).

Along with top-quality skeins, you'll find a good selection of vintage buttons. ✆ **212/989-3030.**

STITCHES EAST
55 E. 52nd St., between Fifth and Sixth aves. (Subway: E or V to Fifth Ave./53rd St.).

A complete knit and needlepoint shop. *Best Bets:* The needlepoint canvases are creative and elegant—and also very expensive. Expect to pay well over $100 for a hand-painted piece. ✆ **212/421-0112.**

DEPARTMENT & SPECIALTY STORES

Things to know:

- Delivery service is available at all stores, but you will be charged for it. Few stores have private delivery service anymore; they usually use UPS or FedEx, except for large pieces of furniture.
- All stores will provide free, simple gift-wrapping services. Elaborate wrapping costs extra. You can usually get a free shopping bag with handles by asking at customer service

or a wrap desk, although stores also have machines that sell outsize shopping bags.

- All stores have buying services and personal shoppers, as well as clean bathrooms. Many have checkrooms for coats and packages. Most now have spas—now you really can shop till you drop.
- Various credit cards are accepted at all stores; some are still pushing their house credit cards and may even offer a 10% discount for purchases made when you sign up for the card. International customers are accepted.

BARNEYS CO-OP
236 W. 18th St., between Seventh and Eighth aves. (Subway: 1 to 18th St.).

This offshoot of Barneys (see below) sells the young, trendy, and really exciting stuff. There are also locations in SoHo (116 Wooster St., near Prince St.) and on the Upper West Side (2151 Broadway, at 75th St.). © **212/593-7800.** www. barneys.com.

BARNEYS NEW YORK
660 Madison Ave., at 61st St. (Subway: 4, 5, 6, N, R, or W to 59th St./Lexington Ave.).

Uptown Barneys is a legend. Only visitors and uptown girls shop here, as this store is special beyond special. Barneys has re-created itself as times have changed, and is still one of the most exciting retail properties in Manhattan. Indeed, no shopping trip to New York is complete without a visit to this store. Whether you buy anything or not is meaningless—you must see and touch and feel.

The flagship location is actually two different eight-story stores that connect on the street level. You won't want to miss a square inch. I'm keen on the unique bath products, European favorites that I don't see elsewhere, and cult makeup brands.

The Madison Avenue store is open daily until 9pm—hours that help make Midtown browsing an evening sport.

Best Bets: The little-known but sublime brands throughout the store. Don't miss Chelsea Passage for home style. While a lot of the merchandise is very pricey, a lot of it is not. It all looks expensive, but there are plenty of items, especially accessories, that are moderately priced. © **212/826-8900.** www.barneys.com.

BERGDORF GOODMAN
754 Fifth Ave., between 57th and 58th sts. (Subway: N, R, or W to Fifth Ave./59th St.).

BERGDORF GOODMAN MEN
745 Fifth Ave., at 58th St. (Subway: N, R, or W to Fifth Ave./59th St.).

Dramatic things have been done to this store to bring back some of its lost energy. If you haven't been here for a while, do stop in. And drop down under to the lower-level beauty floor. My favorite part of the store is still the seventh floor, with a gift department and antiques; Christmas is a delight. Every day is a delight, actually. Hours are Monday through Friday from 10am to 8pm, Saturday from 10am to 7pm, and Sunday from noon to 6pm. There's a restaurant, with a view of the park, on the home-furnishings floor. **Bergdorf Goodman Men** is across the street. *Web Tip:* Shopping online couldn't be easier; however, don't miss visiting the store in person if at all possible. © **212/753-7300.** www.bergdorfgoodman.com.

BLOOMINGDALE'S
1000 Third Ave., at 59th St. (Subway: 4, 5, 6, N, R, or W to 59th St./Lexington Ave.).

A trip to Bloomies is a trip to the moon on gossamer wings. You start off filled with energy and excitement, loving everything you see; but as you wear out, you wear down, and suddenly you realize you're lost, the store is difficult to shop, and you can't remember all the departments. *C'est le Bloomies.* Still, it's one of the best department stores in the world.

I cannot tell you that Bloomingdale's lives up to the hype, but I can tell you that for massive amounts of merchandise and for selection, this store is possibly the best in town.

Some tips: The store has many entrances: You can enter from Lexington Avenue, even though the official street address is Third Avenue. There's also a subway stop right under Bloomies. And finally: A smaller branch of the store is located in SoHo, at 504 Broadway, between Spring and Broome streets. **Best Bets:** The designer boutiques are excellent, and second markdowns can make you very happy. It's not unusual to find prices slashed 70% during final sales. © 212/705-2000. www. bloomingdales.com.

HENRI BENDEL
712 Fifth Ave., near 56th St. (Subway: F to 57th St.).

From a merchandise point of view, this store has changed dramatically and is a little less exclusive and less chic than it once was. Visually, Bendel's is still fun to stare at and shop, although you may not really buy much.

Prices vary from outrageous to quite moderate. The makeup department is good—Bobbi Brown and M.A.C. cosmetics, as well as Chanel and a few big brands, plus the store's own famous brown-and-white-striped logo travel cases. Bendel's does good windows, has a wonderful Christmas tree, and frequently changes the front of the store on the ground floor so you always get a sense of adventure. Be sure to check out the original Lalique windows in the cafe.

Here's one of the best parts—this store does zillions of parties and promotional events, many of which are after-hours. You usually get a goody bag when you attend; at the last event I went to, the goodies even included a $25 gift certificate for any purchase at Bendel's. These events are worth attending; get on the mailing list and party like crazy. *Web Tip:* Sign up for Bendel's Style Bulletin online to receive announcements and

invitations to exclusive store events. © **212/247-1100**. www.henri
bendel.com.

JEFFREY NEW YORK
449 W. 14th St., between Ninth and Tenth aves. (Subway:
A, C, E, or L to 14th St./Eighth Ave.).

I'll spare the comparisons to Barneys or even Colette in Paris.
Jeffrey has done some very interesting things. Architecturally,
this is a temple of moderne set in contrast to the grunginess
of the surrounding district. There's a live DJ most of the time,
and the salespeople have been poached from the best stores in
New York and are thus fabulous beyond belief.

Jeffrey carries shoes, accessories, some cosmetics, menswear,
and several types of women's clothing for just about any look.
Although some of the names are also sold uptown, Jeffrey's
stock is in keeping with his taste, and I find his taste much more
exciting than uptown sensibilities—he tends to be less safe and
take more risks.

This is one of the most exciting stores in New York if you
know who you are. If you're just browsing and don't have a
finely tuned understanding of the ironies of glamour, the store
isn't worth the time it takes to get downtown. Let's pray there
are enough people who get it to keep this store thriving. *Web
Tip:* The website sucks. You can't order online, nor can you
get a feel for the store or what it sells. © **212/206-1272**. www.
jeffreynewyork.com.

LORD & TAYLOR
424 Fifth Ave., between 38th and 39th sts. (Subway: B, D,
F, or V to 42nd St./Bryant Park).

If you haven't shopped at Lord & Taylor recently, you may
think you've taken a wrong turn as you walk into their Fifth
Avenue flagship. Under new ownership, this formerly old-
fashioned, traditional, and, yeah, frumpy department store has
come back to life and is bursting with new energy after a complete multimillion-dollar overhaul. Boring midpriced brands

have been replaced by trendy upscale labels, including Nanette Lapore, Hugo Boss, Tracy Reese, and Ted Baker; in fact, over three-quarters of the brands in the store now weren't there 2 years ago. One thing hasn't changed: The selection of well-priced cashmere knits is still one of the best in town.

The jury's still out on the destiny of this venerable 182-year-old institution. Fifth Avenue real estate is so valuable that if the revamp and upgrades don't bring new shoppers, the store could close. Watch this space.

Best Bets: The wide selection of cashmere knits come in trendy styles and colors, and are reasonably priced at around $100 per piece. And that's before they go on sale. *Web Tip:* The website's been redesigned, just like the store. Ordering is now easier than ever; check out "What's Hot" for the latest designs and "Promotions" for sale items. ✆ **212/391-3344.** www.lordandtaylor.com.

MACY'S

151 W. 34th St., at Broadway (Subway: B, D, F, N, Q, R, V, or W to 34th St./Herald Sq.).

I'm not sure why there are other stores in New York, or the world. And I'm also not sure how anyone can be strong enough to shop the whole store and even grasp what it has. Because it has everything. This is the largest retail store in America—and one of the largest in the world. It's so big you can get a headache here.

Macy's is two buildings joined together, so the front and the back of the place don't necessarily feel related. The designer floor is pretty good; the kids' floor is great; and the selection of anything, from petites to juniors to cute but inexpensive clothes, is vast.

Check out the mezzanine shops, which are often over-looked. Don't miss the Cellar, the downstairs section devoted to housewares and gourmet food. There's a small shopping area in the basement that I find very interesting, including great New York souvenirs. ✆ **212/695-4400.** www.macys.com.

SAKS FIFTH AVENUE
611 Fifth Ave., at 50th St. (Subway: E or V to Fifth Ave./ 53rd St.).

Even though there may be a Saks in your hometown, try to visit the Saks in New York. It has expanded and glitzed up its store to sail into the new century with a modern look that I think is just the right size—not too big, not too small.

In fact, if I personally need something and don't have time to try my bargain resources, or if I just want to shop in one department store to get a feel for what's happening in the world of style, I invariably choose Saks. This is my favorite department store in New York because it's easy and convenient. Saks's average customer is 48 years old, so there's a great selection of clothing for "older" women.

There's a wonderful desk on the first floor that provides free sightseeing information. Best of all, the ladies' room is large and clean, and possesses banquettes, tons of phones, a change machine, and everything except a fax machine. You may find me there.

The fragrance department is world renowned as the best in America and is trying very hard to keep that reputation now that Sephora is across the street. Saks has a special deal with most perfume houses, so it launches new fragrances as soon as they come out. The store also has a variety of unique gift and purchase promotions.

There's a wonderful cafe for lunch, Cafe SFA, as well as London import Charbonnel & Walker, which serves upmarket chocolate treats. *Best Bets:* Saks has opened a new shoe department on the eighth floor that has garnered its own zip code (10022-SHOE). Honest. ✆ **212/753-4000.** www.saksfifth avenue.com or www.saks.com.

ZITOMER
969 Madison Ave., near 76th St. (Subway: 6 to 77th St.).

Since Zitomer now calls itself a department store, who am I to blow against the wind? The former fancy-pants drugstore now sells children's fashions upstairs and accessories (for people and pets) in the next-door store. The doggy bakery is gone, but the selection of dog accessories is strong—Toffee always has fun here and chooses a toy from the bins on the floor, including a Chewy Vuitton purse, a Coco Chewnel squeaky toy, and a rubber French poodle pal. © 212/737-2016. www. zitomer.com.

FABRICS, NOTIONS, TRIMS & MORE

If you have nerves of steel, you might want to wander in the 200 block of West 40th Street, where all the fabric stores are lined up. The most famous of these is B&J Fabrics, but there are dozens of them; you can get a headache in no time at all. It's great fun.

B&J FABRICS
525 Seventh Ave., at 38th St., 2nd floor (Subway: 1, 2, 3, 7, N, Q, R, or W to Times Sq./42nd St.).

They've moved! The new store is slightly larger than the old one, and everything is on one floor. A Garment District icon, this place can be overwhelming, but a good eye can find the best. Though B&J is primarily a fabric resource, it also sells some trims. *Web Tip:* Don't waste your time; there's nothing to see. © 212/354-8150. www.bandjfabrics.com.

DULKEN & DERRICK
12 W. 21st St., 2nd floor, between Fifth and Sixth aves. (Subway: N, R, or W to 23rd St.).

This firm has been manufacturing exquisite silk flowers for over 60 years. Eleanor Roosevelt was a regular customer, and today, stylists for the city's opera, ballet, and Broadway productions continue to rely on D & D for the best faux blooms. Custom work is a specialty.

Best Bets: The velvet flowers are gorgeous, and I love the custom flower pins made from fabric you supply. These blooms are pricey: $50 to $75 each, but *très* chic. *Web Tip:* If you can't visit in person, try the website; it's colorful, it's complete, and it makes ordering a breeze. © **212/929-3614.** www.flowers inthecity.com.

HYMAN HENDLER & SONS
67 W. 38th St., between Fifth and Sixth aves. (Subway: 1, 2, 3, 7, N, Q, R, or W to Times Sq./42nd St.; or B, D, F, or V to 42nd St./Bryant Park).

So fancy, so special, so much a scene of a New York from days past—this is an old-fashioned ribbon broker, now mostly serving the trade. However, anyone can buy. It's like a museum here—you will go nuts over the colors, the quality, and the possibilities. *Web Tip:* The website isn't worth the log-in. The few graphics don't begin to depict the gorgeous stock. © **212/840-8393.** www.hymanhendler.com.

M&J TRIMMING
1008 Sixth Ave., near 38th St. (Subway: 1, 2, 3, 7, N, Q, R, or W to Times Sq./42nd St.; or B, D, F, or V to 42nd St./Bryant Park).

This branch of M&J specializes in trims only: buttons, gems, feathers, braids, and other trims of all kinds, as well as all other sorts of fun gewgaws. The walls are lined with cards wrapped with yards of trim. If you buy the whole card, you get a 10% discount. *Best Bets:* This is where to find your Chanel-style braid. Prices start at around $5 per yard. © **212/204-9595.** www.mjtrim.com.

MOKUBA NEW YORK
55 W. 39th St., between Fifth and Sixth aves. (Subway: 1, 2, 3, 7, N, Q, R, or W to Times Sq./42nd St.; or B, D, F, or V to 42nd St./Bryant Park).

This Japanese ribbon resource, with stores in Paris and Tokyo, is in the same geographic location as Hyman Hendler (see above), but a block over—so I am always confused. Ribbons and trimmings freaks should see them both, although Mokuba tends to be very, very expensive. © **212/869-8900.** www.mokubany.com.

TENDER BUTTONS

143 E. 62nd St., between Lexington and Third aves. (Subway: 4, 5, 6, N, R, or W to 59th St./Lexington Ave.).

If it's buttons you need, or even cuff links, this small and wondrous shop can occupy you all day. Even if you don't need buttons, you'd need your marbles examined if you didn't stop by. *Tip:* You can buy Chanel-style buttons here, but you can't buy any fake Chanel buttons or the sorts with the interlocking Cs on them. (If you are missing a genuine Chanel button, take the garment to the boutique and they will give you a missing button if they have it in stock.) © **212/758-7004.**

TINSEL TRADING COMPANY

47 W. 38th St., between Fifth and Sixth aves. (Subway: 1, 2, 3, 7, N, Q, R, or W to Times Sq./42nd St.; or B, D, F, or V to 42nd St./Bryant Park).

More ribbon, trim, appliqué, and accessories. *Best Bets:* The company's specialty is vintage ribbons and trims, which run $50 to $250 per yard. © **212/730-1030.** www.tinseltrading.com.

FASHION CHAINS & MULTIPLES

Most of these chains have additional locations throughout the city. Go online, check a phone book, or ask your hotel concierge for a complete selection to find the branch most convenient to you or your hotel.

ABERCROMBIE & FITCH
720 Fifth Ave., at 56th St. (Subway: E or V to Fifth Ave./ 53rd St.; or N, R, or W to Fifth Ave./59th St.).

Now residing on Fifth Avenue and fresh from a mall near you, Abercrombie & Fitch must feel that it has it made and can attract international shoppers with its spiffy flagship. There's ample space to show off the must-have uniform of high-school and college kids: preppy with a touch of cool; fratty with panache. In truth, the store basically just sells jeans—but then again, there's the attitude and a wannabe lifestyle that goes with it all. ✆ **212/306-0936.** www.abercrombie.com.

ANN TAYLOR
645 Madison Ave., at 60th St. (Subway: 4, 5, 6, N, R, or W to 59th St./Lexington Ave.).

This is specialized retailing at its finest, with private-label merchandise now leading the way for a solid career look. There are also weekend looks, accessories, shoes, and a complete fragrance and bath-and-body line. Additional branches are located all around town, but this is the flagship. *Web Tip:* Special sizes for tall and short gals are available on the website. Call ✆ **800/DIAL-ANN** (342-5266) for other addresses in Manhattan. ✆ **212/832-9114.** www.anntaylor.com.

ANN TAYLOR LOFT
488 Madison Ave., at 52nd St. (Subway: E or V to Fifth Ave./53rd St.); multiple other locations.

LOFT was Ann Taylor's answer to Gap opening Old Navy— it's a less expensive line that mimics the thought of the real line, but at lower prices and lower quality. I am not impressed, but check it out for yourself. There's a LOFT store in every neighborhood these days, including SoHo (560 Broadway, near Prince St.) and Rockefeller Center (1290 Sixth Ave., near 51st St.); call ✆ **800/DIAL-ANN** (342-5266) for other locations. ✆ **212/308-1129.** www.anntaylorloft.com.

BANANA REPUBLIC

626 Fifth Ave., at 50th St. (Subway: B, D, F, or V to Rockefeller Center); multiple other locations.

Banana Republic has been a huge hit ever since the company rebuilt its image as the poor person's Ralph Lauren. This place is all brushed steel and marble floors and glorious lighting. Yes, the lighting helps; this store is a shrine. There are about a dozen branches in the city (check the website for addresses), but if you're visiting from out of town, the flagship store is the one to gawk at. *Web Tip:* Standard shipping rates on Web orders are low, usually about $6 per order regardless of the number of items. ✆ **212/974-2350.** www.bananarepublic.com.

CLUB MONACO

6 W. 57th St., between Fifth and Sixth aves. (Subway: E or V to Fifth Ave./53rd St.).

This Canadian chain is expanding and moving into the limelight due to its purchase by none other than Ralph Lauren. The firm specializes in translating fashion looks into affordable clothing without doing the cheapie trendy thing. New merchandise comes in every month; the turnover is extraordinary. A firm, solid resource for classic yet hip young things. Other locations include 520 Broadway (near Spring St.), 121 Prince St. (near Greene St.), 160 Fifth Ave. (near 21st St.), and 1111 Third Ave. (near 65th St.). ✆ **212/459-9863.** www.clubmonaco.com.

FOREVER 21

40 E. 14th St., between Broadway and University Place. (Subway: 4, 5, 6, L, N, Q, R, or W to 14th St./Union Sq.).

A California chain that I liken to the poor girl's H&M (see below)—in other words, very trendy clothes at extremely low prices. There's less for the middle-aged mom here than at H&M, but the style is undeniable. My fave: T-shirts that say "Last night's nightmare: I dreamed I was blonde!" *Note:* Do not confuse with **Century 21.** There's another branch at Herald Square, 50 W. 34th St. *Web Tip:* Click on "Brilliant

Buys" for value-priced merchandise. ✆ **212/228-0598.** www.forever21.com.

GAP
With stores too numerous to list, you're likely to see one every few blocks while walking around Manhattan.

If you are British or French, you'll die laughing when you realize how much you've been overpaying for this merchandise. Furthermore, everyone should know that Gap specializes in moving its stock, so it has very good and very regular sales. You'll see stores in every imaginable neighborhood; call ✆ **800/427-7895** to find the location nearest you. www.gap.com.

H&M
640 Fifth Ave., at 51st St. (Subway: B, D, F, or V to Rockefeller Center).

H&M stands for Hennes & Mauritz, a Swedish firm that has taken New York by storm and now has several stores around Manhattan. This one is the flagship, and it's a great source for men's, women's, and children's clothing inspired by the styles on the catwalks. New merchandise arrives every few weeks, sold at very good prices.

In the past few years, H&M has contracted famed designers to do limited-edition collections. Names such as Karl Lagerfeld and Stella McCartney have attracted around-the-block lines and much pushing and shoving for their store debuts. I have not been overly impressed with the designer collections and prefer the regular old workaday stuff. Log on to the website for other locations. ✆ **212/489-0390.** www.hm.com.

J. CREW
347 Madison Ave., at 45th St. (Subway: 4, 5, 6, 7, or S to Grand Central/42nd St.).

There was a time in recent fashion history when J. Crew ruled the world. Things have been difficult lately, maybe because all the preppies have gotten hip. To compete, the brand has gone more lifestyle and now even does bridal. In addition to the Madison Avenue flagship, there are locations at South Street Seaport (203 Front St.), 99 Prince St. (near Mercer St.), 91 Fifth Ave. (near 17th St.), the Time Warner Center (10 Columbus Circle), and Rock Center (near 50th St.) hidden in the rear. ***Best Bets:*** There's almost always a sale in progress; prices are often up to 75% off retail. You'll find the best deals on classic shirts, often found on a sale rack for $15 or less. © **212/949-0570.** www.jcrew.com.

LACOSTE
134 Prince St., near Wooster St. (Subway: C or E to Spring St.; or R or W to Prince St.).

While I am very impressed by the remarkable comeback of this brand with its little alligator logo, I am also horrified that anyone would pay $65 and up for a polo shirt. Great colors, though, and controlled distribution to enhance the value. A teenage must-have. There are other branches at 608 Fifth Ave., near 49th Street; and 575 Madison Ave., near 56th Street. © **212/226-5019.** www.lacoste.com.

OLD NAVY
150 W. 34th St., between Broadway and Seventh Ave. (Subway: B, D, F, N, Q, R, V, W, 1, 2, or 3 to 34th St.).

My goal in life is to take the Old Navy franchise to France and retire as a zillionaire. One look at the flagship on West 34th Street and you will forget that this brand started life as the cheapie line from Gap. All of the locations are good, but the flagship is one of the best stores in New York. There's a diner in the basement, too. Other locations include SoHo (503 Broadway, near Spring St.) and Ladies' Mile (610 Sixth Ave., at 18th St.). © **212/594-0049.** www.oldnavy.com.

TALBOTS
525 Madison Ave., near 53rd St. (Subway: E or V to Fifth Ave./53rd St.).

Attention, conservatives, preppies, and traditionalists: This New England company has gone from mail order to retail, and now has stores all over the U.S. Besides its new men's line, Talbots also has kids' stores (1523 Second Ave., near 79th St.) and petites' sections. *Web Tip:* There's usually a Web-only sale in progress; discounts average 50% on end-of-season and overstocked merchandise. © 212/838-8811. www.talbots.com.

UNIQLO
546 Broadway, between Prince and Spring sts. (Subway: N, R, or W to Prince St.).

This Japanese chain is the home of inexpensive colorful basics; think $50 cashmere sweaters, $60 quilted jackets. . . . The store's not for the faint of heart. Fitting-room lines can be long and tedious and the sales staff isn't sophisticated; but you'll love the prices and selection. *Web Tip:* You can scroll through the new looks online but can't place Web orders. © 212/966-5374. www.uniqlo.com.

ZARA
689 Fifth Ave., at 54th St. (Subway: E or V to Fifth Ave./ 53rd St.).

This Spanish chain has been hidden in Manhattan for a decade, with a store across the street from Bloomingdale's, at 750 Lexington Ave. Now, with the success of H&M, Zara has come out of the closet to open a flagship right under Liz Arden. The clothes are moderately priced interpretations of more expensive styles for men, women, and children—for weekend and work. More fashion-forward than Banana Republic, but not as hip as H&M. Other stores are in Midtown (39 W. 34th St., near Fifth Ave.), near Union Square (101 Fifth Ave., near 17th St.), and in SoHo (580 Broadway, near Prince St.). *Web Tip:* This site is very slow. Don't waste time online; head straight to one of the stores. © 212/371-2555. www.zara.com.

FOODSTUFFS

There are entire guidebooks written about food resources (and I don't mean restaurants) in New York. Below are some sources that are part of the tourist experience.

Farmers' Markets

The best of them all is the Union Square **Greenmarket** (Broadway, between 14th and 17th sts.), held on Monday, Wednesday, Friday, and Saturday. The best day is Saturday; see p. 102 for details.

In the West Village, the Saturday-only **GreenFlea P.S. 41** flea market with farmers' market is held at Greenwich Avenue and Charles Street, April through October. It's nice but not extraordinary. On Sunday, the action shifts (year-round) to the **GreenFlea M.S. 44** market on the Upper West Side, at Columbus Avenue and 77th Street. A small greenmarket sells fruits, pies, pretzels, and honey—but nothing to write home about. See p. 301 and p. 302 for details on the GreenFlea markets.

Specialty Foods

New York is a city of foodies, and these are the stores that tide them all over.

Amish Market
240 E. 45th St., between Second and Third aves. (Subway: 4, 5, 6, 7, or S to Grand Central/42nd St.).

This is not an Amish-a hamischa market from Pennsylvania as you may be expecting, but a deli and takeout source with a handful of branches around town. It focuses on high quality and is especially a godsend down in Battery Park City (17 Battery Place, near West St.). Also at 731 Ninth Ave. (near 49th St.) and 53 Park Place (near West Broadway). *Best Bets:* Choose from over 100 restaurant quality meals-to-go, all ready to

Shopping Adventure: Foodie Neighborhoods

If you are a foodie looking for ethnic markets, you'll want to hop onto the E, F, R, V, or 7 train and jump off at Roosevelt Avenue/Broadway in Jackson Heights, Queens, where you'll find a 1-mile stretch of the United Nations of grocery stores. Just prowl Roosevelt Avenue: It'll change from Irish to Filipino to Colombian to Korean.

If you want to stick to Manhattan, an old standby is what I call the Spice Neighborhood (on Ninth Ave. in the upper 40s), which is home to many Italian markets as well as specialty food shops. Browse. Don't overdress. Here you'll find burlap bags laden with spices and coffee beans. And I'm not talking Starbucks, my dears.

With the arrival of several new chefs in Manhattan and the rebirth of the Columbus Circle area as foodie land, note that the largest Whole Foods in the U.S. is now in the Time Warner Center. Also check out the Union Square area, home to another Whole Foods, the city's first Trader Joe's, and the excellent Greenmarket.

heat and serve. Most entrees are under $10. © **212/370-1761.** www.amishfinefood.com.

BALDUCCI'S
155 W. 66th St., between Broadway and Amsterdam Ave. (Subway: 1 to 66th St./Lincoln Center).

A new version of the old neighborhood market, with branches in the 'burbs as well. Yep, Balducci's has taken over the suburban Hay Day stores. There are locations at Lincoln Square (155A W. 66th St.), and in the grand old New York Savings Bank building at 81 Eighth Ave. (at 14th St.). © **212/653-8320.** www.balduccis.com.

DEAN & DELUCA
560 Broadway, at Prince St. (Subway: R or W to Prince St.).

For the uninitiated, Dean & DeLuca is the dean of fancy food markets, the fanciest of the chic purveyors of things imported and sublime. Need I say it's expensive? In addition to a well-rounded selection of everything you might want to eat, to cook, or to take to go, there's some cookware and a few cookbooks. My problem with Dean & DeLuca is that I've seen the same foodstuffs in other markets for a lot less money, and I won't pay outrageous prices for the privilege of being chic. Nonetheless, it's a landmark, an icon, and a statement in food and fashion.

Besides the original location in SoHo, Dean & DeLuca has additional stores, including one at 1150 Madison Ave. (near 85th St.), and several cafes, such as at 75 University Place (at 11th St.), 9 Rockefeller Plaza (near 49th St.), and the Time Warner Center (10 Columbus Circle).

Best Bets: The D&D cafes are good choices for shopping breaks, and the new Flagship Café at 1 Rockefeller Center (between Fifth and Sixth aves.) has become the silent star of the *Today Show.* © **212/226-6800.** www.deananddeluca.com.

DYLAN'S CANDY BAR
1011 Third Ave., near 60th St. (Subway: 4, 5, 6, N, R, or W to 59th St./Lexington Ave.).

Maybe no one would care if Dylan weren't Ralph Lauren's daughter. Still, this modern candy shop boasts an old-fashioned soda fountain and two floors of penny-candy–style containers filled with all sorts of goodies. *Web Tip:* There's a good selection of sugar-free sweets available online. © **646/735-0078.** www.dylanscandybar.com.

E.A.T. & E.A.T. GIFTS
1062 and 1064 Madison Ave., between 80th and 81st sts. (Subway: 6 to 77th St.).

E.A.T. is another operation from the famous Eli Zabar food family. This creative branch, consisting of a market, a cafe, and a gift shop, is truly super—it's one of the best destinations in Manhattan. The gift shop is really adorable and filled with items in all price ranges. ✆ 212/772-0022. www.elizabar.com.

FAIRWAY
2127 Broadway, near 74th St. (Subway: 1, 2, or 3 to 72nd St.).

This place is great fun. Fairway is a grocery store with so-so regular produce but great exotics. It also carries many imported foodstuffs. Upstairs is an enormous health food department and a cafe. Prices range from extravagant to very fair. There's another location in Harlem (2328 132nd Ave.), if you're planning a picnic with Bill.

Best Bets: The Fairway label olive oils, balsamic vinegar, and chili paste make great gifts. As direct importers, they're able to offer these top-quality products at reasonable prices; a large bottle of extra-virgin olive oil is under $20. ✆ 212/595-1888. www.fairwaymarket.com.

ITO EN
822 Madison Ave., near 69th St. (Subway: 6 to 68th St./Hunter College).

Over 30 kinds of green tea from a supplier who has begun to branch into retail; this is the flagship store. ✆ 212/988-7111. www.itoen.com.

JUAN VALDEZ CAFE
140 E. 57th St., at Lexington Ave. (Subway: 4, 5, 6, N, R, or W to 59th St./Lexington Ave.).

I have not listed the multitudes of Starbucks or even the Illy boutique that opens during Fashion Week, but this one I simply cannot resist. Juan Valdez, as you remember, was a fictional character created to represent coffee growers. Now some smart businessmen are trying to cash in on the coffee craze. But wait, it gets better—this brew is marketed toward those who prefer coffee that's not as strong as what is currently sold in cafes and parlors around America. There are Juan Valdez cafes at Times Square, 1451 Broadway (at 41st St.), and 245 Park Ave. (near 47th St.); watch Juan conquer the world. © 917/289-0981. www.friendsofjuan.com.

LA MAISON DU CHOCOLAT
1018 Madison Ave., between 78th and 79th sts. (Subway: 6 to 77th St.); 30 Rockefeller Center (Subway: B, D, F, or V to Rockefeller Center).

There are plenty of chocolate shops in New York and most of them are good, if not great; however, this French import has it all—divine candy, smart boutiques, clever packaging, and good customer service. *Best Bets:* Their fabric-covered hatboxes full of sweets make great gifts. You choose the box, and then they'll fill it with your favorite chocolates. Prices start at about $60. © 212/744-7117. www.lamaisonduchocolat.com.

M&M'S WORLD
1600 Broadway, between 48th and 49th sts. (Subway: N, R, or W to 49th St.).

This three-story monument to chocolate features an interactive kids' area and a 17-foot green-M&M Lady Liberty. *Web Tip:* Personalized M&M candies are available on the website. Choose two lines of print and 1 of 22 colors. It's pricey ($40 for three 7-oz. bags) but unique. © 212/295-3850. www.mms world.com.

OLIVIERS & CO.
Grand Central Terminal, 412 Lexington Ave., at 43rd St., at Graybar Passage (Subway: 4, 5, 6, 7, or S to Grand Central/42nd St.).

The same man who created the beauty chain L'Occitane founded O&Co., which features olive oil from all over the world, with an emphasis on Mediterranean sources. This place also sells many French foodstuffs. Prices are twice what they are in France, but if you don't mind spending $36 for a tin of olive oil, you won't be disappointed. There's another branch in the West Village (249 Bleecker St., near Carmine St.). *Web Tip:* There's a good tutorial on the website if you're interested in learning about oils from different regions. There are oils to order in every price range. © **212/973-1472.** www.oliviers andco.com.

PAPABUBBLE
380 Broome St., between Mott and Mulberry sts. (Subway: 6 to Spring St.).

This is an old-fashioned confectioner with contemporary tastes, so to speak. Everything is made from scratch and they will even work with your sweet tooth to create a special product or flavor. House specialties are lollipops, ribbon candy, and custom creations. *Web Tip:* The website is one of those click-quick numbers with dancing dots and designs. I couldn't find prices, but the photos are pretty. © **212/966-2599.** www.papabubble.com.

TRADER JOE'S
142 E. 14th St., between Third and Fourth aves. (Subway: 4, 5, 6, L, N, Q, R, or W to 14th St./Union Sq.).

This California chain of food stores has finally come to New York in what is fast becoming one of the foodie havens of the city, Union Square. Not as expensive as a lot of gourmet food stores, and funkier in its choices of fresh and frozen foods. © **212/529-4612.** www.traderjoes.com.

WHOLE FOODS
4 Union Sq. S., between Broadway and University Place (Subway: 4, 5, 6, L, N, Q, R, or W to 14th St./Union Sq.); Time Warner Center, 10 Columbus Circle (Subway: A, B, C, D, or 1 to 59th St./Columbus Circle); multiple other locations.

Whole Foods is a health food store with far more than just organic chicken breasts. It's a virtual department store, and the shoppers are worth picking over also. Note that there are now stores in all up-and-coming residential and shopping districts, such as the Time Warner Center, Chelsea, and Union Square.

Downtown branches: in Chelsea (250 Seventh Ave., at 24th St.), plus another location at 95 E. Houston (between Bowery and Chrystie sts.). © **212/673-5388** for Union Square; © **212/823-9600** for Time Warner Center. www.wholefoods market.com.

ZABAR'S
2245 Broadway, at 80th St. (Subway: 1 to 79th St.).

For New York food mavens, this has been a stop for every specialty food and takeout item for decades. Some dry goods and cooking equipment are available as well. Not to be confused with Eli Zabar and his similar (but different) food markets. © **212/787-2000**. www.zabars.com.

FURS

I am here to state that I believe in ranched fur; I wear both ranched fur and synthetic fur. If you're ready to turn in your good Republican cloth coat, you should be ready for the thrill of your life—Milan and New York are the fur-wearing cities of the world, and New York is the best place to buy and buy well. The only way to make sure you are getting the kind of quality you deserve is to buy from a reputable furrier. The real value in a New York fur-buying spree comes in buying a top-of-the-line coat for $5,500 to $10,500 at wholesale.

CORNICHE FURS & LUXURY OUTERWEAR
345 Seventh Ave., at 30th St., 20th floor (Subway: 1 to 28th St.).

To get a quick grasp on how the fur business has changed, note that this old faithful resource now prides itself on "luxury outerwear," though the business is still in the hands of Leonard Kahn. If the name sounds slightly familiar, it could be because Ben Kahn is one of the world's most famous furriers. Leonard Kahn is his nephew.

While Leonard has been in the fur business for decades, the business he is in now is relatively new, and his products are very new and hot; in fact, he is always bragging that they have the youngest team in the business. Their business is mostly wholesale—they make coats for big-name designer labels and for department stores (no names, please), but they also sell to some private customers like you and me.

A custom mink coat will be about $10,000. Coats off the rack are less expensive than custom-made, and there are sales. A jacket is less than a coat, of course. A cashmere trench-style coat with a plucked mink collar and cuffs and nutria lining costs about $3,500; a shearling coat ranges from $1,450 on up, depending on quality—the reversible ones cost about $2,250.

Note: Every January there is a sale, and the prices are so low you will weep from greed and delight.

I trust Leonard Kahn 100%, and I send you here knowing you will get the best deal in New York. Call for an appointment, serious shoppers only: © **212/564-1735**.

HANDBAGS

Even in New York, a woman is first judged by her handbag, then her shoes, and then her hands (watch, rings, and manicure). So think about these tips:

- If you're looking for a moderately priced handbag, one of the department stores is your best bet.
- All the big-name European leather-goods stores that carry shoes also sell handbags. These include **Bottega Veneta,**

Fendi, Ferragamo, and Prada. I must say that sale times in these big-name shops may make the goods seem fairly priced.

- For something different, check out the little-known Euro names such as **Anya Hindmarch.** For the ultimate one-of-a-kind creation, visit **Anthony Luciano.**

- All discount sources sell handbags; often they carry name-brand handbags. Try **Daffy's** (p. 292)—especially its location at 125 E. 57th St. (between Park and Lexington aves.)—which often has a good selection of leather goods. **Loehmann's** (p. 294) can be good, too.

- There are a few sources on the Lower East Side that will sell or even order big-name handbags at a 20% discount. I really haven't found it worth the trouble, but many do. **Fine & Klein** (p. 124) is the most famous; it's closed on Saturday.

- During big sale seasons, bags are likely to be marked down 50% . . . except at Vuitton, which never marks down merchandise. If you want a big-name bag and aren't picky about which name, check out **Bergdorf Goodman** or **Saks** during sale season.

- A few upmarket stores sell what look like designer bags (check out Suarez on p. 188) without the labels. They usually cost $500 instead of $1,500. Phew.

ANTHONY LUCIANO
347 W. 36th St., Ste. 1400, between Eighth and Ninth aves. (Subway: A, C, or E to 34th St./Penn Station).

You have money to burn. You have a yen to toss your ego to the wind and show the world why you are special. You want what no other person has. Step this way. Luciana makes mostly framed handbags but will do a tote and/or a custom order. If you go to the showroom, you can get a 25% discount. © **212/ 563-2223,** by appointment.

ANYA HINDMARCH

29 E. 60th St., near Madison Ave. (Subway: 4, 5, 6, N, R, or W to 59th St./Lexington Ave.).

I am conflicted about stores like this—the designs are creative, but the prices are over-the-top; and while I am not against expensive handbags, these are so trendy that they date themselves rapidly. Note that the weak dollar has sent prices soaring, but during sale periods, the handbags may be less than in London. Go figure. There's a second location in SoHo (115 Greene St., near Spring St.).

Web Tip: You can design a custom version of the popular Be A Bag online. Send in your favorite jpeg image to be copied onto the bag, then choose size, handles, and so on. Plan on spending around $400 and waiting 8 to 12 weeks. © 212/750-3974. www.anyahindmarch.com.

BULGARI

730 Fifth Ave., at 57th St. (Subway: F to 57th St.).

After a dramatic closure to retool, this Italian icon has moved back to its original flagship location on Fifth Avenue. To bring in the young crowd, they've launched seasonal collections of handbags, mostly in leather. There's another branch at 783 Madison Ave., between 66th and 67th streets.

Best Bets: Actually I think their bathroom amenities, available for free in assorted luxury hotels, are the best, but they do have some handbags that could just be worth the two grand or more that they cost. Absolutely stunning. © 212/315-9000. www.bulgari.com.

CROUCH & FITZGERALD

400 Madison Ave., near 48th St. (Subway: E or V to Fifth Ave./53rd St.).

A new owner has reinvented this store, made it smaller but redirected it, and brought it back as a strong resource for business luggage, travel gear, and tote bags for working women. There's a good combination of name brands mixed among the house brand, which is made in Europe. The emphasis is on the kind of handbags that can contain everything for travel; there's also **The Sherpa Shop** (p. 213) for doggy accessories. ℂ **212/ 755-5888.** www.crouchandfitzgerald.com.

DOONEY & BOURKE

20 E. 60th St., between Madison and Park aves. (Subway: 4, 5, 6, N, R, or W to 59th St./Lexington Ave.).

Dooney & Bourke—in new digs—is no longer preppy or simple. It has a logo print that is very popular, as well as, every now and then, a leather handbag that is so chic, so stylish, and so hot that I drool thinking about it.

Insider's Secret: I saw several D&B bags being off-loaded at T.J. Maxx on Sixth Avenue (p. 295). *Web Tip:* I searched the online catalog for several new handbags; across-the-board, they were out of stock in every size and color. You can register to be notified when the bags are available, but they give no time frames. ℂ **212/223-7444.** www.dooney.com.

JAMIN PUECH

247 Elizabeth St., between Houston and Prince sts. (Subway: 6 to Bleecker St.).

This French designer embellishes brightly colored handbags with beads, embroidery, feathers, and faux jewels. Choose from tiny evening bags, satchels, and totes, all quirky and unique. ℂ **212/ 431-5200.** www.jamin-puech.com.

KIESELSTEIN-CORD

1058 Madison Ave., at 80th St. (Subway: 6 to 77th St.).

From animal-shaped belt buckles to eyewear to handbags with feet, these distinctive (and pricey) designs are now even being copied in Hong Kong. Look for the lizard, frog, or horse-hoof belt buckles as the biggest status symbol this side of a $500 pair of shades. ℂ **212/744-1041.** www.kieselstein-cord.com.

LANA MARKS

645 Madison Ave., near 60th St. (Subway: 4, 5, 6, N, R, or W to 59th St./Lexington Ave.).

The bags here begin around $1,000 (more often $4,000–$6,000). They are like financial statements and icons to those in the know. Styles are classic yet cutting edge. The colors of leather are remarkable; you should go just to stare. *Best Bets:* This is the best source in NYC for bags made from exotic skins—alligator, crocodile, ostrich, and lizard. And yes, these are the $6,000 ones. © 212/355-6135. www.lanamarks.com.

LULU GUINNESS

394 Bleecker St., near W. 11th St. (Subway: A, C, E, or L to 14th St./Eighth Ave.).

This British designer creates handbags that are whimsical enough to make you smile—pots of flowers, tiny storefronts, and dress-up minibags for nights on the town. *Best Bets:* I'm crazy about her clutches—available in many styles, sizes, and colors. Most are in the $300 range. © 212/367-2120. www.luluguinness.com.

SUAREZ

5 W. 56th St., between Fifth and Sixth aves. (Subway: 4, 5, 6, N, R, or W to 59th St./Lexington Ave.).

Suarez uses factories in Italy to ship designer-like goods that aren't copies and don't have designer labels. Prices are not low, but they are less than in the big-name stores. This is the most famous discount source in New York for shoes, bags, and small leather goods. Discount is a relative term, however. Frankly, I find the prices very high—about $600 for a leather handbag, possibly more, maybe a little less. Of course, these are the same bags you'd pay double for if they had their designer logos on them. © 212/315-3870. www.suarezny.com.

HIP & HOT FASHION

. . . .

AUTO
805 Washington St., between Horatio and Gansevoort sts.
(Subway: A, C, E, or L to 14th St./Eighth Ave.).

This Meatpacking District shop offers industrial design for the home and office; it's the talk of the town since it gives you some place other than Jeffrey (p. 166) to see when you come to this part of Manhattan. *Best Bets:* The ($150–$200) Missoni pillows are stunning and they also carry a good variety of Marimekko. ✆ **212/229-2292.** www.thisisauto.com.

INTERMIX
125 Fifth Ave., near 19th St. (Subway: 4, 5, 6, L, N, Q, R, or W to 14th St./Union Sq.).

This store has hot stuff from cutting-edge designers in all price ranges. Sizes tend to run small; prices run moderate. Some accessories. Other locations are at 98 Prince St. (near Mercer St.), 365 Bleecker St. (near Charles St.), 210 Columbus Ave. (near 68th St.), and 1003 Madison Ave. (near 77th St.). *Web Tip:* Sizing for most items is described on the website; for example, you're advised to order large when buying Missoni, as it runs small. ✆ **212/533-9720.** www.intermixonline.com.

MAYLE
242 Elizabeth St., between Houston and Prince sts.
(Subway: 6 to Spring St.; or R or W to Prince St.).

The trendy one in the family is no longer her dad, Peter. Jane is becoming known not only for her store, but also for her lifestyle. She is often seen with the "in" crowd wearing her snappy designs. *Best Bets:* Shop for vintage-inspired designs with a downtown edge. Her signature off-the-shoulder blouses begin at $300. ✆ **212/625-0406.**

PUMA BLACK STORE
421 W. 14th St., near Washington St. (Subway: A, C, E, or L to 14th St./Eighth Ave.).

This Meatpacking District shop features the designer division of Puma, with shoes, clothes, and active sports gear. Considered awesome by those who use words like that. © **212/206-0109.** www.puma.com.

SCOOP NYC
1275 Third Ave., near 73rd St. (Subway: 6 to 77th St.).

This place is small and hip and filled with trendy clothing and accessories for fashionistas. There are additional branches in the Meatpacking District (430 W. 14th St.) and SoHo (473 Broadway, between Broome and Grand sts.). *Best Bets:* The Meatpacking location spans an entire city block with free-standing men's, women's, and kids' stores. © **212/535-5577.** www. scoopnyc.com.

THEORY
40 Gansevoort St., at Ninth Ave. (Subway: A, C, E, or L to 14th St./Eighth Ave.).

No fashionista worth her Jimmy Choos would admit to not knowing the Theory line, this year's flavor of the must-have kind. The clothes are sometimes simple to look at, but the line has a great fit and specializes in fitting tiny women (it goes down to a size 00). There's another branch at 151 Spring St., in SoHo. If you're going to Woodbury Common (p. 298), don't miss the Theory and Theory Men's outlets. © **212/524-6790.** www. theory.com.

JEANS

All department stores carry a bevy of choices, but specialty stores are holding their own in the new- and used-jeans markets, and some denim purists are quick to point out that designer jeans pale when compared to **Levi's.** Those in the market for Levi's should see the Original Levi's Store, described below. You'll find denim boutiques including **Tsubi** (219 Mulberry St., between Prince and Spring sts.) and **True Religion** (132 Prince St., at Wooster St.) downtown.

CHIP & PEPPER
250 Mulberry St., near Prince St. (Subway: 6 to Spring St.; or R or W to Prince St.).

Another L.A.-based jeans company, now open in Nolita to sell you the look. Along with denim, the brand includes Chip & Pepper University, a line of knits incorporating logos from over 75 U.S. universities. *Web Tip:* Expectant moms can choose from several styles of maternity jeans online. ✆ **212/343-4220.** www.chipandpepper.com.

DIESEL
770 Lexington Ave., at 60th St. (Subway: 4, 5, 6, N, R, or W to 59th St./Lexington Ave.).

This place has Italian jeans known to fit the butt, plus other fashions and trends as well. The superstore near Bloomingdale's has jeans, jeans, and more jeans. There are downtown flagships, too, at Union Square (1 Union Sq. W., at 14th St.) and in SoHo (135 Spring St., near Greene St.), as well as the Diesel Denim Gallery (68 Greene St., near Spring St.), Diesel Kids (416 West Broadway, near Spring St.), and an outlet store at Woodbury Common (p. 298). ✆ **212/308-0055.** www.diesel.com.

THE EARNEST SEWN CO.
821 Washington St., near Gansevoort St. (Subway: A, C, E, or L to 14th St./Eighth Ave.).

I buy Lee Slim jeans whenever I can find them and usually for less than $10 a pair. They make me feel 30 years young and look 20 pounds lighter. I have no need for expensive jeans, although I understand the concept.

I can't quite understand paying several hundred dollars for a pair of jeans, let alone even more than that, but I do grasp the idea of denim made to custom-fit and provide just the right lift and give in just the right places. Along with custom denim, you can also choose from several styles of low-cut ready-to-wear jeans, all available in different washes and colors.

Note that the store sells more than jeans and is a sort of hangout for the cool in the Meatpacking District. *Web Tip:* Some styles are available to order online; however, I couldn't find detailed size info such as rise and inseam length. © 212/242-3414. www.earnestsewn.com.

JEAN SHOP
435 W. 14th St., at Ninth Ave. (Subway: A, C, E, or L to 14th St./Eighth Ave.).

Check out the Jean Shop's own brand, which you can customize to be distressed to your liking. *Web Tip:* Don't bother. © 212/366-5326. www.jean-shop.com.

LUCKY BRAND JEANS
38 Greene St., between Broome and Grand sts. (Subway: 6 to Spring St.).

Wall-to-wall denim, with other branch stores dotted around town. Also on the Upper East Side (1151 Third Ave., at 67th St.) and near Union Square (172 Fifth Ave., at 22nd St.); there's an outlet at Woodbury Common (p. 298) as well. © 212/625-0707. www.luckybrandjeans.com.

ORIGINAL LEVI'S STORE
750 Lexington Ave., near 60th St. (Subway: 4, 5, 6, N, R, or W to 59th St./Lexington Ave.).

Levi's opened its first New York store across the street from Bloomingdale's. The "Original" is a large and excellent shopper's delight. There's another location at 536 Broadway (near Spring St.), plus an outlet at Woodbury Common (p. 298) as well. As we go to press, a new flagship store is scheduled to open at 1501 Broadway, at Times Square. *Web Tip:* All styles including standard 525s are available online, and there's always a promotion to get free shipping. © 212/826-5957. www. levis.com.

JEWELRY

....

Jewelry shopping in New York, as in any other place in the world—big city or small—is a matter of trust. The big, fancy jewelers exist not only because their designs are so irresistible, but also because the house has provided years (maybe centuries) of trust. True, every now and then you hear about a trusted jeweler of 50 years going to the slammer for passing off bottoms of Coke bottles as emeralds. But it's rare.

The big-name New York jewelers, whether they are American, South American, or European, have no such scandals attached to them. I'm ready to stake my reputation on their big reputations. That's why I recommend the big stores. Yes, you pay top-of-the-line prices, but you get something very worthwhile: reliability. Never be afraid to walk into a big-name fancy jeweler; you needn't be in the market for a $106,000 bracelet to be a customer. You may find something for as little as $50; surely you will find many choices at $500. How you are treated is a function of how well dressed you are and how you demand to be treated.

Some places pride themselves on having a fancy name but being accessible to regular people like us; **Tiffany & Co.** (p. 259) is one of those places. They don't want you to come for breakfast, but they do want you to buy something as a souvenir of your trip to New York.

The reliability of the big jewelers is also related to resale. You can always sell a piece of jewelry made by a status firm, such as **Tiffany, Bulgari, Cartier,** and **Harry Winston.** No matter how old it is, a genuinely fine piece of jewelry from a trusted house is a good investment. As my friend, the late Hans Stern, internationally famous jeweler, explained to me:

"Buying from a well-known jeweler is like buying a painting. You are paying for the quality of the art as well as the quality and the reputation of the signature."

There is a jewelry district on 47th Street between Fifth and Sixth avenues, and you are welcome to shop there. You may find many wonderful things; Sarah's husband bought her engagement ring there, and she's also had good luck with other shops on the street (see her report below). The prices on 47th will be better than at **Van Cleef & Arpels** (p. 197), for sure. However, like all other businesses, insiders run the jewelry business. Strangers off the street can, and do, get taken. Industrial-grade diamonds may be sold to you; and color-enhanced stones may be touted as the best money can buy—irradiated stones will not give you cancer, but they may not be what you had in mind. Dealers know what they are doing; I do not. Consider yourself warned. If you want to buy in the diamond district, go to a recommended, trusted source.

Tip: It pays to know something about what you are doing, but you can have a perfectly good time and walk away satisfied even if you don't know what you are doing. Remember that fun and big-time investments are two different things.

Faux jewelry is, of course, socially acceptable. It's always been worn, but fewer people used to talk about it, that's all. Almost all important jewels are copied—to fool the burglar. Even Elizabeth Taylor has admitted that there are paste copies of her gem collection. Cheap faux often looks blatantly fake—the gold is too brassy, the gems are lackluster, the fittings are not fine. If you plan on passing off your collection as something related to the crown jewels, choose carefully and pay the extra money. If you want a bad copy of a good watch, they are currently sold on every street corner for about $25. A good eye can see that the watches are too thick to be real. These same watches, by the way, cost $10 on Canal Street, but their reliability is obviously not ensured.

Used and antique jewelry can be bought at auctions, in certain jewelry shops, and in antiques shops. But even earrings from the 1950s are pricey these days, so have a good eye and

Sarah's Findings on 47th Street

Frank Gabriel is located at 55 W. 47th St., in Booth no. 30 ✆ 212/575-1902. He's at the front of the collective as you walk in and you'll see his booth immediately; Frank's the only dealer with no bling in his case. He's so busy, he doesn't have time to fuss with displays. Tom bought my engagement ring from Frank 30 years ago, and I've been buying from him and sending friends to him ever since.

In addition to my engagement ring (an emerald-cut diamond set in platinum with baguettes), I've bought diamond stud earrings and two diamond-and-platinum eternity bands from Frank. After I destroyed my first wedding band in the garbage disposal, Frank settled my insurance claim and replaced the band—no hassle.

I've had all of my jewelry from Frank appraised in San Francisco and all replacement values have been almost double what I paid for the jewelry.

I've also purchased earrings and bracelets from **Maurice Badler**, 578 Fifth Ave., at the corner of 47th Street. This booth is a good resource for SoHo, Hidalgo, and Roberto Coin at discount prices, and it offers a 30-day no-risk guarantee on all purchases. You can also order from the extensive website. www.mauricebadler.com.

—SRL

know what you are buying. For old and used watches, check out **Aaron Faber** (666 Fifth Ave., near 53rd St.), and **Tourneau** (12 E. 57th St., at Madison Ave., along with three other Manhattan locations), which has a retro department.

As for contemporary jewelry, sterling silver with semiprecious gemstones is a great look; it's also immensely affordable. Tiffany sells this look, and many smaller boutiques have come to specialize in it. **David Yurman** (729 Madison Ave., at 64th St.) has become famous for his combinations of silver and gold.

Big Names

New York is famous for big-name jewelers, from Americans to international names from around the world. While luxury is more in style than ever before (at least since the Depression), one of the most interesting trends is that these big names are cultivating a younger image and offering affordable items to bring you into the family. **Bulgari** (see below) has added silks, handbags, and sunglasses to its range; its Madison Avenue shop is less intimidating than its spiffed-up and really-drop-dead Fifth Avenue rehab. The late Hans Stern turned his business over to his sons, who have retooled the Fifth Avenue store and come up with a very kicky gimmick—the rings have stars cut into the undersides of the gold. A dazzling notion! **Ivanka Trump** (see below) has opened a Madison Avenue boutique to show-case her Art Deco–inspired jewelry collection. All of New York sparkles a little bit more now that we have more options and a range that suits more budgets.

BULGARI
730 Fifth Ave., at 57th St. (Subway: F to 57th St.).
© 212/315-9000. www.bulgari.com.

783 Madison Ave., near 67th St. (Subway: 6 to 68th St./ Hunter College).
© 212/717-2300. www.bulgari.com.

CARTIER
653 Fifth Ave., near 52nd St. (Subway: E or V to Fifth Ave./ 53rd St.).
© 212/753-0111. www.cartier.com.

828 Madison Ave., at 69th St. (Subway: 6 to 68th St./ Hunter College).
© 212/472-6400. www.cartier.com.

DAVID YURMAN
729 Madison Ave., at 64th St. (Subway: 4, 5, 6, N, R, or W to 59th St./Lexington Ave.).
✆ **212/752-4255.** www.davidyurman.com.

HARRY WINSTON
718 Fifth Ave., at 56th St. (Subway: F to 57th St.).
✆ **212/245-2000.** www.harrywinston.com.

H. STERN
645 Fifth Ave., near 52nd St. (Subway: E or V to Fifth Ave./ 53rd St.).
✆ **212/688-0300.** www.hstern.net.

IVANKA TRUMP
683 Madison Ave., between 61st and 62nd sts. (Subway: N, R, or W to Fifth Ave./59th St.).
✆ **212/756-9912.** www.ivankatrumpcollection.com.

TIFFANY & CO.
727 Fifth Ave., at 57th St. (Subway: F to 57th St.).
✆ **212/755-8000.** www.tiffany.com.

37 Wall St., between William and Nassau sts. (Subway: 2 or 3 to Wall St.).
✆ **212/514-8015.** www.tiffany.com.

VAN CLEEF & ARPELS
744 Fifth Ave., at 57th St. (Subway: F to 57th St.).
✆ **212/644-9500.** www.vancleef.com.

A Discounter

FORTUNOFF
3 W. 57th St., at Fifth Ave. (Subway: E or V to Fifth Ave./ 53rd St.).

They moved, so don't freak. This store is not as sophisticated as I would like, but the walk-in vault part is fun, and the store has been built into a former bank.

This is a good source for discounted basics such as pearls, simple contemporary gold earrings, chains, silverware, and the like. Brides and babies are the house specialty.

For those who have been working the Diamond District, come with your pen and paper and don't be shy. I was set to buy a pair of seashell earrings (don't ask) at a discount source in the district for $750, which I considered quite good. Then I found a similar pair at Fortunoff for $550. The pair at Fortunoff was not as well made as the pair I wanted, but they made me lose faith in my original jeweler. Don't buy from any no-name jewelry source until you have at least educated your eye and your budget at Fortunoff. ✆ **212/758-6660.** www.fortunoff.com.

Midrange Midas

JADED
1048 Madison Ave., near 80th St. (Subway: 6 to 77th St.).

Awash in a sea of jewels, Manhattan also has an ocean of imitations out there. For the rare piece that is part faux and part art (original creations that are not made with precious stones), stop by Jaded, where the designs are private label and the action is uptown. This is the classiest faux in town.

Prices begin at about $100 for earrings, but the workmanship is excellent and the pieces are unique. This is the "in" place for the Ladies Who Lunch who want to look fashionable and yet different. If you're looking to make just one Manhattan splurge that defines the essence of New York, this could be the place.

Web Tip: You'll get an idea of what's in store from the website, but individual pieces are not featured, prices are not given, nor can you place an online order. ✆ **212/288-6631.** www.jadedjewels.com.

REINSTEIN/ROSS

*29 E. 73rd St., near Madison Ave. (Subway: 6 to 77th St.);
122 Prince St., between Wooster and Greene sts. (Subway:
C or E to Spring St.; or R or W to Prince St.).*

I think I like this firm because it does a look that is similar to
Elizabeth Gage of London; the rings are made of brushed gold
in 18 or 22 karat and often have unusual stones in them. The
look is sort of neoclassical baroque, although you can also find
a more or less traditional gold wedding band inset with little
sparkle diamonds. I'm the kind that prefers the white and yellow diamonds, the orange and yellow sapphires, and so on.
© 212/772-1901 for uptown location; © 212/226-4513 for
SoHo location. www.reinsteinross.com.

TAMBETTI INC.

*509 Madison Ave., at 53rd St., upstairs (Subway: E or V to
Fifth Ave./53rd St.).*

This is a private showroom for which you need an appointment; it is located in an office building and everything is put
away. There are two house specialties—you look through the
drawers of existing works, ooh and aah, and eventually buy
a chunky, hunky, to-die-for boho necklace of beads and
stones for about $1,200; or you bring in your tired, your old,
your tattered jewelry yearning to be free, and the designer,
D'vora, makes you something totally new and hot with what
you've got.

　　She is often called the Queen of Re-Cycling, although I
bought new and am over the moon with my 13-strand pearls
and garnets and smoky quartz dingle dangles. To avoid New
York sales tax, I paid $18 for shipping.

　　Insider's Secret: Bring your strands of stones and beads from
foreign markets, tell D'vora if you want real gold or gold-plated,
and let her string and create. © 212/751-9584.

Fancy Fauxs

ERWIN PEARL
697 Madison Ave., at 63rd St. (Subway: F to Lexington Ave./63rd St.).

This faux jewelry chain specializes in travel jewelry, fabulous fakes in classic styles ranging from pearls to cubic zirconia studs to gold necklaces and earrings. Prices are reasonable, with earrings starting at around $100. You'll see branches of this store in most large airports, including JFK (terminal 3). There are also other shops in Manhattan, including 70 W. 50th St., at Rockefeller Center, Grand Central Station, and 3 World Financial Center, at Wall Street. *Best Bets:* The reversible huggie earrings are available in more than 40 size and color combos, $50 to $85. © 212/753-3155.

GALE GRANT
485 Madison Ave., near 52nd St. (Subway: E or V to Fifth Ave./53rd St.).

Avoid this place at lunch hour, when every other chic woman in New York is trying to buy her fakes. Some of it sparkles a bit too much, but you can get great costume jewelry and some fabulous imitations here. One of my spies was recently in the store, musing over a necklace that might or might not work with a specific dress for an upcoming Important Event. The owner suggested she take the necklace and try it with her dress. If it wasn't quite right, she could return the necklace to the store to have a new one strung to her exact needs within 48 hours. Now that's service! © 212/752-3142. www.gale grant.com.

MARIKO
998 Madison Ave., between 77th and 78th sts. (Subway: 6 to 77th St.).

See p. 134. © 212/472-1176.

RENE
786 Madison Ave., near 67th St. (Subway: 6 to 68th St.).

See p. 134. © **212/249-3001.**

Vintage

ERIE BASIN
388 Van Brunt St., near Dikeman, Red Hook, Brooklyn (Subway: F or G to Smith/9th sts.).

Owner Russell Whitmore's specialty is taking old watch chains and turning them into stunning new necklaces. You'll also find eclectic pieces from the 19th and 20th centuries in this Brooklyn boutique. © **718/554-6147.**

PIPPIN VINTAGE JEWELRY
112 W. 17th St., between Sixth and Seventh aves. (Subway: 1 to 18th St.).

Shop here for Bakelite, cameos, and one-of-a-kind costume jewels. Most pieces are from the '60s and '70s, but there's also some earlier jewelry mixed in with the batch. © **212/505-5159.**

KIDS & TOYS

Shopping for kids in Manhattan is a bit of a Catch-22: You have to be crazy to spend time in New York shopping for kids, but you'd be crazy not to think about it because there are so many great places. So think carefully. If price, or the combination of price and acceptable style, is your main concern, then the truth is that you can do better through catalogs and at suburban discounters. If you want to splurge, however, that's another story. Welcome to a city where you can spend $200 for a pair of party shoes for your kids.

I am assuming that you have chains such as **Gap Kids** and **Baby Gap** in your neck of the woods; if not, they are great fun, and sale prices are moderate. Should you be able to hit the outlet malls, please note that **Carter's** has outlets in Woodbury Common as well as the New Jersey malls. See p. 296 for more on outlet stores. In town, the source for discounted kids' everything is **Burlington Coat Factory** (707 Sixth Ave., at 23rd St.), on Ladies' Mile.

A few thoughts to help you:

- All of the big department stores have excellent children's departments.
- The Lower East Side is good for bulk in layette at a 20% discount.
- Madison Avenue is dotted with fine and funky boutiques that sell unusual specialty items that no one has ever seen before (read: very expensive). The area of Madison Avenue from 86th to 96th streets houses many private schools and is therefore jammed with boutiques catering to young ones—many are branches of international big names such as **Bonpoint** (1269 Madison Ave., at 91st St.) and **Jacadi** (1296 Madison Ave., at 92nd St.). Also check out **Marie-Chantal** (1992 Madison Ave., near 88th St.) and **Magic Windows** (1186 Madison Ave., near 87th St.) for the cat's meow in this genre.
- Mini hip-boho clothing can be found at **Calypso Enfant** (426 Broome St., between Crosby and Lafayette sts.) and **Yoya** (636 Hudson St., between Horatio and Jane sts.).
- There's a **Toys "R" Us** branch at 1514 Broadway, at 44th Street. Note that Toys "R" Us has closed out its clothing divisions.
- Some of the big names, especially in what I call conservative fashion, make kids' clothes—check out **Brooks Brothers** and **Talbots**. Even **Ralph Lauren** now has a toddler line.
- **Daffy's** (p. 292), **Loehmann's,** and **Century 21,** the discounters, sell kids' clothes at all of their locations.

AMERICAN GIRL PLACE
609 Fifth Ave., at 49th St. (Subway: B, D, F, or V to Rockefeller Center).

If you have a young daughter, you know about this amazing series of dolls and the marketing concept that goes behind them. This new store has dolls, a tearoom, and a theater for events. ***Best Bets:*** Just Like You dolls can be custom-made to match your daughter's eyes, skin tone, hair color, and personal style. $90 and up. ***Web Tip:*** Check the website to get dates for special events including author appearances and cooking classes. © 212/371-2220. www.americangirlplace.com.

F.A.O. SCHWARZ
767 Fifth Ave., at 58th St. (Subway: N, R, or W to Fifth Ave./59th St.).

The most famous toy store in America has scaled down enormously, but you can still jump on the floor-mat piano, just as Tom Hanks did in *Big*. ***Best Bets:*** The large selection of items at all prices. There are wild and crazy and stupidly expensive items, but also many items under $25. ***Web Tip:*** You can shop online and even order a couture tutu. At certain times of the year there are promos for free shipping on orders of $75 or more. © 212/644-9400. www.fao.com.

GREENSTONES
442 Columbus Ave., near 81st St. (Subway: B or C to 81st St./Museum of Natural History).

One of the most famous residents of the Upper West Side, Greenstones, thankfully, is not one of those kiddie stores that's as big as a closet with prices as high as a condo. I mean, prices aren't low, but the range of looks is wide, from Chanel-style suits for your young miss to leather bomber jackets. There are almost a hundred different European lines sold here, as well as standard American faves such as OshKosh. There are two other locations on the East Side at 1184 Madison Ave., near

86th Street, and at 1410 Second Ave., at 73rd Street. © 212/
580-4322.

MAGIC WINDOWS
*1186 Madison Ave., at 87th St. (Subway: 4, 5, or 6 to
86th St.).*

Expanded now to include the teenage debutante and party set,
this store features mostly dress-up clothes, because the clients
all wear uniforms to school. Doesn't everyone? *Best Bets:*
Dresses for flowers girls, first communions, or dinner at the
country club. Expect to pay over $200 for a frilly frock. © 212/
289-0028. www.magic-windows.com.

OILILY
*820 Madison Ave., between 68th and 69th sts. (Subway: 6
to 68th St./Hunter College).*

This is a Dutch chain with stores all over the world and prices
that break my heart because I am so attracted to the clothes,
the colors, and the look: happy splashy designs, bright mixed
patterns, and all the celebration a garment can take. There are
children's, women's, and accessories. *Best news:* There's now
an outlet store at Woodbury Common (p. 298). © 212/772-
8686. www.oililyusa.com.

SECOND CHILDHOOD
*283 Bleecker St., near Seventh Ave. (Subway: 1 to
Christopher St.).*

Now you can buy the same toys for your children that you had
as a child, but you'll pay the price; these playthings are for serious collectors. This shop's cases are full of antiques, all cate-
gorized by pedigree and condition. Inventory focuses on early-
to mid-20th-century items. © 212/989-6140.

THREADS
*1451 Second Ave., between 76th and 77th sts. (Subway: 6
to 77th St.).*

This Pottery Barn Kids offshoot carries clothing for children up to age 36 months. They have an in-store monogramming service to customize just about everything they sell. © 212/737-0104. www.potterybarnkids.com.

ZITOMER
969 Madison Ave., near 76th St. (Subway: 6 to 77th St.).

Take the elevator from the pharmacy part of this store and go up to little-girl dreamland. Some child actors have admitted that their Oscar gowns come from Zitomer. © 212/737-2016. www.zitomer.com.

LINGERIE & SWIMWEAR

Like most women, I never know from month to month, bra to bra, what size I wear. Sometimes it's a 36D, sometimes a 38C. Fortunately, New York has a great selection of specialty lingerie shops where I can go to be fitted with bras in styles ranging from sports to everyday to lacy décolleté.

BRASMYTH
905 Madison Ave., at 72nd St. (Subway: 6 to 77th St.).

The bras in this shop are very expensive, and the service can be spotty, especially if they're busy; however, there's good stock on basic bras in all sizes. *Best Bets:* Swimsuits. You can buy the tops and bottoms separately, most in the $100-per-piece price range. © 212/772-9400.

ERES
621 Madison, between 58th and 59th sts. (Subway: N, R, or W to Fifth Ave./59th St.).

This reigning queen of French swim togs has another location at 98 Wooster St., between Prince and Spring streets. © 212/431-7300.

INTIMACY
1252 Madison Ave., at 90th St. (Subway: 4, 5, or 6 to 86th St.).

You'll find a lot of imported (read expensive) labels in this boutique; however, you won't find prettier, sexier, or more unique styles elsewhere. Prepare to go up a couple of sizes. These European bras run smaller than U.S. brands. ✆ **212/860-8366.**

TOWN SHOP
2273 Broadway, at 82nd St. (Subway: 1 to 79th St.).

This is the place for bra selection; they've been in business for over 20 years and have it all. *Best Bets:* Good midprice everyday brassieres are available for $20 on up, and you'll be properly fitted. ✆ **212/724-8160.**

MATERNITY

Even when apparel sales were in the dumps, maternity wear was booming. Besides the specialty shops below, check out www.gap.com for Gap's maternity line.

BELLY DANCE MATERNITY
548 Hudson St., between Charles and Perry sts. (Subway: 1 to Christopher St.).

This West Village branch of the Chicago chain supplies fashionista moms-to-be with designer maternity wear from top designers including Japanese Weekend, Chip & Pepper, and Serfontaine denim. *Best Bets:* There's lots of stock for future moms who are size 0 to 6 before pregnancy. Large ladies need not apply. ✆ **212/645-3640.** www.bellydancematernity.com.

DESTINATION MATERNITY
575 Madison Ave., at 57th St. (Subway: E or V to Fifth Ave./53rd St.).

This three-story emporium is one-stop shopping for all the best-known maternity brands, including Motherhood, Mimi Maternity, A Pea in the Pod, and Edamame Spa. And yes, there's a good selection of plus sizes. © **212/588-0220.**

MENSWEAR

There's no question that Manhattan is the men's shopping capital of America. Furthermore, it's one of the few cities where there is so much bargain merchandise that even a man who hates to shop will be astonished by the opportunities to save. International businessmen and dignitaries, step this way. Special-size men, turn to p. 224; New York is your place, too.

Almost every man who lives in New York (and many who have just visited) has been to **Barneys** and has an opinion about it. Barneys is surely the most famous men's store in New York. Some men exclaim that they need no other store in Manhattan.

If you still want more, stroll the area I call Men's Mad—Madison Avenue in the mid-40s—where there is a cluster of men's shops (most of them famous names), many of which specialize in conservative business attire. This is where you find your **Brooks Brothers, Jos. A. Banks,** and more.

For those willing to go for the gusto and get in some discount shopping, see p. 296.

ALFRED DUNHILL
711 Fifth Ave., at 55th St. (Subway: E or V to Fifth Ave./ 53rd St.).

The shop for the man who has everything, can't stand to shop, and wants to drop in at "his" store to fulfill his needs for suits, accessories, and smokes. It's very much a private club. © **212/ 753-9292.** www.dunhill.com.

ASCOT CHANG
110 Central Park S., between Sixth and Seventh aves.
(Subway: F to 57th St.).

Ascot Chang is a famous institution in Hong Kong and, indeed, around the world. He is one of the world's best-known and best-loved shirt makers. Now he's come to New York (well, his son has) to open a shop for those who know how comfortable a custom shirt can be. Prices are higher than in Hong Kong, but not unreasonable—you'll pay about $150 for a custom shirt. The shop also has ready-made shirts, as well as made-to-measure; you can choose from about 2,000 fabrics. Women's shirts are not available ready-made as in Hong Kong, but can be custom-ordered. There are also suits, suspenders, ties, tennis togs, and the usual apparel for a well-dressed gent.

Web Tip: You can access the special-order catalog online, where you'll be able to create a custom-made shirt from the convenience of your computer. © 212/759-3333. www.ascot chang.com.

BARNEYS NEW YORK
660 Madison Ave., at 61st St. (Subway: 4, 5, 6, N, R, or W to 59th St./Lexington Ave.).

The Madison Avenue men's store connects to the main part of the store on the first floor only (look for the doorway behind the fragrance counter). You then go up escalator after escalator to layers of men's tailoring, a boxing ring, various health and grooming services, and furnishings.

Web Tip: Click on "Mens" and you can shop online; however, for such a fabulous store, this is not an exciting website nor does it offer much in selection. © 212/826-8900. www. barneys.com.

BERGDORF GOODMAN MEN
745 Fifth Ave., at 58th St. (Subway: N, R, or W to Fifth Ave./59th St.).

I don't know how this store has stayed in business: It is gorgeous and wonderful and special and filled with designer names but, alas, few customers. I think Bergdorf's should just call it a museum and charge admission. This is where the Masters of the Universe shop for the ultimate in power dressing for meetings, weekends, bedroom, boardroom, and even bathroom. Check out the cafe upstairs for a quick bite. © 212/753-7300. www.bergdorfgoodman.com.

BROOKS BROTHERS
346 Madison Ave., at 44th St. (Subway: 4, 5, 6, 7, or S to Grand Central/42nd St.); 666 Fifth Ave., at 53rd St. (Subway: E or V to Fifth Ave./53rd St.).

It's not that I'm a traditionalist, a conservative dresser, or anything old-fashioned or uptight, but I'm sorry to say that I don't get it when it comes to the Brooks Brothers on Fifth Avenue. I mean, I understand it conceptually—a young, modern, hip store to lure in young customers and convert them to a brand that has a reputation for being old-fashioned. Great. It's just that the store leaves me bored.

Go see for yourself. It carries men's and women's clothing, mostly for the workplace. Note that the clothes and the look are not the same as those at the regular store on Madison Avenue where, thankfully, little has changed.

You can tell a proper Brooks Brothers suit by the square, boxy cut, which is why it's a uniform for a certain kind of businessman. The cut is also great on an American body, a large man, or a man with a little extra weight on him.

Brooks Brothers does a steady business in these ultraconservative, always-correct suits, but this is actually a better store for sportswear and casual clothes. It does have boys' and women's departments as well—in fact, it has beefed up the latter in hopes of making a major statement in women's career clothing.

There's also a factory outlet at Woodbury Common (p. 298). *Web Tip:* You can order custom shirts online. © 212/682-8800 for Madison Avenue; © **212/261-9440** for Fifth Avenue. www.brooksbrothers.com.

F. M. ALLEN
962 Madison, between 75th and 76th sts. (Subway: 6 to 77th St.).

This Safari outfitter (yes, even Clark Gable was outfitted here) is located in a tiny uptown store where you buy clothes and gear and things a gentleman will need when he goes to ground, such as the right Dunhill flask. The brand is old, the look is classic. There's bush luggage, trips and safaris to book, and mood and adventure and millions of miles of bloody Africa. *Best Bets:* Gentlemen's sporting antiques. © **212/737-4374.** www.fmallen.com.

HICKEY
96 Grand St., between Mercer and Greene sts. (Subway: A, C, or E to Canal St.).

This is a division of Hickey Freeman, one of the most famous American suiters that serves well-dressed and well-heeled men and boys. This is a middle space for young men, a little bit hip but still traditional. © **212/219-0230.**

JOHN VARVATOS
122 Spring St., at Green St. (Subway: 6 to Spring St.); 315 Bowery, between 1st and 2nd sts. (Subway: 6 to Bleecker St.).

After brief stints at Ralph Lauren and Calvin Klein, John Varvatos broke away to design a signature line of comfortable and sporty yet luxurious clothing for men. His black two- and three-button suits and tuxedos are favorites of fashion-conscious grooms. © **212/965-0700** for Spring Street location. © **212/358-0315** for Bowery. www.johnvarvatos.com.

JOS. A. BANK
366 Madison Ave., at 46th St. (Subway: 4, 5, 6, 7, or S to Grand Central/42nd St.).

This is a Boston retailer with a look that's very similar to Brooks Brothers, but at lower prices. The store isn't very big or splashy, but for conservative dressers looking for traditional clothing, this amounts to almost a price war. © 212/ 370-0600. www.josabank.com.

LORD WILLY'S
223 Mott St., between Prince and Spring sts. (Subway: N, R, or W to Prince St.).

Lord Willy's puts a contemporary spin on classic bespoke clothing; this isn't your dad's tailor. A second location at 102 Christopher sells ready-to-wear. The name of the store makes me blush. *Best Bets:* The boxers, which are sized from "big willy" to "massive willy," make excellent gifts ($40). © 212/ 691-0888. www.lordwillys.com.

ROTHMAN'S OF UNION SQUARE
200 Park Ave. S., at 17th St. (Subway: 4, 5, 6, L, N, Q, R, or W to 14th St./Union Sq.).

This is an old-fashioned traditional department store with good customer service (including personal shoppers) and all the big brands you can imagine. The only difference is that all prices are 20% off retail. There are departments for dress-up and dress casual, as well as boys' and boys' ceremonial (bar mitzvahs, first communions) and, of course, weddings and formal events. *Web Tip:* You can sign up for advance notification of sales online. © 212/777-7400. www.rothmansny.com.

THOM BROWNE
100 Hudson St., at Franklin St. (Subway: 1 to Franklin St.).

Thom Browne's flagship atelier in TriBeCa, with its custom fittings, is as unique as his finely crafted suits. Not for traditionalists, his designs are in demand by creative young hedge-funders who order the close-cropped jackets and too-short trousers by the dozens. Comfortable and chic, the suits are also in the hedge fund price range; expect to pay upwards of $3,500 for a two-piece suit. *Web Tip:* There's not much information on the website, but you can preview the latest collection by scrolling through the link at the bottom of the page. ✆ 212/633-1197. www.thombrowne.com.

VILEBREQUIN
1070 Madison Ave., at 81st St. (Subway: 6 to 77th St.).

The celebrity swimwear of choice, these colorful print boxers have been spotted on Hugh Grant, George Clooney, and Brad Pitt, just to name a few. Originally made in St. Tropez out of quick-drying sailcloth, the trunks feature a patented waterproof wallet. They're also available for infants and boys. Another store is located at 436 West Broadway, at Prince Street. ✆ 212/650-0353. www.vilebrequin.com.

MUSEUM SHOPS
....

METROPOLITAN MUSEUM OF ART STORE
Fifth Ave., at 82nd St. (Subway: 4, 5, or 6 to 86th St.).

In addition to the grand flagship inside the museum, there are branches around town, including one inside Macy's and one at Rockefeller Center. *Best Bets:* The shop in the museum is the largest and the best. ✆ 212/570-3894. www.metmuseum.org/store.

MOMA DESIGN AND BOOK STORE
44 W. 53rd St., between Fifth and Sixth aves. (Subway: E or V to Fifth Ave./53rd St.).

This is one-stop gift shopping. Don't miss the wall of postcards and the book section. The crowds take over after 5pm, when the museum closes and the gift shop's still open. ✆ 212/767-1050. www.momastore.org.

PETS

....

CANINE STYLES
43 Greenwich Ave., between Charles and Perry sts.
(Subway: A, C, E, or L to 14th St./Eighth Ave.).

This small but chic boutique serves cat and dog owners. It's where I found a Statue of Liberty toy and a polka-dot collar for my dog. Oh yes, I think I also bought pet aromatherapy, but don't tell anyone. There are also branches at 1195 Lexington Ave., at 81st Street, and at 830 Lexington Ave., between 63rd and 64th streets. ✆ **212/352-8591.** www.caninestyles.com.

THE SHERPA SHOP
Crouch & Fitzgerald, 400 Madison Ave., near 48th St.
(Subway: E or V to Fifth Ave./53rd St.).

This is the place for fabulous doggy gear—totes and carrying bags and travel items, all at prices around $100 for big and fancy, $50 for small and easy to schlep. The quality of the bags is so high that there is now a cult surrounding them, and the brand name Sherpa is fast becoming generic. The line is also sold in most pet stores and pet chains, but this is the mother shop. Approved by airlines. ***Best Bets:*** Toffee recommends the Ultimate Sherpa bag, $115. ✆ **212/755-5888.** www.crouch andfitzgerald.com.

SEX TOYS

....

Sex toys have really come out of the closet. While the Ricky's beauty-supply chain seems to have dropped its Adults Only department, most drugstores now carry a wide range of products and even toys. What's more, designer sex toys are readily available, along with a new range of condoms and accessories designed specifically for women and called Elexa, made by the friendly guys who brought us Trojans.

BABELAND

94 Rivington St., between Ludlow and Orchard sts.
(Subway: F, J, M, or Z to Delancey/Essex sts.); 43 Mercer
St., between Grand and Broome sts. (Subway: A, C, or E to
Canal St.).

You'll find all the basics—vibrators, videos, bondage tape, plus a few gizmos you may not be familiar with. *Web Tip:* The "how to" links leave nothing to the imagination. ℂ 212/375-1701. www.babeland.com.

CONDOMANIA

351 Bleecker St., between Charles and W. 10th sts.
(Subway: 1 to Christopher St.).

Believe it or not, this store has great gift ideas, even souvenirs from New York. While the main, uh, thrust, is condoms, there are many unique and adorable gift items. "Plastics, Benjamin, plastics." *Web Tip:* If you're shy, you can buy almost everything online. The site offer promotions, free stuff, and gift certificates. ℂ 212/691-9442. www.condomania.com.

MYLA

20 E. 69th St., near Madison Ave. (Subway: 6 to 68th
St./Hunter College).

This is a British import; I will not comment on the address except to say that expensive real estate like this demonstrates the upscale intent of the product line. Lingerie as well as toys are available. *Web Tip:* Call the online help desk at **212/327-2676** if you have questions or need help ordering online. ℂ 212/570-1590. www.myla.com.

PLEASURE CHEST

156 Seventh Ave. S., between Charles and Perry sts. (Subway: 1 to Christopher St.).

I got this listing from the TV show *Sex and the City;* so there. ℂ 212/242-2158. www.pleasurechesttoys.com.

SONIA RYKIEL
*849 Madison Ave., near 70th St. (Subway: 6 to 68th St./
Hunter College).*

This shop is mostly a fashion boutique, but following a trend begun by Sonia's daughter Nathalie, there are also some fancy girl things meant to give lasting pleasure. Ask. © **212/396-3060.** www.soniarykiel.com.

SHOES

Shoe stores come in all flavors in Manhattan: department stores (which usually have at least two different shoe departments), boutiques, teenage cheapie shoe stores (just take a look at W. 8th St. next time you're downtown), and, of course, temples to the athletic shoe.

Entire clothing empires and fashion statements have grown from houses that originally manufactured just shoes and small leather goods (**Ferragamo, Gucci, Prada,** even **Bally**).

Big Names in Shoes & Leather Goods

Here are some of the best-known places in the city to attire your feet in style.

BALLY
*628 Madison Ave., at 59th St. (Subway: 4, 5, 6, N, R, or W
to 59th St./Lexington Ave.).*
© **212/751-9082.** www.bally.com.

BOTTEGA VENETA
*699 Fifth Ave., between 54th and 55th sts. (Subway: E or V
to Fifth Ave./53rd St.).*
© **212/371-5511.** www.bottegaveneta.com.

Gucci
*725 Fifth Ave., at 56th St. (Subway: E or V to Fifth Ave./
53rd St.).*
© 212/826-2600. www.gucci.com.

*840 Madison Ave., near 70th St. (Subway: 6 to 68th St./
Hunter College).*
© 212/717-2619. www.gucci.com.

Longchamp
*713 Madison Ave., near 63rd St. (Subway: 4, 5, 6, N, R, or
W to 59th St./Lexington Ave.).*
© 212/223-1500. www.longchamp.com.

Louis Vuitton
1 E. 57th St., at Fifth Ave. (Subway: F to 57th St.).
© 212/758-8877. www.louisvuitton.com.

*116 Greene St., between Prince and Spring sts. (Subway: R
or W to Prince St.).*
© 212/274-9090. www.louisvuitton.com.

Manolo Blahnik
*31 W. 54th St., between Fifth and Sixth aves. (Subway: E or
V to Fifth Ave./53rd St.).*
© 212/582-3007.

Prada
*45 E. 57th St., between Park and Madison aves. (Subway:
4, 5, 6, N, R, or W to 59th St./Lexington Ave.).*
© 212/308-2332. www.prada.com.

*724 Fifth Ave., near 56th St. (Subway: E or V to Fifth Ave./
53rd St.).*
© 212/664-0010. www.prada.com.

*841 Madison Ave., at 70th St. (Subway: 6 to 68th St./
Hunter College).*
© 212/327-4200. www.prada.com.

*575 Broadway, near Prince St. (Subway: R or W to
Prince St.).*
© **212/334-8888.** www.prada.com.

ROGER VIVIER
750 Madison Ave., at 65th St. (Subway: F to 63rd St.).
© **212/861-5371.**

SALVATORE FERRAGAMO
*655 Fifth Ave., near 52nd St. (Subway: E or V to Fifth Ave./
53rd St.).*
© **212/759-3822.** www.ferragamo.com.

STUART WEITZMAN
*Time Warner Center, 10 Columbus Circle (Subway: A, B, C,
D, or 1 to 59th St./Columbus Circle).*
© **212/823-9560.** www.stuartweitzman.com.

*625 Madison Ave., near 59th St. (Subway: 4, 5, 6, N, R, or
W to 59th St./Lexington Ave.).*
© **212/750-2555.** www.stuartweitzman.com.

Specialty Shoes

BELGIAN SHOES
*110 E. 55th St., between Park and Lexington aves.
(Subway: 4, 5, 6, N, R, or W to 59th St./Lexington Ave.).*

Belgian Shoes are handmade moccasins with a distinctive look
that has made them a status symbol. These shoes fit differently
from others, so you may be a different size. They either fit you
or they don't—mine bit me—and the store will not take returns.
Still, many swear by them. © **212/755-7372.** www.belgian
shoes.com.

CHRISTIAN LOUBOUTIN
941 Madison Ave., near 75th St. (Subway: 6 to 77th St.).

The darling of Paris tootsies has opened two Manhattan boutiques, where his wild and witty work is showcased. The red sole is his trademark, which is especially hot when you see a celebrity on a late-night chat show who is swinging her legs so that you can casually see the soles of her shoes. There's a second shop at 59 Horatio St. (at Greenwich St.). *Web Tip:* This site is very slow; in the time it takes to open, you could take a taxi to one of the boutiques. © 212/396-1884. www.christianlouboutin.fr.

SIGERSON MORRISON
28 Prince St., between Mott and Elizabeth sts. (Subway: 6 to Spring St., or R or W to Prince St.).

For the Manolo crowd. Another location is devoted to handbags, right around the corner at 242 Mott St., at Prince Street. The new uptown store is at 987 Madison Ave., between 76th and 77th streets. *Tip:* These catch-me-if-you-can high heels, ballet flats, and mules go up to size 11. *Best Bets:* Comfortable shoes that look uncomfortable. © 212/219-3893. www.sigersonmorrison.com.

TARYN ROSE
681 Madison Ave., between 61st and 62nd sts. (Subway: N, R, or W to Fifth Ave./59th St.).

Created by a doctor, an orthopedic surgeon no less, these shoes were originally meant to be high-end walking shoes for women who shop on Madison Avenue. The brand has grown and they now offer heels and dressy shoes, but the "comfort" factor remains the same. © 212/753-3939. www.tarynrose.com.

TÉ CASAN
382 West Broadway, between Broome and Spring sts. (Subway: C or E to Spring St.).

This SoHo boutique features limited edition shoes from a rotating list of designers including Alexander McQueen, Natalie Portman, and Versace. New styles are introduced weekly and inventory has a quick shelf life; so if you see a pair that you like, grab 'em. They have private fitting rooms if your pedicure's not up to par. The store specializes in vegan shoes. Honest. © **212/584-8000.** www.tecasan.com.

TOD'S
650 Madison Ave., at 60th St. (Subway: 4, 5, 6, N, R, or W to 59th St./Lexington Ave.).

Tod's does stylish flat and driving shoes; they are handmade and last forever. I would pay anything for mine because they are the only shoes I can walk all day in. Tod's has many styles, including high heels and a line of sport shoes called Hogan (which has its own store at 134 Spring St., at Wooster St.). It also does handbags, and will even custom-engrave your initials into your shoe. Hot damn. I have found that there is a universal uniform among chic women who sport jeans, Tod's, a good watch, and an expensive handbag. Just do it. *Best Bets:* The classic driving mocs with pebble soles. Prices are over $300 for all styles. © **212/644-5945.** www.todsonline.com.

Moderate to Mass-Market Big Names

You're sure to find something to suit you at one of these stores.

AEROSOLES
168 Fifth Ave., between 21st and 22nd sts. (Subway: R or W to 23rd St.).

Tip: Aerosoles has outlet stores around the country, including one at Woodbury Common (p. 298), but prices in the outlets are the same as in the stores and the catalog. The only difference: At the outlet, you get the second pair of shoes at half-price. There's another location at 709 Lexington Ave. *Best Bets:* Comfortable boots that you can walk in all day. Most are in the $100 range, but there's often a promotion offering the first pair at retail, with additional pairs at a discount. The sale racks always offer good buys. © **212/755-0683.** www.aerosoles.com.

CAMPER

125 Prince St., at Wooster St. (Subway: R or W to Prince St.).

This Spanish brand is equally known for the architectural design of their boutiques and for their fashion-forward and comfortable shoes. *Web Tip:* Note that some styles run small; a 44 is more like a 42. © **212/358-1842.** www.camper.com.

DSW (DESIGNER SHOE WAREHOUSE)

40 E. 14th St., near University Place (Subway: 4, 5, 6, L, N, Q, R, or W to 14th St./Union Sq.).

See p. 293. © **212/674-2146.** www.dswshoe.com.

GALO

895 Madison Ave., at 72nd St. (Subway: 6 to 68th St./Hunter College).

Classic comfy shoes sold at several locations, including 1296 Third Ave. (at 74th St.) and 825 Lexington Ave. (at 63rd St.). © **212/744-7936.** www.galoshoes.com.

NINE WEST

750 Lexington Ave., near 59th St. (Subway: 4, 5, 6, N, R, or W to 59th St./Lexington Ave.); multiple other locations.

This mall standby is everywhere in New York, including SoHo (577 Broadway, near Prince St.), Union Square (115 Fifth Ave., near 19th St.), and Rockefeller Center (1258 Sixth Ave., near 50th St.); call © **800/999-1877** for other addresses. © **212/486-8094.** www.ninewest.com.

STEVE MADDEN

540 Broadway, near Prince St. (Subway: R or W to Prince St.).

Funky women's and men's footwear, with a few locations around town. Call © **888/762-3336** for addresses. © **212/343-1800.** www.stevemadden.com.

UNISA
701 Madison Ave., near 62nd St. (Subway: N, R, or W to Fifth Ave./59th St.).

Reasonably priced sandals, flats, mules, and pumps—and even the espadrilles you may recall from the '80s. ✆ **212/753-7474.** www.unisa.com.

Sneakers

ALFIE RIVINGTON CLUB
158 Rivington St., at Clinton (Subway: F, J, M, or Z to Essex St./Delancey St.).

This is an excellent choice for Adidas's top-of-the-line styles. ✆ **212/375-8128.**

DAVE'S QUALITY MEAT
7 E. 3rd St., at Bowery (Subway: 6 to Astor Place).

Buyers for Dave's find the latest and most exclusive releases from Nike and Adidas. You'll also find '80s-style basketball and retro skateboard sneakers. *Web Tip:* New arrivals are listed on the website. ✆ **212/505-7551.** www.davesquality meat.com.

SOHO LAB
530 Broadway, at Spring St. (Subway: 6 to Spring St.).

High-tech designs by the folks who make Skechers. *Best Bets:* Don't overlook the flip-flops for $30; they're as comfortable as the sneakers. ✆ **212/431-8803.** www.skechers.com.

SHOPPING CENTERS

The big malls are in the metropolitan areas outside of Manhattan. In New York City, all you get in terms of a mall is several floors of retail space in an office complex—such as "the

Shopping Adventure: Mitsuwa Marketplace

595 River Rd., Edgewater, New Jersey.

This mall's so much fun that you must give it a little consideration. Mitsuwa Marketplace is in New Jersey, where everyone who craves a mall should be going. But wait, this is no mall or ordinary shopping center. It's a small strip village that is totally Japanese!

The largest store is a supermarket that includes eateries, and a row of shops sells cosmetics and gift items as well as clothes. The supermarket, which also carries some American items, has a combination of Japanese goods that you can't find in too many other places. Definitely check out the section devoted to Japanese rice steamers, teapots, and so on. The packaging alone will make you nuts with glee. This is a shopping and artistic adventure if ever there was one.

You can drive from Manhattan (the complex is almost right under the George Washington Bridge), you can take a ferry from Eleventh Avenue and 34th Street in Manhattan to the Port Imperial ferry terminal and get a taxi there, or you can catch the $3 Mitsuwa shuttle bus across the street from the north exit of the Port Authority Terminal on West 42nd Street. ☎ 201/941-9113. www.mitsuwa.com.

Market" at Citicorp, "the Atrium" at Trump Tower, or Time Warner Center on Columbus Circle. All are boring. Don't laugh, but the best of the mall-like spaces in Manhattan is Rockefeller Center.

PIER 17 PAVILION
South Street Seaport, Fulton and South sts. (Subway: 1, 2, or 3 to Fulton St.).

This is actually part of the South Street Seaport complex, and if you are just wandering happily around the area, you will probably discover it for yourself. But if you aren't paying much attention, or if the crowds are too dense, you might not realize that besides the Faneuil Hall–like South Street Seaport complex, and the short stretch of street-level shops on Fulton Street, there is an additional building along the water next to the lightship *Ambrose* that is really a mall on its own. It's complete with escalators and a branch store of many of the major chains in America. © **212/732-8257.** www.southstreet seaport.com.

ROCKEFELLER CENTER

Fifth Ave. to Seventh Ave., from 47th to 51st sts. (Subway: B, D, F, or V to Rockefeller Center).

On rainy days, you can make your way across Midtown underground if you know how to work the city of halls and shops that lies beneath Rockefeller Center. This is more than a mall; it's a village.

Besides fast-food restaurants and a few nice eateries, there are food markets, party stores, candy shops, newsstands (with great magazine selections), and many service-related businesses—banks, a post office, travel agencies, the UPS Store, and men who shine your shoes—all underground. Most of the stores are not anything you haven't seen before.

Aboveground is quite another story—one of New York's revolutions in retail happened right here. A tiny avenue of storefronts leads to the Christmas tree and the ice-skating rink (in season) at Rockefeller Plaza, as well as a spacious branch of the **Metropolitan Museum of Art Store.**

Around the corner, on Rockefeller Plaza, there's a small branch of gourmet-food purveyor **Dean & DeLuca,** which features a coffee bar and snacks to eat in or take out. This place is especially hot since hanging out in front of the studio for NBC's *Today Show* has become such a popular activity.

Web Tip: Check the website for merchants' special offers and coupons. © **212/332-6868.** www.rockefellercenter.com.

TIME WARNER CENTER
10 Columbus Circle (Subway: A, B, C, D, or 1 to 59th St./ Columbus Circle).

I like this mall, also referred to as the Shops at Columbus Circle, for all the wrong reasons—I like it simply because it's there and it has changed the face of New York. It is not a good mall, however; it has no soul and surely no warmth and, on top of that, it has an odd layout. But the **Whole Foods** on the lower level is indeed fabulous (and fabulously crowded; go during off hours). There are mostly big-name designer shops and upscale restaurants here, with a few of the everyday names you need on a regular basis, like **Sephora** for makeup (though not a great one) and a large **Borders** for books and music. *Best Bets:* This Borders is one of the best in the city and it's usually not crowded. © **212/823-6300.** www.shopsatcolumbuscircle.com.

TRUMP TOWER ATRIUM
725 Fifth Ave., at 56th St. (Subway: F to 57th St.).

The problem with the Trump Tower is that everybody wants to see it, but nobody thinks they can afford anything in there—so little actual shopping is going on while the mobs come and go. Donald Trump has gone on to other adventures, but still gets a lot of mileage out of his luxury tower, which has apartments in addition to the stores. The atrium space is Glitz City, with five levels (complete with lots of marble and brass) devoted to retail. *Best Bets:* The flagship **Gucci.** Even if you can't afford to buy, go to see the fab new boutique.

SPECIAL SIZES FOR MEN

BARNEYS NEW YORK
660 Madison Ave., at 61st St. (Subway: 4, 5, 6, N, R, or W to 59th St./Lexington Ave.).

Barneys has one of the most complete ranges of clothing sizes in New York. It also does alterations on the premises. The famous warehouse sale (p. 106) has a large selection in all size ranges, too. See p. 163 for more about Barneys. © 212/826-8900. www.barneys.com.

ROCHESTER BIG & TALL
1301 Sixth Ave., at 52nd St. (Subway: B, D, or E to Seventh Ave./53rd St.).

Rochester carries hot brand names in large and tall sizes, though I must say that the prices make me shiver—and I found it a better value to have my husband's clothes made to order by our tailor in Hong Kong. But if you like to buy ready-made, there is a very good selection of quality looks and makes here. *Web Tip:* Shop the online sales. You'll often find merchandise not available in the store. © 212/247-7500. www.rochester clothing.com.

TOM AUSTIN
20 W. 43rd St., between Fifth and Sixth aves. (Subway: B,D, F, V, or 7 to 42nd St./Bryant Park).

This men's shoe emporium specializes in hard-to-fit feet. Classic styles such as tassel loafers are available in many colors and sizes. © 212/687-1635.

SPECIAL SIZES FOR WOMEN
....

New York is one of the best cities in the world for specialty sizes; most of the department stores have made it their business to stock well-developed petite and plus-size women's wear. Even the store catalogs now feature garments available in a range of sizes. Most designers, retailers, and boutiques want to help you look as elegant as possible, no matter how big or small you may be. In fact, many established names, such as **Liz Claiborne** (petites only), have special sizes, which are sold at their outlet stores; see Woodbury Common (p. 298).

If you can get in over a weekend, or can buy wholesale, try 498 Seventh Ave. (at 37th St.) for its showrooms for plus-size women. Also try **Forman's Coats/Plus Sizes** (78 Orchard St., between Grand and Broome sts.), and don't forget that any couture garment can be made to measure.

See the "Maternity" section, earlier in this chapter, for special sizes in that category.

TALL GIRL SHOP
46 W. 39th St., between Fifth and Sixth aves. (Subway: B, D, F, V, or 7 to 42nd St./Bryant Park).

This shop isn't visually striking, but once you go in and start inspecting the goods, you'll be impressed. There are jeans in all styles, sportswear, jackets and coats, workout gear, and business suits, all proportioned for a tall fit. Both Junior (3–19) and Misses (6–20) sizes are stocked.

Tall Girl carries lines specially tailored to accommodate a taller woman's longer proportions. Small details such as zipper length and pocket placement are all given the same close attention as sleeve and overall length, and their team of fit specialists ensures that every garment meets their rigorous fit specifications.

Best Bets: There's a good selection of Pendleton classics and denim in contemporary styles. Most jeans are under $100. ✆ 212/840-9005.

STATIONERY

DEMPSEY & CARROLL
136 E. 57th St., 4th floor, between Lexington and Third aves. (Subway: 4, 5, 6, N, R, or W to 59th St./Lexington Ave.).

This firm has been around since 1878, but was recently sold and relaunched as a more customer-friendly venue. That doesn't mean the quality has changed; every invitation and notecard is still manufactured to the company's original standards. All are rendered on sturdy cotton-fiber papers with hand-cut copper dies. *Best Bets:* There's a once-a-year sale when prices are slashed across-the-board. © 212/750-6055. www. dempseyandcarroll.com.

GREENWICH LETTERPRESS
39 Christopher St., between Sixth and Seventh aves. (Subway: 1 to Christopher St.).

Sisters Beth and Amy Salvini stock their small shop with a wide array of gorgeous cards, stationery sets, and wrapping paper manufactured by small presses across the country. Their custom line is made on 75-year-old letterpresses and includes cards, stationery, invitations, and paper gifts featuring quirky retro-modern images. *Best Bets:* Notecards are a steal at $16 for a box of eight, and the innovative custom wedding invitations are a good bet for value-conscious brides. © 212/989-7464. www.greenwichletterpress.com.

MRS. JOHN L. STRONG
699 Madison Ave., at 62nd St., 5th floor (Subway: 4, 5, 6, N, R, or W to 59th St./Lexington Ave.).

Flora Strong (Mrs. John to you) began supplying exquisite hand-engraved invitations and writing papers to the world's elite 80 years ago, and her firm continues to set the standard for clients who expect the very best. If you're planning a custom order, please call ahead for an appointment. In fact, even if you want to browse, call ahead. The environment is very hoity and somewhat toity. *Best Bets:* The wedding invitations are in a class by themselves; prices begin in the thousands. © 212/838-3775.

SMYTHSON OF BOND STREET
4 W. 57th St., between Fifth and Sixth aves. (Subway: F to 57th St.).

This hoity-toity British firm has opened in New York with extremely expensive products, some of them very imaginative.

Look for notepapers and diaries, as well as small leather goods and some travel items. If you're British, the must-have gift item is the passport cover. If you're American, you can write old-fashioned thank-you notes on these letter papers and know that all your friends will think you're hot stuff. *Web Tip:* Online orders are processed in the U.K., but shipping to the U.S. is reasonably priced, beginning at $10 for a small order sent air-mail. ✆ **212/265-4573.** www.smythson.com.

TEENS

Teen buys include vintage clothing and jeans, cutting-edge street fashion that must be cheap, and lots of accessories, including whatever shoes are of the moment. Also see "Hip & Hot Fashion," on p. 189. A few more affordable sources are listed below.

LOUNGE
593 Broadway, at Houston St. (Subway: B, D, F, or V to Broadway/Lafayette St.).

With a live DJ spinning the shopping music, this store is either the poor man's Jeffrey or the hipster's H&M. The clothes are moderately priced and slightly more edgy than what you'd find uptown or in a mass-market chain. Men's and women's as well as shoes and boots; some accessories, too. It's a lifestyle store, dude. *Web Tip:* The website is well designed and quick, but there's not much information as to what's in stock. No Web orders. ✆ **212/226-7585.** www.loungesoho.com.

MISS SIXTY
386 West Broadway, between Spring and Broome sts. (Subway: C or E to Spring St.).

Teens and 'tweens go crazy for the sexy urban-chic looks in this shop. *Best Bets:* The great-fitting Italian jeans are available in over 50 styles; all are priced under $200, which is a bargain for those who worship designer denim. © 212/334-9772. www.misssixty.com.

RUGBY
99 University Place, at 12th St. (Subway: 4, 5, 6, L, N, Q, R, or W to 14th St./Union Sq.).

If you can't beat 'em, join 'em—so none other than Ralph Lauren has launched yet another spinoff: a store on the front yard of NYU that sells the casual look teens and 'tweens have been wearing and buying from the likes of Abercrombie & Fitch (p. 172). The look has a preppy edge to it, keeping with Mr. Lauren's well-defined style. The physical space is also pure Lauren—men's and women's clothes in a store that is so atmospheric as to almost be a movie set. © 212/677-1895. www.polo.com.

STRAWBERRY
129 E. 42nd St., at Lexington Ave. (Subway: 4, 5, 6, 7, or S to Grand Central/42nd St.); multiple other locations.

These very inexpensive clothes copy the looks made popular by the biggest names in fashion. Yes, Gucci. A lot of it is definitely junky, but if you are patient and use that eagle eye of yours, you will be rewarded. Other locations include 501 Madison Ave. (near 52nd St.) and 49 W. 57th St. (near Sixth Ave.). © 212/986-7030.

URBAN OUTFITTERS
526 Sixth Ave., at 14th St. (Subway: F, L, or V to Sixth Ave./14th St.).

Urban features boho-chic styles at modest prices, making it a strong source for teens and 'tweens. There are lots of ethnic fashions and trendsetting styles here. Branches are popping up everywhere, including the Upper East Side (999 Third Ave., near 59th St.), NoHo (628 Broadway, at Houston St.), and the East Village (162 Second Ave., at 10th St.). *Web Tip:* Visit the

Web catalog to find online-only items. They offer free shipping on orders over $150. Call © **800/282-2200** for info. © **646/638-1646**. www.urbanoutfitters.com.

VINTAGE

....

Vintage clothing has never been more chic, thanks to a steady stream of celebrities who wear vintage—Julia Roberts at the Academy Awards, anyone? Teens wear vintage jeans, models wear vintage slips, fashion editors wear vintage Pucci. The **Manhattan Vintage Show** is held two to three times a year at the Metropolitan Pavilion, 125 W. 18th St., www.manhattanvintage.com (download a coupon for discount admission). You'll find 80 to 100 booths selling textiles, clothing, and some fur.

In addition to the following listings for vintage men's and women's clothing, see p. 307 for resale shops.

Funky Vintage

ANDY'S CHEE-PEES
18 W. 8th St., between Fifth and Sixth aves. (Subway: A, B, C, D, E, F, or V to W. 4th St.).

Mostly jeans, cords, and tatty T-shirts with some gems in there if you hunt. For the teen and 'tween crowd. There's another location at 37 St. Marks Place, at Second Avenue. *Web Tip:* Download discount coupons online. © **212/420-5980**. www.andyscheepees.com.

DAVID OWENS VINTAGE CLOTHING
154 Orchard St., between Stanton and Rivington sts. (Subway: F or V to Second Ave.).

Part of the new Lower East Side, this small store sells men's and women's vintage clothing from the 1940s through the 1980s. © **212/677-3301**.

WHAT COMES AROUND GOES AROUND
351 West Broadway, between Broome and Grand sts.
(Subway: C or E to Spring St.).

This source in the heart of SoHo is a great place for spotting celebs who like to wear vintage. The store has been so successful that it now has a wholesale showroom in TriBeCa, where regular retail customers can also shop; call ✆ **212/274-8340** for an appointment. *Best Bets:* Shop here for vintage Levi's. Prices vary depending on age and condition. ✆ **212/343-9303.** www. nyvintage.com.

Expensive Vintage

FROCK
148 Orchard St., between Stanton and Rivington sts.
(Subway: F or V to Second Ave.).

This low-key shop specializes in designers from the '60s, '70s, and '80s, and it carries clothing in a full range of sizes. There's also a good selection of accessories, including shoes, jewelry, and handbags. Designers include names such as Pierre Cardin, Norma Kamali, Gucci, Pucci, Yves St. Laurent, and Manolo Blahnik. *Web Tip:* In-stock items are listed on the website with measurements and prices. ✆ **212/594-5380.** www.frocknyc. com.

KENI VALENTI RETRO-COUTURE
155 W. 29th St., at Sixth Ave., 3rd floor, room C5 (Subway: 1 to 28th St.).

Knock three times and whisper low. But wait, make sure you've called first for an appointment. This is a secret celebrity resource; serious collectors only. *Web Tip:* Some of the stock is shown online. Sizes run very small; I couldn't find anything larger than a 6. ✆ **212/967-7147.** www.kenivalenti.com.

RARE VINTAGE

24 W. 57th St., between Fifth and Sixth aves. (Subway: F to 57th St.).

This is another celebrity find; Angelina Jolie found a stunning bump-concealing Halston gown here to wear to the SAG Awards. The emphasis is on formalwear, and most gowns are collectors' items that come with a card detailing the history of the garment. Expect to see labels such as Halston, Dior, and Chanel. © 212/581-7273. www.rarevintage.com.

RESURRECTION

217 Mott St., between Prince and Spring sts. (Subway: 6 to Spring St.; or R or W to Prince St.).

Much Pucci. © 212/625-1374. www.resurrectionvintage.com.

Chapter Nine

....

NEW YORK BEAUTY

Beauty may only be skin deep, but it's a huge business in New York. Stores are battling with one another for the chance to carry the best and newest beauty brands—the odder the better. Day spas are everywhere in New York, be they famous names or neighborhood finds. French hairdressers are celebrities here—actually, all hairdressers are celebrities. Hotels are competing to out-spa one another. Quick—where's my spinning class?

No city—not even Paris—has the beauty energy that Manhattan now has thanks to stores and spas from **Aveda** to **Bergdorf Goodman** to **Bliss.** Downtown firms have branches uptown and in Midtown (see Bliss on p. 252).

This chapter incorporates such diverse subjects as cosmetics, hairdressers, bath goods, perfumes, and even spa listings. So light up a Diptyque candle, rub a little Origins energizing oil on your brow, and have your eyebrows threaded while you read on.

THE GEOGRAPHY OF BEAUTY

....

There are beauty businesses on just about every block of Manhattan; certainly every neighborhood has its own mom-and-pop shops, so to speak. The largest concentration of hip and hot sources is in SoHo, which many people in the industry have nicknamed the Lipstick District.

Upper Madison Avenue has several sources for beauty products, but it's best known for its string of very fancy pharmacies, which carry hard-to-find European brands. Midtown is dotted with the city's major department stores as well as flagships of many specialty stores. Midtown also has some of the small specialty multiples, such as **Crabtree & Evelyn** (p. 242) and **L'Occitane** (p. 243), many of which began life in another country (although, despite what you may think, Crabtree & Evelyn is an American firm).

THE BIG NAMES IN BEAUTY

AVEDA

Time Warner Center, 10 Columbus Circle (Subway: A, B, C, D, or 1 to 59th St./Columbus Circle); 509 Madison Ave., at 53rd St. (Subway: E or V to Fifth Ave./53rd St.); 456 West Broadway, between Houston and Prince sts. (Subway: C or E to Spring St.); multiple other locations.

This cult fave is a leading brand in aromatherapy, with haircare and beauty products made from high-quality, all-natural ingredients. Call © **800/644-4831** for more locations; also see the listing below. www.aveda.com.

AVEDA INSTITUTE

233 Spring St., between Sixth Ave. and Varick St. (Subway: 1 to Canal St., or C or E to Spring St.).

Some of the best low-priced gifts in Manhattan ($10–$12) come from this tiny SoHo shop. The Aveda Institute is both a store and a spa, featuring aromatherapy treatments and an array of products for men and women, including various hair cocktails that have been created especially for colored and problem hair.

The line is sold in salons around the country, and sometimes you'll see a few items in drugstores. However, if you want to experience the full range of products, including candles, aromatherapy, and makeup, you should hit an Aveda store in New York.

Best Bets: Make an appointment at the hair salon for a cut and color by a student stylist. Haircuts are $20 and foils start at $45. The price is right! © 212/807-1492. www.aveda instituteny.com.

THE BODY SHOP
509 Madison Ave., at 53rd St. (Subway: E or V to Fifth Ave./53rd St.); multiple other locations.

Just when I say that I'm tired of the line, I find something new to interest me. **Note:** Some The Body Shop stores in the U.K. offer spa services; this trend will eventually come over to the U.S. © 800/289-8603. www.thebodyshop.com.

H2O PLUS
511 Madison Ave., at 53rd St. (Subway: E or V to Fifth Ave./53rd St.).

This Chicago firm has taken the malls of America by storm. As the name would imply, it sells goodies for the bath—gels, shampoos, travel kits, and more. You can find great gifts (some in the $10 range!) for just about every age, though the kiddie bath toys and products are the best. © 212/750-8119. www.h2oplus.com.

LATHER
127 E. 57th St., near Lexington Ave. (Subway: 4, 5, 6, N, R, or W to 59th St./Lexington Ave.).

Consider this a not-yet-big name but on the way, and head into the small store in expensive real estate. Lather sells men's and women's bathing (and shaving) products and has a spa too. It's a fresh take on the same old stuff; great for gift packs. **Web Tip:** You can search for gifts by price range; the selection is divided into three groups: under $30, $30 to $60, and more than $60. © **212/644-4449**. www.lather.com.

LUSH
1293 Broadway, at 34th St. (Subway: B, D, F, N, Q, R, V, or W to 34th St./Herald Sq.).

For the uninitiated, LUSH makes bath balls that snap, crackle, and fizz when you drop them in water, plus natural beauty products ranging from shampoos to skin creams. Everything is sold deli style—the soaps are in loaves, the products are in refrigerator cases. Not every product is fabulous, but the presentation is adorable and the novelty factor is high. Great gift items, especially if you live in a town that has no LUSH. Now then, prices are about $5 per bath ball, which I find expensive, but call me irresponsible. Surely you are paying for the novelty factor and the razzmatazz, of which there is much.

Other locations have opened at 2165 Broadway (near 76th St.), 531 Broadway (at Prince), and 7 E. 14th St. (Union Sq.). Be sure to get a copy of the company newspaper *(Lush Times)* and check out the website if there is no LUSH in your hometown.

Insider's Secret: U.S. and Canadian LUSH recipes are the same to meet legal requirements. Products elsewhere in the world can be different. *Web Tip:* Go to the quick-order link on the website to see what's in stock and place your order with a quick click. © **212/564-9120**. www.lush.com.

ORIGINS
402 West Broadway, at Spring St. (Subway: C or E to Spring St.); Grand Central Terminal, 42nd St. and Park Ave. (Subway: 4, 5, 6, 7, or S to Grand Central/42nd St.); multiple other locations.

While this line of natural-ingredient beauty aids, shampoos, aromatherapy treatments, and cosmetics is also sold in traditional department stores, the Origins store has a wider selection as well as some products that are not available elsewhere. I love this line and often send out gifts from here.

Limited items (discounted, of course) are available at Woodbury Common (p. 298) at the Cosmetics Company Store (an outlet for the various Estée Lauder brands such as Origins and Clinique).

Best Bets: I use Jump Start in my bath when I can afford it (at $25 a bottle, it's a rather big splurge); this aromatherapy product has a tingle that really seems worth the moola—it makes me giggle and sing in the shower. © 800/ORIGINS (674-4467). www.origins.com.

SABON

93 Spring St., between Broadway and Mercer St. (Subway: R or W to Prince St.); 434 Sixth Ave., near 10th St. (Subway: A, B, C, D, E, F, or V to W. 4th St./Washington Sq.); 1371 Sixth Ave., near 55th St. (Subway: F to 57th St.); multiple other locations.

Sabon means soap, and it is *bon*. This Israeli firm has several shops in Manhattan and most likely plans to take over the world, much like LUSH. Swanky and sophisticated and a lot of fun—it's an especially good gift headquarters, with its natural products and treatments bespeckled with herbs and flowers. *Best Bets:* Soap shish kabobs—great gifts, $11. © 866/697-2266. www.sabonnyc.com.

SEPHORA

555 Broadway, between Prince and Spring sts. (Subway: R or W to Prince St.); 2164 Broadway, between 76th and 77th sts. (Subway: 1 to 79th St.); Time Warner Center, 10 Columbus Circle (Subway: A, B, C, D, or 1 to 59th St./ Columbus Circle); multiple other locations.

Let's start with a short history of this French firm, which was getting innovative on its own and was then bought by LVMH, which turned it into a global power. New stores are popping up in all neighborhoods—making Sephora kind of like a neighborhood beauty supermarket that carries many lines you've never heard of. Yummy. Furthermore, different stores carry different brands—including lines created for black women and even Sephora's own house brand—so you will never get bored.

Note there is a no-gift-with-purchase policy at this chain; gift-with-purchase is reserved for U.S. department stores only. Sephora also refrains from spritzing customers with perfume or, alas, giving out scads of fancy giveaways. You can, however, ask for samples of anything you'd like to test, and these are not the kind of samples you get at department stores—rather, they're fresh samples, straight from the jar, and put in containers for you to take home.

Best Bets: Sarah loves Sephora's $20 matifying compact foundation. It's lightweight and can be applied wet or dry, depending on how much coverage you need. © 877/SEPHORA (737-4672). www.sephora.com.

Small but Special

LAFCO
285 Lafayette St. (Subway: B, D, F, or V to Broadway/ Lafayette St.).

Double-whammy famous: This is where you can buy the Santa Maria Novella pharmacy skin care and products from Florence—hard to find in the U.S.—as well as assorted other hard-to-find brands, including Portuguese soaps and suds. © 212/925-0001.

MALIN+GOETZ
177 Seventh Ave., at 20th St. (Subway: 1 to 18th St.).

This Chelsea studio and lab represents the new world in skin care—pure prods for men and women, high in quality and low in hype with simple packaging but yet a gorgeous store to appeal to the people in the 'hood. ***Web Tip:*** This well-organized website gives skin-care advice with each product, and ordering couldn't be easier. © 212/727-3777. www.malinandgoetz.com.

PIR COSMETICS
14 Prince St., at Elizabeth St. (Subway: 6 to Spring St.).

This Nolita boutique specializes in hard-to-find luxury brands such as Kevin Aucoin, Sue Devitt, Mario Badescu, and Agragia. The sales staff will treat you like royalty while they recommend what's best for your skin and lifestyle. *Web Tip:* The website's slow but complete, and you can order online. © 212/219-1290. www.pircosmetics.com.

DEPARTMENT STORES

All department stores have enormous makeup-and-perfume departments, usually on the street floor. **Macy's** (p. 167) has expanded its beauty department—still on the ground floor—while **Bergdorf's** (p. 164) has created a totally new department, not on the ground floor but one floor below.

Saks (p. 168) prides itself on having the largest selection of perfume brands in New York; it carries many scent and makeup lines not found anywhere else. **Bloomingdale's** (p. 164) has one of the best cosmetics departments in the city and often has creative promotional events.

It is the specialty stores, though, that really go for the gusto—**Henri Bendel** (p. 165) and **Barneys** (p. 208) carry brands that might not be found elsewhere in the city, even at Sephora. Barneys is the most competitive and now stocks over 30 specialty lines, including **Aesop** and **ReVive.**

MAKEUP BRANDS & STORES

Makeup must be almost as lucrative as perfume, since many stores have launched their own makeup lines.

At the other end of the, uh, spectrum, **Versace** went into color cosmetics before he died—that line is now carried in department stores. Many other big-name designers have color cosmetic lines, too, such as **Giorgio Armani** (the cosmetics are actually made by L'Oreal), **Calvin Klein,** and, of course, **Yves Saint Laurent** (visit the renovated **YSL** boutique at 855 Madison Ave., to see designer Tom Ford's work). Can Donna Karan be far behind?

The stores and brands described below are specialists in the field of makeup; many of them were created by makeup artists or models.

FACE STOCKHOLM
110 Prince St., at Greene St. (Subway: R or W to Prince St.); Time Warner Center, 10 Columbus Circle (Subway: A, B, C, D, or 1 to 59th St./Columbus Circle); multiple other locations.

Face Stockholm, from Sweden (duh), began life as the makeup of choice for many a supermodel in the 1980s. The reason that the stars took to the brand is the range of colors that can be bought ready-made. There are more than 100 shades of nail polish and almost 200 shades of lipstick. Everything is out, so you can test it. Once considered a cult brand, it has become so popular that it's now distributed through some of the fancy department stores. © **212/966-9110.** www.facestockholm.com.

LANCOME
201 Columbus Ave., at 69th St. (Subway: 1 to 66th St./ Lincoln Center).

After test-market studies, this French brand has opened its first flagship on NYC's Upper West Side. This is sort of a PlayStation for girls. The staff will introduce you to all the cosmetics, fragrances, and skin-care products. Ask about treatments. © **212/362-4858.** www.lancome.com.

M.A.C.
113 Spring St., between Mercer and Greene sts. (Subway: R or W to Prince St., or C or E to Spring St.); 175 Fifth Ave., near 22nd St. (Subway: R or W to 23rd St.); multiple other locations.

Ricky's: The Funky Beauty-Supply Store

A small but growing chain of beauty-supply stores that has reached cult status with many in the beauty biz, Ricky's has opened some uptown stores as the chain works its way into middle-class accessibility. Ricky's supplies stars, models, the rich and famous—this is the store where the movers and shakers of the beauty world hang out because it's a semi-professional source of supplies and goods.

Ricky's creates its own house line of products and sells wigs, hair accessories, and just about anything else that's fun, funky, and unusual, including body glitter in every color imaginable. This is a must-stop for Halloween products.

Ricky's is a growing business, with about a dozen branches in Manhattan. The flagship is at 509 Fifth Ave., near 42nd Street (Subway: B, D, F, or V to 42nd St./Bryant Park). Other store locations include 590 Broadway (below Houston St.), 1189 First Ave. (near 65th St.), and many more. There is now a store in East Hampton, at 50 Main St. And yes, your grandmother is right: Ricky's has even opened in Florida. For a complete list, go to www.rickys-nyc.com.

This is a Canadian brand of makeup that is often worn by models. The line has become so enormously chic, and has gathered such a devoted following, that it was snapped up by Estée Lauder. Its products are available at **Henri Bendel** in a totally renovated selling space, at **Saks, Macy's,** and **Bloomies,** and at M.A.C.'s own stores (of course).

People say that the reason this line is so popular is that the makeup lasts longer on the face (and lips) than other brands; I think the reason it's so popular is that the prices are pretty low and the image is very high. The colors are sublime.

Tip: This brand is *muuuch* cheaper than other major U.S. or European brands, yet the quality is top-notch. *Best Bets:* With eye shadow at $14 each, this is the best high-quality makeup deal out there. ✆ 800/588-0070. www.maccosmetics.com.

BATH & BODY STORES

· ·

CASWELL-MASSEY
518 Lexington Ave., at 48th St. (Subway: 6 to 51st St., or E or V to Lexington Ave./53rd St.).

Resembling an old-fashioned British chemist shop (pharmacy), Caswell-Massey is best known for its private-label products, which have been going strong for hundreds of years now: George Washington even used its cologne (no. 6). *Insider's Secret:* The soaps are big and fat and costly ($28 a box), so if you give them as a gift (they are the perfect gift) make sure the recipient is sophisticated enough to know this is serious soap. ℰ 212/755-2254. www.caswellmassey.com.

CRABTREE & EVELYN
Time Warner Center, 10 Columbus Circle (Subway: A, B, C, D, or 1 to 59th St./Columbus Circle); 30 Rockefeller Center, near 49th St. (Subway: B, D, F, or V to Rockefeller Center); 520 Madison Ave., near 53rd St. (Subway: E or V to Fifth Ave./53rd St.); multiple other locations.

I know this will come as a shock, but here goes: Crabtree & Evelyn is not a British firm, nor is it 100 years old. In fact, it was born in the era of the natural 1970s in New England and has become an international soap-and-jam empire based on the old English look. It has stores in suburban malls everywhere, plus an outlet at Woodbury Common (p. 298).

In my weaker moments, I get this line mixed up with Caswell-Massey; then I remember that George Washington used Caswell-Massey, and Crabtree & Evelyn is the line that first seduced me into flavored/scented soaps. The history of my life can be traced through my changes in taste, from avocado to almond scents in soaps and creams and lotions. ℰ **800/CRAB-TREE** (272-2873). www.crabtreeandevelyn.com.

FRESH

1367 Third Ave., at 78th St. (Subway: 6 to 77th St.); 57 Spring St., between Mulberry and Lafayette sts. (Subway: 6 to Spring St.); multiple other locations.

These products are somewhat farm-inspired, made with milk, eggs, honey, and so on. The sugar-cube fizz balls for the bath are a bit pricey but heavenly, and the body salt scrubs may actually be worth $40! New Yorkers from the *Sex and the City* set really eat this stuff up. **Web Tip:** You'll receive free samples with every order. ✆ **212/585-3400.** www.fresh.com.

KORRES

110 Wooster St., between Spring and Prince sts. (Subway: R or W to Prince St.).

Korres is a plant-based line of beauty products made in Greece. Using homeopathic remedies, the company offers a complete hair and skin-care line, makeup, and sun-care products. **Best Bets:** Eco-moms love the herb-based anti-lice treatment and bug balm, both under $20. Don't snicker. ✆ **212/219-0683.** www. korres.com.

L'OCCITANE

1046 Madison Ave., at 80th St. (Subway: 6 to 77th St.); Time Warner Center, 10 Columbus Circle (Subway: A, B, C, D, or 1 to 59th St./Columbus Circle); 92 Prince St., near Broadway (Subway: R or W to Prince St.); multiple other locations.

This is one of my favorite French brands in America, offering perfumes, aromatherapy, soaps, candles, makeup, and body products from the south of France. Honestly, I'm not certain how to classify this one, for L'Occitane does it all: It also sells bedding, bathroom stuff, home sprays, and travel kits. If you don't know this brand, please sniff your way over and inhale deeply. There's an outlet at Woodbury Common (p. 298), too.

Note that L'Occitane is connected by lineage and some moneymen to **Oliviers & Co.,** an olive oil firm, so the stores are often next door to each other. © **888/623-2880**. www. loccitane.com.

LUSH
1293 Broadway, at 34th St. (Subway: B, D, F, N, Q, R, V, or W to 34th St./Herald Sq.).

See p. 236. © **212/564-9120**. www.lush.com.

WHOLE BODY AT WHOLE FOODS
250 Seventh Ave., at 24th St. (Subway: 1 to 23rd St.).

Check out the **Whole Foods** organic market and then pop into adjacent **Whole Body** for natural bath, body, and beauty products. Some lines are a tad underground, while others are famous in Europe and otherwise hard to find in New York, like **Dr. Hauschka,** a German brand that is all the rage in London. (Try the rose oil on your cuticles.) Other Manhattan locations include 95 E. Houston St., between Bowery and Chrystie streets, 4 Union Square South, and 10 Columbus Circle, at Time Warner Center. © **212/924-5969**. www.whole foodsmarket.com.

PHARMACIES WITH A TWIST

CLYDE'S
926 Madison Ave., near 74th St. (Subway: 6 to 77th St.).

The store is spacious, fancy, and low-key, and will appeal to those who don't like to search every nook and cranny to find what they want. © **212/744-5050**.

CONCORD CHEMISTS
485 Madison Ave., at 52nd St. (Subway: B, D, F, or V to Rockefeller Center).

This is an unusual drugstore: It has many Euro lines of makeup and beauty treatments, some accessories, and a few brands of gunks and goops that are hard to find. I used to work in the office building above the store, so I have been dropping in for years (it's near Saks and Burger Heaven). *Web Tip:* Unfortunately, they don't have an online catalog. The website is pretty useless, but there is a link to send an e-mail for more information. © **212/486-9543.** www.concord-chemists.com.

JANET SARTIN INSTITUTE
875 Third Ave., at 53rd St., Mezzanine Level (Subway: E or V to Lexington Ave./53rd St.).

Before day spas were common—in fact, before I even had blemishes—Janet Sartin was one of the most serious specialists in skin care. Call ahead for an appointment, or just drop in to stock up on products. © **212/751-5858.** www.sartin.com.

KIEHL'S
109 Third Ave., at 13th St. (Subway: 4, 5, 6, L, N, Q, R, or W to 14th St./Union Sq.).

This pharmacy is old-fashioned in the most yummy sense of the word; you can actually feel the tradition in this place. Kiehl's offers the kind of ambience other stores can only try to copy. Its products are created from knowledge based on hundreds of years of customer feedback and satisfaction. Okay, so the store is only 150 years old, but you get the point.

Kiehl's goods have become the rage in Europe, so they make excellent gifts for international visitors to take home. These are the sort of "in" products that show people that you know about the very best in beauty and body and face care. Some department stores and European-style drugstores in Manhattan also sell this line. There's another Kiehl's location at 154 Columbus Ave., between 66th and 67th streets. *Best Bets:* Toffee, Beckham, and Bentley are crazy about the Cuddly Coat Doggie Shampoo. One $16 bottle is good for about four shampoos. © **212/677-3171.** www.kiehls.com.

SPACE.NK

99 Greene St., between Prince and Spring sts. (Subway: R or W to Prince St.).

This London import isn't a pharmacy in the traditional sense; rather, it's a luxe boutique specializing in cult brands, many of them Asian and European, and most of them very expensive. They strive to introduce new talent and so the inventory constantly changes. ***Best Bets:*** Call or stop by to get invited to the store's special events. When a new line is introduced, they throw a party and you'll come away with lots of samples. © **212/219-8625.**

ZITOMER

969 Madison Ave., near 76th St. (Subway: 6 to 77th St.).

Zitomer is a virtual department store of great drugstore stuff—it even sells clothing and has a doggy boutique. The store is a bit over-the-top for me, but it's great fun for the first-timer. Zitomer specializes in hard-to-find brands and European skin-care specialties. ***Insider's Secret:*** Use this as a beauty source but do not have prescriptions filled here—they are more expensive than any other drugstore in town. © **212/737-2016.** www. zitomer.com.

PERFUME & SCENT SHOPS

All department stores, many discounters, and many specialty stores sell perfumes. The listings below are specialty houses known for their own lines of scents.

BOND NO. 9

9 Bond St., between Broadway and Lafayette St. (Subway: 6 to Bleecker St.); 399 Bleecker St., at 11th St. (Subway: 1 to Christopher St.); 680 Madison Ave., near 61st St. (Subway: N, R, or W to Fifth Ave./59th St.); 897 Madison Ave., near 73rd St. (Subway: 6 to 68th St./Hunter College).

The NoHo flagship is worth the trip for the decor and ambience alone. Bond No. 9—named after the address of the shop, obviously—is a fragrance line named after various New York neighborhoods, like Park Avenue, Chinatown, and Chelsea Flowers. (One of the latest, however, is somewhat controversially called the Scent of Peace.) *Best Bets:* This line makes a great gift to take overseas as it's very hard to find in Europe. A small 50mL bottle of scent starts at $125. ☏ 877/273-3369. www.bondno9fragrances.com.

CARON AT PHYTO UNIVERSE
715 Lexington Ave., at 58th St. (Subway: 4, 5, 6, N, R, or W to 59th St./Lexington Ave.).

Although nothing will ever be as *charmant* as Caron's store on avenue Montaigne in Paris, this store is great fun, as are the Caron scents, which are largely unknown in the U.S. I wear the one that was created for the first "air hostesses" (in 1947); it's spicy. I used to wear the old version of Fleur de Rocaille, which is more floral. The line has a lot of history and is considered very sophisticated—so sophisticated, in fact, that regulars bring their own perfume bottles in for refills. If you don't want to be part of the wave of commercial scents being spritzed about and inserted into products, then visit Caron for an old-world alternative. All fragrances come only in perfume—nothing is diluted with *eau.* ☏ 212/308-0270.

CHANEL
15 E. 57th St., between Fifth and Madison aves. (Subway: N, R, or W to Fifth Ave./59th St.).

Yeah, yeah, I know: Chanel is sold in every department store in America. But there is a tiny line of fragrances (about five of them), created by Coco herself, which is sold only in Chanel boutiques around the world. I know this because I wear one of them, Cuir de Russie (Russian Leather), which is spicy and a tad heavy—but I am a woman of a certain age and it's a heady scent. ☏ 212/355-5050. www.chanel.com.

JAR Parfums at Bergdorf Goodman
754 Fifth Ave., between 57th and 58th sts. (Subway: N, R, or W to Fifth Ave./59th St.).

Joel Arthur Rosenthal is a French jeweler (formerly of the Bronx) who has made his initials famous among the elite clients who know his Place Vendôme shop. Now he's branching into scent—and Bergdorf's has him. If you're dancing for joy, then you won't mind the price tags that begin at $350 and go up, up and away. ✆ 212/872-2874. www.jar-parfums.fr.

Jo Malone
949 Broadway, at 22nd St. (Subway: R or W to 23rd St.); 946 Madison Ave., near 74th St. (Subway: 6 to 77th St.); multiple other locations.

This British cult scent heroine merged into the Estée Lauder empire in order to go global; her first store in America rests between an **Origins** and a **M.A.C.**—two of Lauder's other brands. I mention all this because it was actually hard for me to find the shop; it is in the Flatiron Building, but proudly faces Broadway rather than Fifth Avenue.

Malone does not do color cosmetics; rather, she does body treatments, bath products, perfumes, and home scents such as linen sprays and candles. Prices are so high here that it's a shame Malone doesn't produce smelling salts. Still, this is the ultimate New York status gift or insider name to drop. *Note:* The products cost less in London.

Best Bets: Try layering the scents; a winning combo is Grapefruit combined with Lime Basil & Mandarin. A 30mL bottle of cologne is $50. ✆ 212/673-2220. www.jomalone.com.

L'Artisan Parfumeur
68 Thompson St., near Spring St. (Subway: C or E to Spring St.).

You'll find scents as well as potpourri and home fragrances— many nice gift items, but you won't get out of the shop for less than $60. Other locations include 222 Columbus Ave., at

70th Street, and 1100 Madison Ave., at 82nd Street. © **212/ 334-1500.** www.artisanparfumeur.com.

PENHALIGON'S
870 Madison Ave., between 70th and 71st sts. (Subway: 6 to 68th St./Hunter College).

This English brand is now expanding around the world. Penhaligon's is old-fashioned yet a cult classic, with fragrance for both men and women. The names of the scents sound like they belong in a Jane Austen novel. What's interesting is that the firm makes colognes, which are water- and alcohol-based, but many people claim they have long-lasting powers. *Web Tip:* Ordering online is easy, but delivery charges are steep and aren't revealed until the order is complete. © **212/249-1771.** www. penhaligons.com.

HAIR SALONS & STYLISTS

AVEDA INSTITUTE
233 Spring St., between Sixth Ave. and Varick St. (Subway: C or E to Spring St.).

Sarah's daughter, Elizabeth, books student stylists here for her haircuts and blond highlights. Liz's color formula is noted, so each visit produces the same fab results. *Best Bets:* Stylists-in-training give $20 haircuts and $45 highlights, and all are supervised by an instructor. © **212/807-1492.**

FRÉDÉRIC FEKKAI
712 Fifth Ave., between 55th and 56th sts., 4th floor (Subway: F to 57th St.).

Okay, read my lips: Fred-er-*reeeek,* that's how we say it. If you say Fred-rick, you give yourself away as a hair novice. This multifloor salon offers the works: hair, beauty, and spa treatments, plus a cafe and retail products. I don't find it very

Blow-Outs & Budget Cuts

Here are the best hair deals in town for little or no money.
Bumble & Bumble (415 W. 13th St., at Ninth Ave., 6th floor;
© 212/728 6253) offers free cuts, color, and styling; sign up
for model calls at www.bbmodelproject.com. Grab a free cut
on either Tuesday or Wednesday at **John Allan** (418 Washington St., at Vestry St.; © 212/334-5358) from a new stylist.

Village Cuts (179 W. 4th St., at Jones St.; © 212/675-6736)
offers $15 cuts, with 10% off to first timers. Guys will want
to try **Frank's Chop Shop** (19 Essex, at Hester St.; © 212/228-
7442) for cuts and straight-razor shaves for $22 to $45.

BLOW STYLING SALON
342 W. 14th St., between Eighth and Ninth aves.

If you need a quick blow-out, this is a good choice ($40).
© 212/989-6282.

DEJA VOUS
38 W. 56th St., between Fifth and Sixth aves.

Twenty minutes, $35, and you're blown away. © 212/581-
6560.

MARITZA'S HOUSE OF BEAUTY
1987 Seventh Ave., at 119th St.

Insiders travel uptown for Maritza's "doobie" ($15), which
includes a quick roller set after the blow-out. The result is
smooth, sexy waves that last 2 to 3 days. © 212/665-8970.

calming, but it sure is fascinating; the models and photographers are what I find so distracting. It's a real trip.

All beauty and spa services are offered; I got hooked on a
lavender rubdown here. Call ahead for an appointment—it takes
about 3 months to get the master himself to give you a hair-
cut and, thus, a new identity.

Fekkai has expanded into accessories such as headbands (adorable) and handbags (very chic), and has written a book as well. There's another location in SoHo at 394 West Broadway, 2nd floor, and as we go to press, a salon is planned for the newly remodeled Mark Hotel. ℂ **212/753-9500.** www. fredericfekkai.com.

JEAN-CLAUDE BIGUINE
1177 Sixth Ave., near 45th St. (Subway: B, D, F, or V to 42nd St./Bryant Park); multiple other locations.

The theory here is French class that's accessible to the American masses. This is a French chain of hair salons; just walk in for a *coupe* (cut), *le brushing* (styling), or whatever Madame needs, for a minimal fee; appointments are optional. Biguine is a bigwig (yuck, yuck) in France, but has only a few salons here in the States. *Web Tip:* Prices are listed on the website so you know what you'll pay before your visit. ℂ **212/921-4484.** www.biguine.com.

SPAS

....

The day-spa business has become so huge that it's hard to know a department store from a spa from a beauty salon these days. **Frédéric Fekkai** (p. 249) has full spa services; I went for the fake tan once. Many hotels have had spas for a while now—some even offer special jet-lag or shopping treatments to rejuvenate you.

AMORE PACIFIC
114 Spring St., between Mercer and Greene sts. (Subway: R or W to Prince St.).

If you think the best we ever got from Korea was the *M*A*S*H* television series, then you haven't checked out Amore, a Korean beauty gallery and spa in SoHo. The space feels like a shrine of peace and simplicity. As these things go, the prices are also sublime—they begin at around $100 for a 1-hour treatment, which is a bargain in New York. *Best Bets:* The skin-care line has been tested by mavens who claim it's among the best (it's sold uptown at Bergdorf's). This line is far more expensive than the spa treatments. ✆ **212/966-0400.** www.amorepacific.com.

Aveda Institute

233 Spring St., between Sixth Ave. and Varick St. (Subway: 1 to Canal St., or C or E to Spring St.).

See p. 234 for more information. ✆ **212/807-1492.** www. aveda.com.

Bliss Spa

568 Broadway, at Prince St. (Subway: R or W to Prince St.); 12 W. 57th St., between Fifth and Sixth aves. (Subway: N, R, or W to Fifth Ave./59th St.); 541 Lexington Ave., at 49th St. (Subway: 6 to 51st St.).

Bliss may be responsible for starting the day-spa craze in New York. The firm became so hot that it was gobbled up by LVMH; it has also morphed into a catalog and website of products. Bliss has clean, modern packaging and offers a look and feel of practical luxury—you feel like you're taking care of yourself, not wasting money or splurging on something silly. The environment is luxe, but the emphasis is on well-being.

Best Bets: The "High Heeler"—a soaking, scrubbing treat for over-shopped feet. One hundred dollars, 60 minutes. *Web Tip:* If you're looking for just the right gift for a bride, or a thank-you to an overworked friend or mom, order a gift certificate online. They're considered, uh, bliss. To book at any New York location, call ✆ **212/219-8970.** www.blissspa.com.

CLARINS

*1061 Madison Ave., near 80th St. (Subway: 6 to 77th St.);
247 Columbus Ave., near 72nd St. (Subway: B or C to
Columbus Ave.).*

Face and body treatments are available at this store-cum-spa,
where all the products are from the famed French brand. To
book, call © **212/734-6100** for Madison Avenue, or © **212/
362-0190** for Columbus Avenue. www.clarins.com.

Chapter Ten

·····················

NEW YORK HOME

HOME SWEET APARTMENT

···

Maybe it's because we're addicted to those home makeover shows on TV, but we're all becoming more and more design conscious. Just as the mass market multiples have knocked off the latest catwalk styles, the designs from glossy home style magazines are becoming accessible to all of us.

For those with gobs of money, it's not hard to get in touch with the great names in interior design and to create digs that should be (and perhaps will be) featured in *Architectural Digest*. I'm usually looking for something less stellar. I did my first apartment in New York with cast-offs found at curbside. I still hate to pay full retail price—especially when it comes to home furnishings and decorative items. In fact, I buy a lot of the things for my house in Provence at **T.J. Maxx** (p. 295) and bring them back to France. I'll search out a Target in any suburb, and I *loooove* Kmart style for basics.

If you're going high-end, toss this book aside and ask your secretary to dial a designer. If you do your own decor, are always looking for a deal, and like to mix mass and class, read on for my suggestions and those of Paul Baumrind, correspondent for *Born to Shop New York* and a real-live interior designer.

SPECIAL PROMOTIONS & EVENTS

Aside from the goings-on in the D&D (design and decoration) industry, there are a lot of tabletop people who are actually in the gift industry or other aspects of design. Many of them hold sample sales. On weekends before Christmas, a large number of warehouses are open to the public; there are ads in the papers and sometimes flyers handed out on the streets. Also check *New York* and *Time Out* magazines for weekly sales.

REGULAR RETAIL

There's hardly such a thing as regular retail anymore, and the days when a family walked into B. Altman and chose a living room set are as dead as B. Altman. Nowadays, most department stores do not even have furniture departments.

Mass merchants who offer style and value have inherited the "regular retail" home-furnishings business: namely, **Pottery Barn** (p. 270), **Restoration Hardware** (p. 264), and **Crate & Barrel** (p. 262). Terence Conran is here with **The Conran Shop** (p. 262), located under the 59th Street Bridge; and the new Japanese-owned design superstore, **Muji** (p. 264), is drawing crowds to SoHo. Manhattanites are willing to drive to the suburbs to get even better buys; **IKEA** (p. 263; in Paramus, New Jersey) is thriving, and, as we go to press, plans to open another branch in Brooklyn's Red Hook in the summer of 2008.

ABC Carpet & Home (p. 261) has become one of the few full-service home-furnishing stores in the city. It's actually one of Manhattan's "showplace" stores, and it's an absolute retail dream. ABC has also created a renaissance in the neighborhood around it.

Most big-name American designers—and many European ones—have gone into the lifestyle business, as have some of the chains. **Calvin Klein** (p. 139) sells home style on Madison Avenue.

There are design concepts that come from Europe and find a place in America; there are copycat firms that charge a lot of money for newly made antiques; there's style, there's wit, there's bad taste—all easily accessible, some easily affordable. But more important, now there's good taste that's affordable. And New York will never be the same.

TRENDSETTERS IN HOME STYLE

ANKASA
135 E. 65th St., at Lexington Ave. (Subway: 6 to 68th St./ Hunter College).

Sachin and Babi Ahluwalia are textile designers whose former clients include Oscar de la Renta and Vera Wang, among others. They have now taken their creative know-how to design a luxurious home-decor collection, catering to clients with a strong sense of color and style. Most pieces in the line feature textiles with hand embroidery and color palettes that vary with the season. ✆ **212/861-6800.** www.ankasa.com.

ARMANI CASA
97 Greene St., between Prince and Spring sts. (Subway: R or W to Prince St.).

Don't let the entryway fool you; this place is very deep and also has a downstairs level. The style here is Zen—not quite Asian, but very minimalist. Besides $50 dishes, there's furniture and bedding. ✆ **212/334-1271.** www.armanicasa.com.

BAKER TRIBECA
129 Hudson St., at Beach St. (Subway: 1 to Franklin St.).

This large showroom, located in trendy TriBeCa, sells mostly traditional American furnishings. I prefer the stuff upstairs—it's more solid and classic as opposed to the newer and edgier designs on the ground floor. ✆ **212/343-2956.** www.baker furniture.com.

B&B ITALIA
138 Greene St., between Prince and Houston sts. (Subway: R or W to Prince St.).

Modern and moderne, and, as the name says, Italian. ✆ **212/ 966-3514.** www.bebitalia.it.

CALYPSO HOME
199 Lafayette St., at Broome St. (Subway: 6 to Spring St.).

The Calypso empire began as ethnic-island ready-to-wear and has expanded into a lifestyle look complete with home store. Located near the original boutique, Calypso Home specializes in tabletop and gift items, plus some furniture. Prices are as varied as the pieces, but the customer is used to paying top dollar for just the right thing. It's perfect, darling, who cares what it costs? *Web Tip:* The online home style selection is very limited. ✆ **212/925-6200.** www.calypso-celle.com.

CHARLOTTE MOSS
20 E. 63rd St., between Fifth and Sixth aves. (Subway: 6 to 68th St./Hunter College).

Don't confuse this shop with Moss, the home store in SoHo. Charlotte Moss is a New York interior designer, author, and society maven who has opened a namesake shop in a fabulous five-story town house on one of the chicest blocks in town. It's designed as a grand residence, so as you walk from floor to floor you'll see all the goods displayed in room settings. The offerings are top-notch, so be prepared to spend big bucks. *Web Tip:* Some accessories and linens featured in the shop are available online, but you really need to visit in person. ✆ **212/308-3888.** www.charlottemoss.com.

FELISSIMO
10 W. 56th St., between Fifth and Sixth aves. (Subway: E or V to Fifth Ave./53rd St.).

Felissimo takes up an entire town house, where it sells artsy-fartsy gifts and tabletop goods in the most sumptuous surroundings in town. This place is a gallery of good taste. The dishes are somewhat in the same style as those at Armani Casa; you'll also find linens, paper, candles, and much more. It's a pleasure to indulge your senses in this tranquil space. Try the store's new scent. © 800/247-5655. www.felissimo.com.

LE FANION
299 W. 4th St., at Bank St. (Subway: 1 to Christopher St.).

If you can't make it to Isle-sur-la Sorgue in Provence, this shop is a good stop for unique French Country hand-turned pottery, crystal chandeliers, hand-painted tiles, weather vanes, and armoires. © 212/463-8760. www.lefanion.com.

PEARL RIVER MART
477 Broadway, between Grand and Broome sts. (Subway: 6 to Spring St.; or R or W to Prince St.).

I'm not sure that you can call this store trendsetting; it features all sorts of Chinese-style products, many of which are now considered chic and fun decor additions, and which are, at this time in style history, also trendy. This stuff has been around forever, though Pearl River itself has moved up the street from Chinatown. The Mao Communist souvenirs are considered cutting edge. You could get inspired here. *Best Bets:* I'm a bamboo nut, so I love the bamboo shelves and benches; most are under $100. © 212/431-4770. www.pearlriver.com.

RALPH LAUREN
867 Madison Ave., at 72nd St. (Subway: 6 to 68th St./Hunter College); multiple other locations.

There isn't a bigger influence on modern mass design in America than Ralph Lauren and his faux-English, old-world, old-style country looks. To see it all in action, stop by the flagship in the old Rhinelander Mansion on Madison Avenue. There are also Ralph Lauren bedroom boutiques in a few department stores and at ABC Carpet & Home. Much of the big-time home-furnishings line is available to the trade; to get the bed linens at discount, try any of the Ralph Lauren outlet stores outside of the city, such as at Woodbury Common (p. 298). ✆ **212/606-2100.** www.polo.com.

SHABBY CHIC
83 Wooster St., between Prince and Spring sts. (Subway: C or E to Spring St.; or R or W to Prince St.).

If you adore comfy, oversize, upholstered furniture that could have come straight from Grandma's, then you've come to the right source. You can pay a fortune here for mismatched faded chintz or a giant cabbage-rose couch complete with slipcovers and throw pillows. *Insider's Secret:* Shabby also does a home line for Target. ✆ **212/274-9842.** www.shabbychic.com.

TAKASHIMAYA
693 Fifth Ave., near 54th St. (Subway: E or V to Fifth Ave./ 53rd St.).

I have raved in other parts of this book about Takashimaya, the elegant Japanese department store. Poke into the atrium, take a look at the French florist's booth, and go upstairs. Make the time—the displays are beautiful and the style is far more country French than Japanese. And, yes, there are a number of affordable items. Well, a few, anyway. *Best Bets:* Prices can be astronomical, but there are some simple items—such as a serving dish from Tibet—in the $25 to $50 range. These make extraordinary gifts because they are stylish and beautifully wrapped by the store in unique packaging. ✆ **212/ 350-0100.** www.ny-takashimaya.com.

TIFFANY & CO.
727 Fifth Ave., at 57th St. (Subway: F to 57th St.).

If you're thinking breakfast at Tiffany's, you should be thinking about the trendsetting tabletop designs for which this store has become famous. In fact, Tiffany has even published a book on its table settings. The store has moderately priced items, so that while the reputation is upscale, just about anyone can afford something or other here. Learn how to mix your flea market finds with Tiffany delights for the perfectly groomed table. *Best Bets:* Tiffany sterling silver flatware still sets the standard for quality and elegance. When I win the lottery, I'll buy up the Audubon pattern and use it every day. ☎ 212/755-8000. www.tiffany.com.

THE COMPLETE LOOK FOR THE HOME

Moss
150 Greene St., between Houston and Prince sts. (Subway: R or W to Prince St.).

The sleek store sells a little of everything, with an emphasis on gift items and home style in the quirky and moderne vein. The 7,000-square-foot space is fun, but I don't live and die by Philippe Starck lemon squeezers (though others do). Moss is somewhat like an art gallery—many products have either an edge or black humor in the subtext. *Web Tip:* New merchandise is posted every day on "The Daily New" link on the website. ☎ 212/204-7100. www.mossonline.com.

WILLIAM-WAYNE & CO.
850 Lexington Ave., at 64th St. (Subway: 6 to 68th St./ Hunter College); 40 University Place, at 9th St. (Subway: R or W to 8th St.).

William-Wayne started out downtown as a funky little resource, and then turned rich and famous. One of the stores features wonderful accessories and tabletop items; Paul adores this place because he says it reminds him of my living room. That's a polite way of saying that it's crammed with fun junk, many with animal themes. The other shop has more of a country look and features garden and outdoor furniture. This is one of those New York cutie-pie stores that you just have to see, even if you don't buy anything. ✆ **212/288-9243** for Lexington Avenue; ✆ **212/533-4711** for University Place. www.william-wayne.com.

MASS PLUS CLASS

Perhaps the biggest change on both the social and design scenes in New York is that good design at low prices not only has become readily available, but is almost de rigueur in every economic bracket.

ABC CARPET & HOME
888 Broadway, at 19th St. (Subway: R or W to 23rd St.).

If you've ever doubted that retail is theater, then you haven't been to ABC Carpet & Home. The street-level floor is an emporium of goods, with items for the home, for kids, and for gifts. Upstairs, there are floors devoted to fabrics, linens, and furniture. The thought that this is a discounter pervades, although frankly, I don't think they know the meaning of the word *discount* here (though there is a great outlet store in the Bronx, at 1055 Bronx River Ave., near Watson Ave.; ✆ **718/842-8772**; Subway: 6 to Whitlock Ave.). They do, however, know the meaning of the words *style, selection,* and *serendipity.* **Best Bets:** The carpet sales. If you can time your visit during one of these events, you'll save up to 75% on top-quality rugs. ✆ **212/473-3000.** www.abchome.com.

BED BATH & BEYOND
620 Sixth Ave., at 18th St. (Subway: 1 to 18th St.); 410 E. 61st St., at First Ave. (Subway: 4, 5, 6, N, R, or W to 59th St./Lexington Ave.); 1932 Broadway, at 65th St. (Subway: 1 to 66th St./Lincoln Center); 270 Greenwich St., at Warren St. (Subway: 1, 2, or 3 to Chambers St.).

This national chain was one of Manhattan's first superstores, and its stores are *packed* with sheets, towels, kitchen items, and everything in the world you can imagine. The New York stores are not unlike the suburban branches, except they're even larger and grander. ✆ **800/GO-BEYOND** (462-3966). www.bedbathandbeyond.com.

CB2
451 Broadway, between Canal and Grand sts. (Subway: N, Q, R, or W to Canal St.).

Crate & Barrel's offshoot offers less expensive, younger, more contemporary designs. They call it affordable modern. ✆ **212/ 219-1454.** www.cb2.com.

THE CONRAN SHOP
407 E. 59th St., at First Ave., under 59th St. Bridge. (Subway: 4, 5, 6, N, R, or W to 59th St./Lexington Ave.).

The point of this store is to be more cutting edge than Crate & Barrel, but not too expensive. I admit that I am often confused between the offerings from Crate & Barrel and Conran's, though I know that the latter believes it is trendier. The Conran Shop also has a greater mix of merchandise, such as luggage, lifestyle gadgets, foodstuffs, and gifts. *Best Bets:* Check out the contemporary Indian home accessories by Rohit Bal, who designed Elizabeth Hurley's wedding outfit. ✆ **212/755-9079.** www.conran.com.

CRATE & BARREL
650 Madison Ave., at 59th St. (Subway: N, R, or W to Fifth Ave./59th St.); 611 Broadway, at Houston St. (Subway: R or W to Prince St.).

Chicago is no second city when it comes to exporting its most famous store to Madison Avenue. Its arrival created almost as much excitement as Barneys did when it opened up here several years back. There's a branch in SoHo as well.

The IKEA Solution

IKEA

1000 Ikea Dr. (New Jersey Tpk., exit 13A), Paramus, New Jersey.

There's free bus service from the Port Authority on weekends; call ✆ 800/BUS-IKEA (287-4532) for details. Another branch is scheduled to open in Brooklyn's Red Hook neighborhood in summer 2008. ✆ 908/289-4488. www.ikea.com.

Items range from plates to sofas, all chic but mass-produced. The look tends to be clean and lean without embellishment—just old-fashioned, simple design in the right colors for the moment. The total lifestyle look seems perfectly designed for the places that New Yorkers inhabit (be they city apartments or country weekend retreats). Plus, the prices are bargains, the displays are great, and the salespeople are friendly. ✆ 212/780-0004 for Broadway, ✆ 212/308-0011 for Madison Avenue. www.crateandbarrel.com.

GRACIOUS HOME

1201, 1217, and 1220 Third Ave., at 70th St. (Subway: 6 to 68th St./Hunter College); 1992 Broadway, at 67th St. (Subway: 1 to 66th St./Lincoln Center).

This place has hardware, bed linens, vacuum cleaners, paint, wallpaper, and everything else you could possibly need as you renovate, restore, or redo your home. Prices are in keeping with regular retail in Manhattan, but most people don't mind because of the selection. Prices on many items are way beyond me—like $100 a sheet. Still, Gracious Home is sort of an institution. ***Best Bets:*** The West Side location is more chic to me (I like the tabletop department). ✆ 800/338-7809. www.gracioushome.com.

HOME DEPOT

980 Third Ave., at 59th St. (Subway: 4, 5, 6, N, R, or W to 59th St./Lexington Ave.); 40 W. 23rd St., between Fifth and Sixth aves. (Subway: R or W to 23rd St.).

The famous suburban home-improvement store has two Manhattan branches. Civilization arrives in Gotham. ✆ **212/929-9571.** www.homedepot.com.

JENSEN-LEWIS

89 Seventh Ave., at 15th St. (Subway: 1, 2, or 3 to 14th St.).

This Chelsea source specializes in a modern home look, especially leather and canvas furniture, and is conveniently located near a few other home stores. Very good prices. ***Web Tip:*** Check the website's Closeout page for the best deals. You'll find lots of stuff not available in the store. ✆ **212/929-4880.** www.jensen-lewis.com.

MUJI SOHO

455 Broadway, between Grand and Howard sts. (Subway: 6, J, M, N, Q, R, W, or Z to Canal St.).

This trendy Japanese chain stocks affordable household goods, including office supplies, furniture, electrical appliances, fabric, and some apparel. The look is sleek, the colors are muted, and the prices are low. BYOB (that's bag) as they discourage the use of paper and plastic shopping bags. ✆ **212/334-2002.** www.muji.com.

RESTORATION HARDWARE

935 Broadway, at 22nd St. (Subway: R or W to 23rd St.).

I wish I could rave about this store the way many people do, but I find the merchandise very bland and so much like Pottery Barn meets Williams-Sonoma with a dash of Archie McPhee that I don't even know how these people stay in business, let alone thrive. Still, it's a popular resource for home stuff. ✆ **212/625-1374.** www.restorationhardware.com.

SMITH & HAWKEN
394 West Broadway, near Spring St. (Subway: C or E to Spring St.).

Smith & Hawken began as a catalog company and now has stores stretched across America. It sells stylish garden and home style with a touch of the green thumb. ***Best Bets:*** I use the canvas gardening tote as an airplane carry-on bag. It's a good size for my laptop and the outside pockets are perfect for boarding passes and passports; $38. ✆ **212/925-1190.** www.smithandhawken.com.

BIG NAMES IN TABLETOP

Go to the following stores for classics in crystal, porcelain, and more.

BACCARAT
625 Madison Ave., at 59th St. (Subway: 4, 5, 6, N, R, or W to 59th St./Lexington Ave.).
✆ **212/826-4100.** www.baccarat.fr.

BERNARDAUD/LIMOGES
499 Park Ave., at 59th St. (Subway: 4, 5, 6, N, R, or W to 59th St./Lexington Ave.).
✆ **212/371-4300.** www.bernardaud.fr.

CARTIER
653 Fifth Ave., near 52nd St. (Subway: E or V to Fifth Ave./ 53rd St.).
✆ **212/753-0111.** www.cartier.com.

CHRISTOFLE
680 Madison Ave., at 62nd St. (Subway: 4, 5, 6, N, R, or W to 59th St./Lexington Ave.).
✆ **212/308-9390.** www.christofle.com.

DAUM
694 Madison Ave., near 62nd St. (Subway: 4, 5, 6, N, R, or W to 59th St./Lexington Ave.).
© 212/355-2060. www.daum.fr.

LALIQUE
712 Madison Ave., near 63rd St. (Subway: 4, 5, 6, N, R, or W to 59th St./Lexington Ave.).
© 212/355-6550. www.lalique.com.

TIFFANY & CO.
727 Fifth Ave., at 57th St. (Subway: F to 57th St.); 37 Wall St., between William and Nassau sts. (Subway: 2, 3, J, M, or Z to Wall St.).
© 212/755-8000. www.tiffany.com.

TRENDSETTERS IN TABLETOP & GIFT ITEMS

Don't forget museum gift shops for excellent and sophisticated tabletop items and gifts.

ADRIEN LINFORD
1339 Madison Ave., at 94th St. (Subway: 6 to 96th St.); 927 Madison Ave., near 74th St. (Subway: 6 to 77th St.).

Paul says that much of the merchandise here—gifts, tabletop, and rich-lady necessities—is also at Barneys. Items are often inventive and always chic. Much of the merchandise is the sort that comes from Vietnam but is identified as chic without being thought of as a souvenir. © 212/426-1500 for 94th Street; © 212/628-4500 for 74th Street.

AGATHA RUIZ DE LA PRADA
135 Wooster St., between Houston and Prince sts. (Subway: R or W to Prince St.; or C or E to Spring St.).

If there's only one Prada in your style lexicon, it's time to learn about this Spanish designer who does bright, hot colors and a very distinctive style that is possibly best loved by the young. The SoHo store—her first in the U.S.—has furniture, kitchenware, housewares, rugs, and bedding. Prices are moderate to low. You get a lot of wham for your buck here, but will you still love yourself in the morning? *Web Tip:* The website's fun and colorful, but very general in nature. No prices, no online catalog. © **212/598-4078.** www.agatharuizdela prada.com.

THE APARTMENT
101 Crosby St., near Prince St. (Subway: R or W to Prince St.; or 6 to Spring St.).

Talk about concept stores—this SoHo fun spot is set up like a real apartment, with fun, funky, and minimalist merchandise appropriately displayed in room sets. Don't miss the bathroom—the stuff in there is for sale, too. © **212/219-3661.** www.theapt.com.

AUTO
805 Washington St., between Horatio and Gansevoort sts. (Subway: A, C, E, or L to 14th St./Eighth Ave.).

Like an art gallery, Auto has a whole lifestyle selection of fashion, beauty, and home items that you might want to stare at but may be afraid to touch until you relax, look around, and see the humor. Do your wackiest gift shopping here. *Best Bets:* The Missoni cushions, pillows, and throws are fab. © **212/ 229-2292.** www.thisisauto.com.

BARNEYS NEW YORK
660 Madison Ave., at 61st St. (Subway: 4, 5, 6, N, R, or W to 59th St./Lexington Ave.).

A marvelous store and a boon to Madison Avenue, but most of all, a fabulous gift and tabletop resource. Chelsea Passage

is the department for home accessories. © **212/826-8900.**
www.barneys.com.

BERGDORF GOODMAN
754 Fifth Ave., between 57th and 58th sts. (Subway: N, R,
or W to Fifth Ave./59th St.).

The seventh floor is the only stop you'll need to make if you
want to get a quick survey of elegant choices for your home:
beautiful china, linens, and stationery, plus nooks and cran-
nies filled with the best-bought wonders of the world—from
hand-painted dinner napkins sprinkled with gold dust to Venetian glass swizzle sticks. Leontine Linens has a shop here for
intricate monogrammed linens. © **212/753-7300.** www.bergdorf
goodman.com.

JOHN DERIAN
6 E. 2nd St., between Second Ave. and Bowery. (Subway: 6
to Bleecker St.; or F or V to Second Ave.).

Don't be afraid of the neighborhood (just take a taxi)—fear
instead the damage you can do to your credit rating here.
Feast your eyes; feast your heart. This decoupage artist began
selling plates to Bergdorf's and now has an empire of tabletop items and assorted other wares. It's truly an art form and
the man is a genius, though an expensive genius. **John Derian
Dry Goods,** the annex at no. 10, focuses more on linens and
home furnishings. This shop keeps limited hours, usually Tuesday through Sunday, from noon to 7pm. *Tip:* Sometimes you
can find copies of his cut-and-paste items at Anthropologie for
less moola. © **212/677-3917.** www.johnderian.com.

MACKENZIE-CHILDS
14 W. 57th St., between Fifth and Sixth aves. (Subway: F to
57th St.).

This is one of my favorite firms but Sarah finds it cloying. It's
all hand-painted and over-the-top cutie pie. Anyone who has

ever dreamed of coming to New York to see the best of American talent has got to step into this place to soak up the glory. You probably can't afford to buy more than a doorknob. But what a doorknob! © 212/570-6050. www.mackenzie-childs.com.

"REAL PEOPLE" TABLETOP

The only resource you really need for tabletop items, whatever your budget, is **Crate & Barrel** (p. 262). **Macy's** (p. 167) carries all leading brands, including a new exclusive line of table- and cookwares by **Martha Stewart.** If you're looking for a few other resources, well, New York's got more. And the more the merrier.

FISHS EDDY
889 Broadway, at 19th St. (Subway: 4, 5, 6, L, N, Q, R, or W to 14th St./Union Sq.).

See p. 101 for the dish on all the dishes at Fishs Eddy. If you're into restaurant supply and funky styles, this is a great stop. Prices are fair; style is high. © 877/347-4733. www.fishseddy.com.

MICHAEL C. FINA
545 Fifth Ave., at 45th St. (Subway: B, D, F, or V to 42nd St./Bryant Park).

All major china, crystal, and silver lines are discounted here— Lenox, Wedgwood, Spode, Noritake, and more. The jewelry counter is boring, but the gift shopping is tremendous fun. On a price-by-price basis, Fina may not always offer the best deals in the world, but for $25 wedding gifts, look no further. © 212/557-2500. www.michaelcfina.com.

PIER 1 IMPORTS
71 Fifth Ave., at 15th St. (Subway: 4, 5, 6, L, N, Q, R, or W to 14th St./Union Sq.); 1550 Third Ave., at 86th St. (Subway: 4, 5, or 6 to 86th St.).

The imports here are from all over the planet and certainly hail from the world of inexpensive. It's a one-stop supermarket of wicker for your beach house or first apartment. You may find the Manhattan stores a little jazzier than many suburban branches, offering a bit more in the way of gift items rather than big pieces. *Web Tip:* Don't count on finding an item you've seen online in the store. Inventory changes daily, and I find the website's often out-of-date. © **212/206-1911** for Fifth Avenue, © **212/987-1746** for Third Avenue. www.pier1.com.

POTTERY BARN
600 Broadway, near Houston St. (Subway: R or W to Prince St.); 127 E. 59th St., between Lexington and Park aves. (Subway: 4, 5, 6, N, R, or W to 59th St./Lexington Ave.); 1965 Broadway, at 67th St. (Subway: 1 to 66th St./ Lincoln Center).

Whenever I need Christmas gifts in the $10 range, this is my first destination. Aside from the holiday specialties, you'll find a host of plates and platters, candlesticks, linens, and furniture. Add it to the resource list for beach homes and first apartments. © **888/779-5176.** www.potterybarn.com.

SUR LA TABLE
75 Spring St., at Crosby St. (Subway: R or W to Prince St.).

Sur La Table is the wonderful tabletop-and-cookware resource that started out in Seattle's Pike Place Market. Now it's in SoHo and giving Williams-Sonoma a run for its money. *Web Tip:* Their online catalog is one of the best, with a huge selection, quick shipping, and great customer service. © **212/966-3375.** www.surlatable.com.

Williams-Sonoma

110 Seventh Ave., at 16th St. (Subway: 1, 2, or 3 to 14th St.); Time Warner Center, 10 Columbus Circle (Subway: A, B, C, D, or 1 to 59th St./Columbus Circle); 121 E. 59th St., between Park and Lexington aves. (Subway: 4, 5, 6, N, R, or W to 59th St./Lexington Ave.); 1175 Madison Ave., at 86th St. (Subway: 4, 5, or 6 to 86th St.).

This cooking-oriented chain continues to pump out housewares, trendy must-haves for entertaining, and even its own cookbooks. *Best Bets:* Fancy cookware, gourmet foodstuffs, and tabletop items are the specialties. © 877/812-6235. www.williams-sonoma.com.

BIG NAMES IN LINENS

Frette

807 Madison Ave., near 68th St. (Subway: 6 to 68th St./ Hunter College).

Frette sells fine and fancy Italian linen. It has also introduced a lingerie line, so you have something to wear between its fancy sheets. © 212/988-5221. www.frette.com.

Olatz

43 Clarkson St., near Hudson St. (Subway: 1 to Houston St.).

Olatz is the wife of the artist/movie director Julian Schnabel (Olatz is her first name) and her eponymous store in the West Village, which sells bed linens made in Portugal. To win the hearts, minds, and credit cards of the young women with serious money, these are not just sheets, they are bed linens that are decadently embroidered, scalloped, laced, or draped in color borders to beat the band. There are some sheets that are so exquisite that you know immediately, innately, that, to paraphrase George Kaufman, this is what Marie Antoinette would have bought if she had money. *Best Bets:* The 100% linen sheets, which start at $1,135 for a queen. That's per sheet, not per set. And don't miss the pajamas, nightshirts, and dressing gowns. *Web Tip:* The website's rather limited in scope; it is lovely to look at but doesn't do much. ✆ **212/255-8627**. www.olatz. com.

PORTHAULT
470 Park Ave., at 59th St. (Subway: 4, 5, 6, N, R, or W to 59th St./Lexington Ave.).

The most expensive beds in America are probably dressed in Porthault prints from France—a set of king-size sheets with standard pillowcases is well over $1,500. Every January, there's a half-price markdown spree. I know some women who treat themselves to one pillowcase a year; as time goes by, they amass a delightful mélange of Porthault prints, which they mix with white sheets (always a style classic) and American quilts— the look is stunning. ✆ **212/688-1660**. www.dporthault.fr.

PRATESI
829 Madison Ave., at 69th St. (Subway: 6 to 68th St./ Hunter College).

More fine Italian linen. A basic sheet set does cost more than $1,000 (but of course); then again, that's less expensive than Porthault. Pratesi has numerous styles that are suitable for the man who doesn't want to sleep in a bed of roses. Sales are held in January and July. ✆ **212/288-2315**. www.pratesi.com.

OFF-PRICE BED LINENS
....

Most of my bed linens come from either **T.J. Maxx** (p. 295) or **Century 21** (p. 291) . . . or the **Pratesi** outlet in Italy. In fact, the thought of paying regular retail makes my nose itch. The department stores often have good sales, though. In addition, many specialty stores have their own look and their own home style departments. Also, if you make the trek to the Lower East

---

Personalize It

ANYBODY'S CUSTOM DESIGN EMBROIDERY
South Street Seaport, Pier 17, 2nd floor (Subway: 2 or 3 to Fulton St.).

Out of the way, yes, but well worth the schlep. This shop will design a custom monogram—choose from over 20,000 designs and 40 font styles—and stitch it onto your linens. Depending on the order, it usually takes 1 to 5 days to embellish your textiles. ℂ **212/267-7070.** www.abcde-embroidery.com.

Side, you may see newer styles than you'd find in off-price stores, though at a mere 20% off regular retail.

While the Lower East Side is trying to transform itself more into a home style area than a discounter's paradise, and many resources have moved out, you can still count on **Harris Levy** (98 Forsyth St.) for 20% off on bed linens.

European shoppers, take note: Bed sizes in the U.S., U.K., and continental Europe are different—know what you are doing! Sheet sizes are frequently marked in centimeters as well as inches, so look at the small print.

KITCHEN CONCEPTS

. . . .

BRIDGE KITCHENWARE CORPORATION
711 Third Ave., at 45th St. (Subway: 4, 5, 6, 7, or S to Grand Central/42nd St.).

Calling all cooks! This is the favorite address of professional chefs in Manhattan. Whatever kitchen utensils you may need, this place will have them. *Web Tip:* The new website is updated daily with new product listings. ℂ **212/688-4220.** www.bridge kitchenware.com.

BROADWAY PANHANDLER
*65 E. 8th St., between Broadway and University Place
(Subway: R or W to 8th St.).*

This housewares store seems ordinary enough at first, but it has become a local legend. Check out the selection of Wilton cake supplies and professional equipment for fancy baking. Also known for great prices on kitchen equipment. ✆ **212/966-3434.** www.broadwaypanhandler.com.

THE CONTAINER STORE
629 Sixth Ave., at 19th St. (Subway: 1 to 18th St.); 725 Lexington Ave., at 58th St. (Subway: 4, 5, 6, N, R, or W to 59th St./Lexington Ave.).

The Container Store is a good source for organizational home style and for getting started in a new home. Its first Manhattan location, across from Bed Bath & Beyond on Ladies' Mile, makes it easy to shop and compare. A second location has opened near Bloomingdale's. ***Best Bets:*** This is one-stop shopping for holiday gift wrap and stocking stuffers. ✆ **212/866-4200.** www.containerstore.com.

DEAN & DELUCA
560 Broadway, at Prince St. (Subway: R or W to Prince St.).

This upscale SoHo grocery store, greengrocer, and cookware shop has the beautiful people (and a coffee counter where you can stare at them), the beautiful fruit, and the prices to match. I love it here and insist that you visit. There's another location at 1150 Madison Ave., at 85th Street, and don't miss the D&L Café at Rockefeller Center. ✆ **212/226-6800.** www.deanand deluca.com.

BATHROOM CONCEPTS

Obviously, **Bed Bath & Beyond** (p. 261) is a good place to start for bathroom accessories. Other fine resources include

The Container Store (p. 274) and discounters like **T.J. Maxx** (p. 295) and **Century 21** (p. 291). If you want to spend more, **Gracious Home** (p. 263) has plenty that will spin your head.

THE APARTMENT
101 Crosby St., near Prince St. (Subway: R or W to Prince St.; or 6 to Spring St.).

See p. 267. © **212/219-3661.** www.theapt.com.

POTTERY BARN BED & BATH
100–104 Seventh Ave., between 16th and 17th sts. (Subway: 1 to 18th St.).

Take a stroll through Pottery Barn Bed & Bath; you'll recognize Waterworks wannabes at a fraction of the designer price. This store will inspire you to remodel. © **646/336-7160.** www. potterybarn.com.

RESTORATION HARDWARE
935 Broadway, at 22nd St. (Subway: R or W to 23rd St.).

Sarah remodeled a guest bathroom using lighting, faucets, and fixtures purchased online at 60% off. She found matching towels in the store (70% off) and the end result is stunning. © **212/625-1347.** www.restorationhardware.com.

WATERWORKS
225 E. 57th St., between Second and Third aves. (Subway: 4, 5, 6, N, R, or W to 59th St./Lexington Ave.); 469 Broome St., near Greene St. (Subway: C or E to Spring St.).

When you care enough to have the very best, shop at Waterworks for everything from fixtures to bathroom design elements. Prices are high, but the selection is unique and sophisticated. They've recently added bath and skin-care products from cult brands such as Cote Bastide and Profumo Farmaceutica Santa Maria Novella. *Best Bets:* The bathtub selection can make you

drool enough saliva to fill said tub. ✆ **212/371-9266**. www.
waterworks.com.

ELECTRONICS CONCEPTS

APPLE STORE
*103 Prince St., at Greene St. (Subway: R or W to Prince
St.); 401 W. 14th St. (Subway: A, C, E, or L to 14th St./
Eighth Ave.); 767 Fifth Ave., at 59th St. (Subway: N, R, or
W to Fifth Ave.).*

The Big Apple now has three extremely hip Apple Stores. The
Fifth Avenue store is your stop for creative or tech help and
special events; workshops are held in the SoHo store's new state-
of-the-art theater. The West 14th Street store is a three-story
wonder with Open and Pro Labs—free in-depth training for
aspiring creative professionals.

   Apple stores tend to have hot architecture and be in high-
traffic destinations where you want to be anyway. The Meatpacking District store anchors the area. The Fifth Avenue store
entrance is down a glass elevator. ***Best Bets:*** The stores' Genius
Bars help us understand tech stuff. ✆ **212/226-3126**. www.
apple.com.

B & H PHOTOVIDEO
*420 Ninth Ave., between 33rd and 34th sts. (Subway: A, C,
or E to 34th St./Penn Station).*

We received a letter from David Hoy, who shops New York's
electronics outlets and recommends this store for photographic
and electronic equipment. He writes, "It's huge and is staffed
by very knowledgeable people only too happy to give advice.
Their prices seem to be excellent, quite the best I could find
in New York." ✆ **212/444-6615**. www.bhphotovideo.com.

BEST BUY

60 W. 23rd St., at Sixth Ave. (Subway: F or V to 23rd St.); multiple other locations.

Here's another instance of the suburban big-box chains coming into Manhattan. This branch of Best Buy is in a great part of town (near The Container Store and many off-pricers) and has electronics for the whole family. There's another location at 622 Broadway, in NoHo. ℂ **212/366-1373.** www.best buy.com.

BROOKSTONE

16 W. 50th St., near Rockefeller Plaza. (Subway: B, D, F, or V to Rockefeller Center); 20 W. 57th St., between Fifth and Sixth aves. (Subway: F to 57th St.).

This is the original big boy's toy and gadget store, with plenty of products to test. There's probably a branch in the mall nearest you. Good source for gifts. ℂ **212/262-3237.** www. brookstone.com.

HAMMACHER SCHLEMMER

147 E. 57th St., between Lexington and Third aves. (Subway: 4, 5, 6, N, R, or W to 59th St./Lexington Ave.).

This is the place for gadgets and toys and travel devices and everything that whirrs and whistles and goes bump in the night. There are floors and floors of fun and novelty items—some of them are even practical and worth the money. *Web Tip:* Once you buy online from these guys, they never stop sending you e-mail offers. ℂ **212/421-9000.** www.hammacher.com.

J&R MUSIC & COMPUTER WORLD

Park Row, between Ann and Beekman sts. (Subway: R or W to City Hall).

The best source for electronics and boy toys—and a homegrown alternative to all the national chains. ℂ **212/238-9000.** www. jr.com.

SHARPER IMAGE
10 W. 57th St., between Fifth and Sixth aves. (Subway: F to 57th St.); multiple other locations.

For the life of me, I can't adequately explain the difference between Brookstone and Sharper Image, except that the gadgets at Brookstone tend to be more health- and relaxation-oriented, while Sharper Image has more technology items and cutting-edge toys. © 212/265-2550. www.sharperimage.com.

SONY STYLE
550 Madison Ave., at 56th St. (Subway: E or V to Fifth Ave./53rd St.).

You can play with all the latest toys and gadgets and technology here. You cannot, however, play with the many boys and young men who hang out here. ***Best Bets:*** Come here to check out the latest gadgets, then compare prices with discounters before you buy. © 212/833-8800. www.sonystyle.com.

HOME-FURNISHING YARD GOODS & WALLPAPER
....

Also see the "Fabrics, Notions, Trims & More" section on p. 169 and take a look at the small shops clustered on East 20th and East 19th streets near Broadway (around the corner from ABC Carpet & Home).

PATERSON SILKS
151 W. 72nd St., between Columbus and Amsterdam aves. (Subway: 1, 2, or 3 to 72nd St.).

This place is pretty funky, and you'll need a bit of a sense of humor to shop here. These guys are mass purveyors of fabrics, curtains, slipcovers, and even fashion fabrics. Last time I stopped by, the selection made my skin crawl. After I got used to the stock, though, and adjusted my sights, I realized there were a lot of simple basics at very good prices. Also at 300 E. 90th St., at Second Avenue. © 212/874-9510.

SECONDHAND ROSE
138 Duane St., between West Broadway and Church St. (Subway: 1, 2, 3, A, or C to Chambers St.).

This shop's specialty is vintage wallpaper in original rolls, dating from the 1860s to 1970. ✆ **212/393-9002.** www.second handrose.com.

SILK TRADING CO.
ABC Carpet & Home, 888 Broadway, at 19th St. (Subway: R or W to 23rd St.).

This chain has stores in various design centers around the country, but has debuted in Manhattan with its own "boutique" within ABC Carpet & Home. It boasts a stunning selection of silks by the yard from international sources, but also sells ready-made draperies along with some furniture and accessories. *Web Tip:* Design your own curtains by clicking on the "Drapery by Design" link. ✆ **212/473-3000.** www.silktrading.com.

AUCTIONS FOR ART & ANTIQUES
....

CHRISTIE'S
20 Rockefeller Plaza, at 49th St. (Subway: B, D, F, or V to Rockefeller Center).

Christie's is a British firm; Sotheby's is based in the U.S. People who shop big-time auctions do not prefer one house to the other; they merely choose the auction they are interested in. Both houses will treat you and your money with equal charm or disdain, depending on your money and your manners. Call to request a catalog. *Web Tip:* Auction calendars with complete inventory listings can be found on the website. ✆ **212/636-2000.** www.christies.com.

DOYLE NEW YORK
175 E. 87th St., between Lexington and Third aves. (Subway: 4, 5, or 6 to 86th St.).

Doyle's is not quite as intimidating to me as the big-timers. The house has important auctions and must get your attention if you are a serious shopper, even though snobs will tell you it just isn't Christie's. *Best Bets:* Doyle's tries to acquire some unusual items not seen in the other houses. ✆ **212/427-2730.** www.doylenewyork.com.

PHILLIPS
450 W. 15 St., between Ninth and Tenth aves. (Subway: A, C, E, or L to 14th St./Eighth Ave.).

Phillips is an international auction house of the same caliber as Christie's and Sotheby's. It is able to acquire lots of good-quality items, some with incredible pedigrees, representing centuries of ostentatious buying or conservative wealth poured discreetly into fabulous collections. ✆ **212/940-1200.** www. phillips-dpl.com.

SOTHEBY'S
1334 York Ave., at 72nd St. (Subway: 6 to 68th St./Hunter College).

Sotheby's is the world's "other" famous auction house, leading the ranks along with Christie's. It publishes a catalog for all sales, national and international. You can subscribe to the catalogs that deal only with your collecting mania (painting, pre-Columbian, furniture, and so on), which is a wonderful way to keep up with the international market in your area.

Sotheby's experts are available for consultation to both buyers and sellers. (Other auction houses also provide this service.) If you have a piece of art that you think is worthy of being put up for auction, you can make an appointment to bring it in or have an expert visit you. I've fallen in love with a few of the Sotheby's experts; they know their stuff and are really fun to be with—especially when you share a common interest. ✆ **541/312-5682.** www.sothebys.com.

SWANN GALLERIES
104 E. 25th St., between Park and Lexington aves., 6th floor (Subway: R or W to 23rd St.).

Specialists in books and paper goods, movie posters, and ephemera, this sixth-floor location is low-key and funky. No, I'm not mixed up—Swann is upstairs, so take the elevator. You'll be thrilled when you get there. © **212/254-4710**. www.swann galleries.com.

HOITY-TOITY ANTIQUES: THE UPPER EAST SIDE

The Upper East Side is home to the best of the best. If you are looking for a Ming vase, Empire chairs, a Federal hutch, or a Louis sofa, and have a well-endowed checkbook, look no further. These shops are superb in both quality and selection. The owners are knowledgeable and willing to help you find what you are in search of. They will also authenticate and help you ship.

Most hoity-toity shops are specialists; many require an appointment and are not even open to the public. (I haven't listed any of those, thank you.) Seek and ye shall find; shop and ye shall spend. If you are buying, dress however you please. If you are browsing, please look the part and dress up in respect for the artworks and the dealers.

NEWEL GALLERIES
425 E. 53rd St., between First Ave. and Sutton Place (Subway: 6 to 51st St.).

This one is in a category by itself and is one of those "Gee, Toto" kinds of places. They do not have one of these in your hometown, no matter where you come from (unless you're from Manhattan). Shocking and wonderful and weird and fabulous and incredible and not to be believed and—well, you just have to go see this for yourself: Newel is an antiques resource of extraordinary proportions. Many pieces are for rent; all are one of a kind. You have to experience the six floors of warehouse space here to appreciate Newel's unusual nature. This is theater. This is what you came to New York for. Closed on weekends. ✆ 212/758-1970. www.newel.com.

NOT QUITE HOITY OR TOITY, BUT FANCY

In the past few decades, East 60th Street in the 200 block has been many things. It's now home to a large number of antiques shops selling mostly Continental antiques, not of the Lord-Rothschild-is-pleased category, but far above the flea market and garden-variety. There are almost two dozen dealers here, so the best thing to do is just walk and wander. Begin at no. 207 and make your way east—a few shops are open to the trade only.

And Don't Forget

MANHATTAN ART & ANTIQUES CENTER
1050 Second Ave., between 55th and 56th sts. (Subway: 4, 5, 6, N, R, or W to 59th St./Lexington Ave.).

This place houses about 100 dealers selling this and that. I have bought here and used to come here often; now I prefer tag sales and flea markets, but this is still fun. These are professional dealers, and they know what they've got. *Web Tip:* Dealers (some with Web links) and their specialties are listed on the website. ✆ 212/355-4400. www.the-maac.com.

NOT-SO-FANCY ANTIQUES

You don't have to grow up in Versailles to want to buy antiques. Even if your budget is limited, you can still find enough selection and enough specialty items to make a trip to the markets worthwhile. Recent college grads and young professionals, take note: You can have your cake and eat it, too.

Enjoy Madison Avenue and the East Side and all the gilt trips you can stand, but take your checkbook when you travel to 12th Street or to Brooklyn—these are the areas where designers go to nose through lots of stuff, hoping to find hidden jewels. The shoppers wear blue jeans or are properly dressed professionals, although Brooklyn on a weekend is decidedly laid-back.

Atlantic Avenue, Brooklyn

Many of the antiques shops that could no longer pay the rent in Manhattan have moved to Atlantic Avenue. The street is incredibly long and houses many, many antiques stores of varying quality and price range. From Manhattan, take the F train to Bergen Street. Walk back along Smith Street and turn right onto Atlantic after 3 blocks. On weekends, there's a flea market–like affair set up by dealers for locals.

The greatest concentration of antiques shops starts at Hoyt Street and continues along Atlantic Avenue for about 10 blocks.

University Place

Located between the Village, SoHo, and the nether regions of Lower Manhattan, University Place is a street that's just filled with the fun kind of antiques shops that I love to prowl. University Place starts right below 14th Street and ends at Washington Square Park; it creates its own little neighborhood, bounded by Broadway, which at this point in its life is now on the East Side.

University Place, along with the little side streets between Fifth Avenue and Broadway, is not the home of the $50 bed frame, but this is where affordable furniture can be yours. You should know your market if you are spending a lot of money or think you have a serious piece; otherwise, just enjoy.

If this sounds like I've just told you about the funkiest little yet-to-be-discovered part of town ever created, think again. Some very sharp dealers have already moved down here and are slowly creating a gentrified zone connected to the renewal

Steve Finds Home Style Inspiration in SoHo

Okay, I can't afford the home style stores in SoHo—but a guy can look and dream, right? These are the shops I continually pop into for apartment inspiration. You can shop them as a walking tour: Start on Broadway with **CB2** (p. 262), **Muji** (p. 264), and **Pearl River Mart** (p. 258)—all affordable—then head west out of my price range and onto Broome Street. Walk past Mercer to **Ochre**, 462 Broome St. (© 212/414-4332), a British shop of gorgeous bespoke lighting and quietly sophisticated furniture, mostly done in pale colors for a sun-faded look. This store reminds you what a relaxed, organic home should feel like. (Disclosure: I know two of the owners, Andrew and Harriet, and their velvety-soft dog, Blue.)

Stay on Broome but double back east a few blocks to **Aero**, 419 Broome St. (© 212/966-1500; www.aerostudios.com). Thomas O'Brien's house of vintage-modern style is tastefully done up in black, grays, browns, and creams. (I'm attempting to re-create this palette in my minuscule bathroom.) I can't do $175 pillows and $8,000 rugs, but I love the look and have bought some of O'Brien's line from Target. Aero has a great 70%-off sale on all smaller items after holiday and summer seasons.

Across the street at **Calypso Home** (p. 257), check out the Maison de Vacances (www.maisondevacances.com) bedding line, some in curious hides (a salmon-skin pillow is $115).

Last but not least: I asked the owners of Ochre which local stores inspire them, and they pointed me to Crosby Street (from Calypso, walk west and south): **Michele Varian**, 35 Crosby St. (© 212/343-0033; www.michelevarian.com), feels like Paris–meets–Park Slope, with silk pillows ($104-plus) and small bird-themed treasures. (Varian is actually from Detroit.) **BDDW**, 5 Crosby St. (© 212/625-1215; www.bddw.com), is a huge white-brick temple for handmade wood furniture (credenzas start at $6,000). The dark, museum-like **De Vera**,

---

1 Crosby St. (© **212/625-0838**; www.deveraobjects.com), offers up exquisite antique decorative art and jewelry, mostly Venetian. Glass beetles start at $400, gem necklaces at $1,100. Someday I'll afford it. For now, I'm "just browsing, thanks."

—by Stephen Bassman

---

of the entire Fifth Avenue area between 23rd and 14th streets and the Gramercy Park area. The area is so well combed by dealers that the diamonds get ferreted out very quickly. You may be forced to make do with rhinestones.

Chapter Eleven

....

NEW YORK BARGAINS

BARGAIN CAPITAL USA

....

New York, with so many retail opportunities, also has a lot of bargain opportunities. And this is the town where the slogan "I can get it for you wholesale" is a way of life. So step this way—have I got a deal for you.

But pardon me first, I'm off to the first-ever Pratesi warehouse sale. I did not learn about it from my friendship with the Pratesi family, oh no! It was in today's *Daily Candy!*

If you're visiting from overseas, no doubt you think New York, even at regular retail prices, is indeed a bargain mecca, because compared to Britain or France in terms of regular retail prices, it is. And you haven't even been to Woodbury Common yet. And you probably don't know about Filene's Basement or Loehmann's. If you're British, you probably do know about T.J. Maxx, but maybe not. And you surely have never heard of Century 21. Don't even know to thank Sy Syms and his firm, Syms, in your nightly prayers? Read on, read on.

I urge all international visitors to New York to read this chapter and highlight the good parts. If your English is spotty, get a dictionary. This is the part where I tell you about the *gangas* (that's "bargains" in Spanish—and, yes, it was one of the first words I learned in that language).

SALES

You can get a good bargain at any good store, but in New York you get an incredible selection during sale times. Since many department stores carry the same merchandise, you may be able to build your wardrobe as you go from store to store, buying part of an outfit at one store and finishing the look off with a component from another store.

Like all parts of the United States, New York has two big sale periods: Spring and summer merchandise is sold at rock-bottom prices mid-July through August, and fall merchandise goes on sale beginning in November, with further reductions December through January.

Some stores have cyclical sale periods—they clean house every 60 to 90 days and mark down automatically, with or without big sale announcements. If a store needs cash, it may host a 1-day sale, with hours from 8am until 11pm (or so), just to bring in as much traffic as possible and boost the bottom line.

Most sales are announced in local newspapers, and some special sales are written about editorially, as in *New York* magazine's "Sales & Bargains" column (also online at www.ny mag.com). *Time Out New York* (www.timeoutnewyork.com) runs a weekly section, "Sales and Sample Sales," as well. Online newsletter *Daily Candy* lists special sales events at small shops and boutiques (www.dailycandy.com). Even factory outlets have sales. Sometimes a store runs a coupon ad in the newspaper that corresponds to a sale—you get a 15% or 20% discount with the use of the coupon. This is not as low-rent as it sounds; some of Manhattan's biggest department stores do it regularly, especially around holidays when they want to jump-start the shopping season.

The conditions of the sale are posted in the store during the sale. Some stores specify a no-return policy during sale periods; if an item is not returnable, the clerk must tell you that it is not returnable, and the sales slip must also state this fact.

One final tip about sales: At the American designer stores and department stores, after-Christmas sales take place, well, after Christmas—either the day after Christmas or else right after New Year's. However, the European designer boutiques in New York tend to have their sales much, much later in January—the third or fourth week of the month, to be exact. I mention this because if you are flying to New York specifically to shop the after-Christmas sales, do not assume that December 26 is the magic day. It may in fact be January 26! Also note that the July sales are now held during the last week of June.

DEPARTMENT STORE SECRETS

New York is the king of department store flagships, so even if you have a branch of these stores in your hometown, you owe it to yourself—and your bottom line—to visit the Manhattan location. With-it department stores have mouthwatering colors, ambience, entertainment, and cachet, in addition to great markdowns (they're often able to offer their shoppers a kind of value not seen elsewhere). You'd be surprised at just what kinds of bargains and treats you may find in New York's department stores.

Besides offering fantastic sales, look to department stores to offer promotions and customer services you just can't find elsewhere. A large department store once gave away a second strand of pearls to customers who bought one strand (a Mother's Day promotion), and cosmetics and perfume gift-with-purchase deals and giveaways are commonplace. There might not be a free lunch in New York, but there certainly are free makeovers. Extras are everywhere you turn in department stores.

When it comes to bargains, remember that department stores have to unload merchandise just like every other retailer does. They do this through the rather old method we all love best: sales. But when the sale merchandise isn't all sold, what happens to it? It does not go to retail heaven. Usually it goes back to the warehouse, to be held for the annual department store warehouse sale—or to the factory outlet. Yep, department stores now have factory outlets. They are all located outside of Manhattan, out of respect for regular retail, but they aren't hard to get to, so read on.

Note: If you are not experienced at negotiating department store sales, ask a salesperson for help. There are often additional markdowns off the last ticketed price, which may be hard to discern.

TIPS FOR BARGAIN-BASEMENT SHOPPING

Here are some tips for shopping the bargain basements:

- Remember that bargain basements may or may not have new merchandise. Some get their goods at the beginning of the season; others don't get new items until traditional stores have dumped their unsold merchandise. Old merchandise is always less expensive than new merchandise.
- Look for damages.
- Know the return policy before you buy.
- Try everything on; actual sizes may be different from the marked sizes.
- If you are shopping in a chain, understand that another branch of that chain will have some of the same merchandise and some different merchandise, the better the zip code, the better the choices. Along the same lines, different factory outlets can have entirely different merchandise in exactly the same time frame.
- Expect communal dressing rooms and sometimes-primitive conditions.
- Be prepared to check your handbag and/or your shopping bags. Security can be offensively tight at bargain basements.
- Remember that few bargain basements will mail packages for you.

Shop a department store before you go to a bargain basement so that you know what kinds of prices to look for. At various well-known bargain basements (all listed in this book), I saw the same designer blouse on the same day for several different prices that covered a range of more than $100. The Saks Fifth Avenue price was $230. I then saw the blouse at different outlets for $180, $163, $142, $109, and $93. It is impossible to know which bargain is the very best bargain when you are shopping, but try to do a little homework first.

Also know that department store prices can be competitive with outlet prices. Try this experience on for size: I was shopping at my beloved Filene's Basement, where I found a truly fabulous, stunning skirt by a Belgian designer for the Filene's Basement price of $49. A sensational bargain. But wait: The Neiman Marcus price tag, still attached, showed all the markdown prices that Neiman's had used in order to sell this little skirt. The last price on the floor at Neiman's was $51! While both prices are great bargains, there ain't much margin here, and department store prices, very frequently, are as good as it gets.

Some bargain basements just don't have bargains. Let the shopper beware.

DISCOUNT STORES & OFF-PRICERS

So what's the difference between a discounter and an off-pricer? The discounter sells some current brand-name merchandise and some private-label merchandise at a 20%-to-25% discount off prices that you'd find in department stores. The off-pricer sometimes sells current merchandise that is gleaned from a warehouse closeout, but often sells older merchandise at a deeper discount.

Just for comparison's sake, remember that sale prices in any department store are 20% to 50% off. The big difference is that the department store offers the sale price after the merchandise has been on the floor for a while. The discounter starts off with the "everyday low price."

Discounters may also have merchandise made for them, specifically created by designers to be sold at low prices—Target is famous for this.

Target and **Kmart** are two of the more famous discounters. **Filene's Basement, Century 21, T.J. Maxx,** and **Daffy's** are off-pricers. I actually think that **Loehmann's** functions as both.

Off-pricers offer the most savings. These stores can be smaller and less fancy than discounters, or as big as a warehouse and very nicely decorated. Have you been to **Century 21** lately?

Easy Access

CENTURY 21
22 Cortlandt St., between Church St. and Broadway
(Subway: R or W to Cortlandt St.).

Words fail me and my palms get sweaty when I think about Century 21. There is no question that this is one of the best bargain resources in New York.

Century 21 sells name brands at discounts—and, my friends, what names! I've seen some heavy-duty designers (Armani, Lacroix, Prada, Sonia Rykiel, Carolina Herrera, Tod's) that I've never spotted at Filene's Basement or anywhere else. The store sells men's, women's, and children's clothing; linens; shoes; luggage; small electronics; and name-brand perfumes and cosmetics. Prices, for the most part, range from 40% to 70% off, depending on the item.

The women's underwear selection is pretty good, and there is a small department for plus sizes. The shoe department separates out the Tod's from the rest. I am addicted to designer sunglasses, which I buy here for about $50 a pair. You can get European designer ties for $40 to $50 each (saving about $70 per tie), and you can even snag Annick Goutal perfumes. The perfumes and cosmetics are not discounted, but Century 21 has an incentive system so that the more you buy, the larger the gift coupon you get for use on any item in the store.

Besides its department store in Lower Manhattan, Century 21 has a store in Brooklyn in the middle of real-people neighborhood Bay Ridge, with a separate home style store behind; it's at 472 86th St., between Fourth and Fifth avenues (© 718/748-3266; Subway: R to 86th St. in Brooklyn). There are also locations in New Jersey and Long Island. *Web Tip:* If you sign up for the C21 Web newsletter, you'll get a heads-up on new arrivals before they hit the racks. Inventory moves fast and there's no online catalog. © 212/227-9092. www.c21stores.com.

CONWAY

1333 Broadway, at 35th St. (Subway: B, D, F, N, Q, R, V, or W to 34th St./Herald Sq.); 11 W. 34th St., between Fifth and Sixth aves. (Subway: B, D, F, N, Q, R, V, or W to 34th St./Herald Sq.).

Conway has many different branches and parts to it; to get the real flavor, you must shop at the giant store on Broadway, near Macy's. The other stores are ordinary and bland, but not this one: It's a real Turkish bazaar (albeit air-conditioned), with tables piled high with merchandise—out-of-season; discontinued, unloved styles; and designer overruns. This branch is the souk of your dreams, but you have to like the jumble. This is not Bendel's. This is a bargain basement in the truest sense of the word; all it lacks is basement space. Only for the strong-hearted. © 212/967-3460 for Broadway store.

DAFFY'S

335 Madison Ave., at 44th St. (Subway: 4, 5, 6, 7, or S to Grand Central/42nd St.); 125 E. 57th St., between Park and Madison aves. (Subway: N, R, or W to Fifth Ave./59th St.); 1311 Broadway, at 34th St. (Subway: B, D, F, N, Q, R, V, or W to 34th St./Herald Sq.); 1775 Broadway, with entrance on W. 57th St. (Subway: A, B, C, D, or 1 to 59th St./Columbus Circle); 462 Broadway, at Grand St. (Subway: R or W to Prince St.); 50 Broadway, between Morris and Exchange Place (Subway: 4 or 5 to Wall St.).

I always check out this source in homage to past bargains and as a tribute to my Gypsy soul—I just can't pass up the idea of a bargain. Daffy's does get some names sometimes, and you can do rather well for yourself. I especially like the idea that one of the branches is almost next door to the Four Seasons.

The store on Madison, though not the biggest, is convenient for Midtown shoppers. The East 57th Street store is the fanciest and easiest to shop. The West Side store, near Macy's, is a many-level splendor inside a mall: It is truly overwhelming. And I am not overwhelmed easily. That branch—and the one at Broadway and West 57th—are my least favorite. Although the old store on Lower Fifth Avenue has closed, there are now locations in SoHo and near Wall Street.

Like all the places listed in this section, it's very much hit-or-miss at Daffy's. *Best Bets:* Daffy's has a good men's department that includes shoes. © 212/557-4422 for Madison Avenue location. www.daffys.com.

DSW (DESIGNER SHOE WAREHOUSE)
40 E. 14th St., near University Place (Subway: 4, 5, 6, L, N, Q, R, or W to 14th St./Union Sq.).

This is an enormous space devoted not only to shoes for men, women, and kids, but also to accessories and gift items. There are tons of brands (and a handful of really, really big-name brands—such as Pucci). Note that the 14th Street store is in the same building as a branch of Filene's Basement. There's another location in Battery Park at 102 North End Ave. *Web Tip:* As we go to press, DSW's online catalog, 24/7@dsw.com, is scheduled to be up and running soon. © 212/674-2146. www.dswshoe.com.

FILENE'S BASEMENT
4 Union Sq. S., near University Place (Subway: 4, 5, 6, L, N, Q, R, or W to 14th St./Union Sq.); 620 Sixth Ave., at 18th St. (Subway: F or V to 14th St.); 2222 Broadway, at 79th St. (Subway: 1 to 79th St.).

Filene's Basement stocks overruns and unsold designer goodies, from shoes to underwear, for men and women. It has departments for petites, plus sizes, and some home style (not much). The Boston stores are better, but that doesn't mean you should ignore the New York branches (heaven forbid). It just means that New York can be spotty; you have to get lucky. I bought an Alberta Ferretti evening skirt for $299. There's also a good selection of Jones New York.

The Union Square store participates in the bridal sale—a total madhouse with a heap of wedding gowns at rock-bottom prices, $250 to $699 each for dresses worth up to $10,000. So here's the deal: You wait in line, then you race in and grab *any* gown. Then you can trade with other people if you want. The sale is announced on the website.

Note that the Union Square store is atop DSW, while the Sixth Avenue location is in the same building as T.J. Maxx, so you can get two birds with one credit card. **Best Bets:** Teen queens will want to check out the Prom Event, usually held in March. Prom dresses from top designers are discounted 50% to 75%. © 212/358-0169 for Union Square location. www.filenes basement.com.

LOEHMANN'S
101 Seventh Ave., at 16th St. (Subway: 1, 2, or 3 to 14th St.); 2101 Broadway, at 72nd St. (Subway: 1, 2, or 3 to 72nd St.).

I've found that the quality of shopping at Loehmann's has improved enormously in recent years; either I've gotten lucky or things are looking up. Now I visit one of these stores as a first stop in my discovery tour of bargains.

The stores are clean and modern—and so crammed with merchandise that racks bulge and items sometimes droop onto the floor. You might want to go first thing in the morning when you have lots of energy to explore. Loehmann's sells men's and women's accessories and designer stuff. On a recent visit, I was shocked by how many French brands were on hand—brands that as an American shopper I probably would not have known. Not that status is everything, but I got things at a fraction of their Paris costs. Sarah found racks of Armani in the men's section of the new Broadway store. *Web Tip:* Join the Insider Club online so you can be rewarded with coupons, including discounts during the week of your birthday. © 212/ 352-0856. www.loehmanns.com.

T.J. MAXX
620 Sixth Ave., at 18th St. (Subway: F or V to 14th St.).

This off-pricer sells a little of everything—clothing for men, women, and children; underwear; shoes; luggage; home accessories; and bed and bath products. It even carries some big-name designers every now and then. My favorite finds here have been home items, dishes, picture frames, and gifts in the $10-to-$15 price range. For serious clothing, you have to be lucky—although there are clothes in all sizes and styles. © 212/ 229-0875. www.tjmaxx.com.

Out of the Way—Slightly

LOEHMANN'S (THE BRONX)
5740 Broadway, at 236th St., Bronx (Subway: 1 to 238th St.).

Note that this listing is for out-of-the-way locations; the Manhattan stores are listed on p. 294. There is also a branch in Sheepshead Bay, Brooklyn, at 2807 E. 21st St., at Shore Parkway (© 718/368-1256).

Naturally, you've heard of Loehmann's and probably shopped in one of its many stores, but this location is its flagship, housed in a former ice-skating rink in a lovely section of the Bronx called Riverdale-Kingsbridge. While this Loehmann's is nice, it's not immensely different from the Loehmann's in your own neighborhood, and might not be worth the trip if you are visiting from out of town. However, I have found designer clothes in this store that weren't in other branches. Impossible to know.

The store itself is clean and spiffy, complete with benches for husbands to sit on and the Back Room, where the big-name designer collections are housed. There are other bargain shops, off-pricers, and discounters nearby, so you can make a day of it.

Directions: To get here by subway, take the 1 to 238th Street. Exit onto Broadway and walk 2 blocks south. By bus, take the regular BX no. 9 to West 236th Street (at Broadway); the Liberty Lines express bus BMX no. 1 (which runs along Third Ave. in Manhattan) to West 239th Street; or the BMX no. 2, which runs up Sixth Avenue in Manhattan, to the same stop in the Bronx.

By car from the West Side: Drive north on the Henry Hudson and exit at West 239th Street. It's probably easier to go from the East Side by taking I-87 North (Major Deegan Expwy.), exiting at West 230th Street or Van Cortland Park South (W. 240th St.), then heading west a block or two to Broadway. Call for more specific directions. © **718/543-6420.** www.loehmanns.com.

Just for Men

ROTHMAN'S OF UNION SQUARE
200 Park Ave. S., at 17th St. (Subway: 4, 5, 6, L, N, Q, R, or W to 14th St./Union Sq.).

Rothman's sells discounted big-name designer clothes and suits in wide variety of sizes, so any man can find the right fit. See p. 211. © **212/777-7400.** www.rothmansny.com.

FACTORY OUTLETS

The factory-outlet business has become so attractive (that means profitable) that many makers are overproducing perfect merchandise for their outlet stores. This capitalizes on the designer's well-known name and expensive advertising campaign, which has already been paid for, and reaches a totally different segment of the market, so it doesn't compete with the traditional retailers.

The prices in factory outlets are usually the same as at discount stores or department store sales—20% to 25% off regular retail. A dress that has a $100 price tag usually sells for $79 at an outlet. But it can sell for $50, and certainly will be marked down as the season draws to a close. The discount may vary on a per-item basis, since irregulars should be less expensive than overruns.

Outlets may or may not offer a better deal than off-pricers. Generally speaking, an off-pricer has better bargains than an outlet store, unless you hit a sample sale or special promotion. On the other hand, if you have the opportunity to spend a day at Woodbury Common, an entire city of outlets, you may indeed do all the shopping and saving you might ever crave.

There are several factory-outlet villages in the greater New York area that offer different types of shopping to the eager public. I feel very strongly that no trip to New York could be called a proper shopping excursion without a visit to at least one of the outlet malls. If you're going to only one, there is no doubt in my mind that it should be **Woodbury Common;** it's both easy to get to and easy to shop.

A few general outlet survival tips:

- Wear comfortable shoes—you'll do a lot of walking.
- Drive if you can; it's worth the price of a rental car. I once saw bargains at the Eileen Fisher outlet that were so great that the trip more than paid for itself. Bring friends and share the cost of the rental.
- Know that weekends are very crowded; a weekday visit is preferable if possible.
- Read the carefully posted signs about return policies before you buy. The rules vary from store to store, but most warehouses allow returns within a 7-day period.
- Sign up on mailing lists if you want. Each warehouse has a mailing list and will honor out-of-state addresses, although it may not send to addresses outside of the U.S.

- If someone is carrying an interesting shopping bag, ask questions. Discount shoppers love to help others.
- Do not assume a bargain or a best-price-in-town price tag.

WOODBURY COMMON
498 Red Apple Court, Central Valley, New York.

Woodbury Common has changed so dramatically in the past few years that I don't know where to begin. Since it will continue to evolve, take a Xanax and dream of renting a golf cart to get around this enormous village-mall. The additions at Woodbury make it so exciting that it cannot be compared to its sister malls in New Jersey, or anywhere else. It has more high-end stores than those others, and *oui,* the only **Chanel** factory outlet in the world. This is, hands down, the king.

If you are an international visitor to the United States, you'd better take notes or videotape—your friends at home just won't believe this place. Bring your station wagon, bring your van, bring your pals. And for heaven's sake, bring your credit cards.

I guess the most important thing I should do is warn you that the area is now too big to do in a day, so you might want to consider spending a night nearby. If you get overwhelmed easily, do research when you arrive so you can hit the places that interest you the most.

Visually speaking, Woodbury Common is the most attractive of the outlet villages. Its core is a fake Colonial village, and each shop (you enter from outdoors) is a different pastel shade—it's so cute that you may want to move in. The new additions are not as cute as the center part. They aren't uncute, they're just more economically built. With the new additions, the village has grown a little wild—it sprawls here and there and you could do well with a golf cart to get to all the outlets. Consider moving your car once or twice, although this is impossible on weekends and could be impossible any day— the later in the day it gets, the harder it is to find a parking space.

There are 220 outlets in the village, including many big-name shops like **Barneys, Burberry, Chanel, Calvin Klein, Coach, Crate & Barrel, Dior, Ellen Tracy, Frette, Gucci, J. Crew, Loro Piana, Neiman Marcus Last Call, Off 5th Saks Fifth Avenue Outlet, Space (Prada, Miu Miu), Theory, TSE, Tumi,** and **Ugg.**

Stop by the information center for a free map and newspaper upon arrival. You may want to join the VIP Shopper Club (www.premiumoutlets.com/vip). There are several clean restroom stations scattered around the mall. Of course, there are places to have coffee or a bite. What they really need is a hotel on the premises.

Directions: The drive is easy (on a gorgeous highway) and beautiful almost any time of the year, especially autumn. It takes approximately 1 to 1½ hours from Manhattan. Hop on the New York State Thruway (I-87) and get off at exit 16. Almost immediately after going through the tollbooth, you will see the mall to your right.

If you are visiting from Connecticut, not Manhattan, you may wonder about the best route because of the limited number of bridges across the Hudson River. Again, it depends on which part of Connecticut you are coming from, but I saved a half-hour by using the Tappan Zee Bridge in my drive from Fairfield County.

You can also get here via **Gray Line** (© **800/669-0051** or 212/397-2620), which operates bus tours from the Port Authority, at 42nd Street and Eighth Avenue. There are several morning buses and afternoon/evening return buses each day; all riders get a discount coupon booklet. The cost is about $40 per person.

Hours are usually daily from 10am to 9pm, except for some holidays. © **845/928-4000**. www.premiumoutlets.com/woodburycommon.

WAREHOUSE SALES

A warehouse sale is not a sample sale but a once-a-year, once-in-a-lifetime, or every-now-and-then event most often held in a real warehouse. Perhaps the most famous is the **Barneys Warehouse Sale,** which is held in the Barneys offices downtown, advertised in the newspapers *(New York Times),* and held regularly twice a year. Others may be one-off events. I just saw an ad for the **Donghia Warehouse Sale** (Donghia is a home style and fabric line) that included a shuttle bus from the Milford, Connecticut, train station. Sometimes the design firm will rent public space for the sale; Vera Wang has held her sales in a hotel; others are held at one of the city's armories. A few businesses keep warehouses open to the public on regular hours, such as **ABC Carpet & Home** with a warehouse in the Bronx.

FLEA MARKETS

Just because you buy it at a flea market does not mean it's a bargain—or that the price is any better than in a store. Know your prices and comparative values, and keep in mind that this is alternative retail—vendors may tell you any old hogwash in order to get you to buy. We've heard "antiques" vendors say some outrageous (false) things about their wares. Be careful. You should also know that cash is preferred (especially if you are bargaining), most markets are held on weekends (and some vendors appear on only one of those days), outdoor markets are held "weather permitting" (which means there's no market in a downpour or when it's freezing), and some markets do not operate on the weekend between Christmas and New Year's.

Special-event flea markets, such as the **Pier Shows,** are sensational, especially when money is tight and dealers want to raise cash. Watch the trade newspapers for announcements of these shows and other markets.

THE ANNEX/HELL'S KITCHEN FLEA MARKET
W. 39th St., between Ninth and Tenth aves. (Subway: A, C, or E to 42nd St.).

The Annex, the best flea market in New York, got driven out of Chelsea by the neighborhood's own success: The parking lot that it called home was sold to make room for new construction. Now it has relocated and joined forces with the Hell's Kitchen Flea Market. This is one of the best in terms of getting the adrenaline running and the heart pumping fast for a few hours of shopping fun. I must warn you, however, that this place was "discovered" a while ago; so the prices can be very high, and vendors may not know their stuff. The crowd that shops, however, is as much fun as the dealers and the goods. Open Saturday and Sunday from 9am to 5pm. © 212/243-5343. www.hellskitchenfleamarket.com.

THE ANTIQUES GARAGE
112 W. 25th St., between Sixth and Seventh aves. (Subway: F or V to 23rd St.).

This market attracts thousands of shoppers each weekend with over a hundred vendors on two floors selling everything from rugs and furniture to fine silver. There's a shuttle bus from the Hell's Kitchen Flea Market to the Antiques Garage, $1 per ride. Another market is located in Chelsea, just steps away, on the uptown side of West 25th Street, between Sixth and Seventh avenues. This one's junky.

GREENFLEA M.S. 44
Columbus Ave., between 76th and 77th sts. (Subway: 1 to 79th St.).

This is a varied market with several parts to it so, as a whole, it's got something for everyone. You'll see a small greenmarket—don't miss the pretzels—and both an outdoor and an indoor portion of the flea market.

The outdoor portion brims with colors, energy, and style. You'll find lots of arts and crafts and, of course, traditional flea market–esque "antiques." A large percentage of people seem to have just returned from some exotic destination and offer wares from wherever they traveled to (Ecuador, Mexico, Bali).

There's also a small amount of new and basic merchandise (socks, underwear, pet needs). Nothing beats a gorgeous day, a hot pretzel, and all this fun.

Inside the school is a jumble of "antiques"—I get claustrophobic from it all. I'm happy enough with the used treasures sold outside; on a pretty day, it seems like a sin to be indoors, but the crowds don't agree with me. Open Sunday only, from 10am to about 5:30pm. © 212/239-3025. www.greenflea markets.com.

GreenFlea P.S. 41
Greenwich Ave., at Charles St., between Sixth and Seventh aves. (Subway: 1, 2, or 3 to 14th St.).

This schoolyard extravaganza comes complete with greenmarket. It gets going late, so don't arrive before 11am. This is part of the Village's glory. Open Saturday only. *Web Tip:* This market's open only in fair weather, so check the website on Wednesday, Thursday, or Friday to see if the market will open on Saturday. © 212/239-3025. www.greenfleamarkets.com.

STREET MERCHANTS

The street merchants in Manhattan are really best for beads and trinkets—and should only amuse you, not take your shopping budget. In good weather, there's someone at every other corner selling a small selection of something: watches, sunglasses, handbags, books, pearls, ties, sweaters, and so on. In bad weather, there are folks selling things like umbrellas, gloves, and scarves.

The quality of all this merchandise is suspicious, but if you take it with a grain of salt, you may find that the shoe fits. The umbrella will last long enough to get you through the storm, the pearls won't turn, and the watches may work for quite some time.

Street hawking, especially of fake or counterfeit merchandise, is essentially illegal, so most hawkers are on the lookout for the police and will roll all of their merchandise into a ball and be gone in less than 30 seconds should anyone look at them suspiciously. Street hawkers are abundant or scarce depending on the police presence at any given time. They try to work popular areas and to attract visitors—Fifth Avenue in Midtown boasts a fair number; Sixth Avenue in the Village (near Bleecker St.) and Lower Broadway (near Astor Place) are other good places to find street merchants. I've also noticed that there are more folks out on the streets on weekends than on weekdays.

When I really need something fake, I simply pop onto the subway and go to Canal Street, where prices and selection are superior.

Buyer Beware: Counterfeits & Imitations

If you're talking street merchandise, you have to be thinking of the most nontraditional retailing ploys of them all: counterfeit. Or stolen. Or merely "lost." The watches are no doubt counterfeit, while the sweaters may have just gotten "lost" from their original warehouse. It's so hard to keep track of all those trucks, you know.

There is some room for debate as to when an item becomes a counterfeit, a copy, or a knockoff, and at what point it's illegal. If the intent is to defraud the true maker, the item is a counterfeit. Thus, all those $25 Gucci, Rolex, Dunhill, and Cartier watches that street merchants sell are counterfeits. It is illegal to sell them and probably illegal to buy them.

Most brand names that are sold on the street are frauds, so look carefully at the way the signatures are made. Some Gucci fakes look like Gucci from afar, but careful inspection reveals that those aren't even Gs in the pattern. That's not a fake. It's an attempt to take advantage of your bad eyesight or inattention to detail. But it's legal.

New York does not have the sophisticated counterfeits that can be found in Italy or China or Bangkok—most U.S. fakes scream "fake" and are just for fun. A few of them are cute enough as joke presents, even though they don't really look that much like the real thing when you inspect them carefully.

I would never, ever give a fake and attempt to carry it off as the real item. Blatantly fake merchandise is rather easy to spot. It looks cheap, feels cheap, and may even smell cheap. Good copies take a more practiced eye:

- Know what the real thing looks and feels like.
- Know if the real maker even has the same style. Those phony Chanel-style sunglasses sold on Canal Street? Sure, they look cute, but as it turns out, Chanel sunglasses don't even come in that particular style! See those silly Chanel-style earrings that are studs for pierced ears? Chanel does not manufacture studs. And so on.
- Check the weight of the goods (good watches are very thin, for example), the texture of the fabrics, the lining, the stitching, the make of the label, the way the trademark is made. Real Ray-Ban sunglasses not only say Ray-Ban on them (as do the fakes), but also have little RB initials smoked into the lens near the temples. This is difficult or impossible to fake. Most big-name designer goods have the name of the firm etched into the mold for the hardware. It says Gucci or Hermès right in the brass. Fixings and hardware are good clues to fakes, even in terms of quality, if not in terms of engraving.
- Ask if the product comes with an ID card. Ho, ho, ho. Real designer goods now come with their own credit card–like ID card, some with a serial number. Even a tie at Prada comes with such an animal. They don't have ID cards in the Prada-style bags sold on Canal Street.

If you are purposely choosing an imitation, consider the light in which your fake will be shown. If all your friends have the real thing, and you are wearing the fake out to brunch, you'd better believe that sooner or later someone will discover your secret. However, if you are making a one-time appearance at the Oscars, or if your gemstone will be seen only by candlelight, no one will know the difference unless you tell. Do remember, however, that high-quality fakes are not cheap, and that inexpensive fakes always look fake.

SAMPLE MADNESS & SPECIAL SALES

A few designers and manufacturers keep their samples of items in an archive. They lend these clothes out to friends or family (many of the evening clothes you see photographed in society pages are loaners), but they do not sell them. Other designers figure that any amount of cash they can bring in is worthwhile, and realize that the cost of storing decades' worth of samples can get to be exorbitant. What to do? Have a sample sale!

Many sample sales require cash, though some of the big ones take credit cards. Note that some sample sales are held in boutiques (**Eileen Fisher**), private parties, or shindigs for best customers or fashion elite (**Chanel, Fendi, Yves Saint Laurent**); **Vera Wang**'s is at the Penn Plaza Pavilion Exhibit Hall.

Market NYC (268 Mulberry St., between Houston and Prince sts.; 490 Hudson St., at Christopher St.; © 212/580-8995; www.themarketnyc.com) takes place every weekend where local young designers showcase their wares. For big-name designer sales, contact **Soiffer-Haskin,** a local company that hosts sales events in their offices at 317 W. 33rd St., near Eighth Avenue. Recent sales include **Escada, Pratesi, Dennis Basso,** and **Ralph Lauren Home.** Log on to www.soiffer haskin.com to be notified of upcoming events by e-mail or snail mail.

Sample Savvy

To get lots of details on sample sales, subscribe to the *S&B Report* (it stands for "Sales & Bargains"). Note that the subscription rate goes up every year; a subscription presently costs $75 a year for the online version and $124 for the print version. What you get in return is a monthly booklet with names, addresses, and short descriptions of what's for sale. For information, call © **877/579-0222,** or visit the website (which does have e-commerce!) at www.lazarshopping.com.

If you don't want to subscribe, or if you are in town for just a few days but still want to get in on the action, try these tips:

- Walk down Broadway or Seventh Avenue near the Garment District, and you will more than likely be given handouts touting a variety of sample sales.
- The best way to find a special sale or a sample sale is simply to ask. Call your favorite designers, especially in April and October, and ask, "Do you sell samples or extra stock to the public?" If the answer is no, you might next ask, "Do you have a factory outlet where you sell samples or extra stock?" It never hurts to ask.
- Read the local events magazines like *New York* (www.nymag. com) and *Time Out New York* (www.timeoutny.com). Both announce many sales; *New York* has totally redone its shopping coverage, and bargain announcements and many sales are now listed each week.
- Check out **TopButton.com** and the **SSS Sample Sales** hot line (© **212/947-8748;** www.clothingline.com), free resources with thousands of sale listings. *Daily Candy* often has sample sales listed (www.dailycandy.com).
- Watch advertisements in the *New York Times* for the latest sales; pay close attention around gift-giving seasons.
- Sign up for mailing lists, and ask about future shows.

And while you're at the sale, remember these tips:

- Try to avoid the lunch-hour crush; get there when the doors open if possible.
- Whenever possible, try it on.
- Don't give a sample-sale gift to someone in a box from a real department store. The items are usually coded with a red X on the tag so that people can't return them to the department store for full price.
- Don't buy something just because it's cheap.

USED MERCHANDISE

....

People often put perfectly good pieces of furniture out on the street for garbage collectors to haul away. Honest. I happen to have pieces of furniture that were rescued from the curbs of New York City.

Also, many people give their cast-offs to charity to get a tax deduction for the donation. Scads of thrift shops and charity-related stores sell previously worn merchandise. I happen to like the **Posh Sale** (p. 312) because of the high quality of the designer merchandise. I must note, though, that some of my younger friends—women ages 25 to 35—tell me that the clothes sold at the Posh Sale are too matronly for them.

Not to worry. These days, used clothing is so chic it's called "vintage"—and even Saks sells it. For the young crowd, there are plenty of East Village sources and even flea markets for vintage. For those who want gently used designer clothes, there are resale shops galore.

Resale Shops

Manhattan's resale shops are a special breed unto themselves, each with its own rules and regulations and secrets. Generally speaking, resale shops pride themselves on fashionable merchandise that is only a year or two (at the most) old. All things considered, if you want to wear Chanel, resale is the only way to go. Well, it's not the only way to go, but it's the only way that I can contemplate.

Also note that with the revival of many '60s and '70s fashion looks, it's getting harder and harder to tell vintage from resale. Try both.

Designer Resale
324 E. 81st St., between First and Second aves. (Subway: 6 to 77th St.).

This place is small, but the clothes are frequently brand-new, and there are indeed designer names to be found. Its occasional color-coded sticker system is a bit unclear, so when you go to pay, the price turns out to be much less than you thought it was. Ask!

There's another branch, **Designer Resale Too** (311 E. 81st St., near Second Ave.), and a men's branch, **Gentlemen's Resale** (322 E. 81st St.), on the same block. © **212/734-3639.** www.resaleclothing.net.

ENCORE
1132 Madison Ave., between 84th and 85th sts., 2nd floor (Subway: 4, 5, or 6 to 86th St.).

This store got attention about 30 years ago when it was rumored that Jacqueline Kennedy Onassis was turning in her used clothes here. I had been coming by for years and finding zilch, and then suddenly I hit pay dirt. Would you like to hear about the Yves Saint Laurent Rive Gauche dress for $90? For the past year or so, Encore has been one of my regular sources.

The first floor sells dressy gowns, shoes, and handbags, while the second floor houses more casual items.

Open Monday, Wednesday, Friday, and Saturday from 10:30am to 6:30pm; Thursday from 10:30am to 7:30pm; and Sunday from noon to 6pm. *Best Bets:* If you've ever dreamed of interlocking Cs, this could be the start of something big: There are always a few Chanel suits priced from $500 to $750. A Chanel suit at $500 is really an outstanding buy, as the average price for a used Chanel suit is usually higher. (The average price for a new Chanel suit is $4,500, in case you were wondering.) © **212/879-2850.** www.encoreresale.com.

LA BOUTIQUE
1045 Madison Ave., between 79th and 80th sts., 2nd floor (Subway: 6 to 77th St.).

This shop is next door to Michael's (see below) but miles away in attitude and finesse. La Boutique's sales staff is professional and courteous and helped me find several pieces in my size that I had missed on the rack. On my last visit, I saw some Chanel and Prada, but the real finds were pieces by Eskandar, St. John, and Armani, all marked 40% off the shop's already low price. A new vintage department features designers from the '60s and '70s including Pucci, Halston, and Mary Quant.

There are other locations at 160 W. 72nd St., between Broadway and Columbus Avenue, and at 803 Lexington Ave., at 62nd Street, 2nd floor. © 212/517-8099. www.laboutique resale.com.

MICHAEL'S
1041 Madison Ave., between 79th and 80th sts., 2nd floor (Subway: 6 to 77th St.).

Over the years, I've personally done better at Encore, but the last time I did some "thrifting" around the city, I had a ball at Michael's and got a whole new wardrobe for about $90—and found nothing at Encore. That's life in the big city. Anyway, this store is close enough to Encore and right next door to La Boutique, so you can hit all three in the same trip.

I saw a pair of red-and-white Chanel slingbacks that I'll never get over as long as I live—they were worthy of a museum. I'm shrinking my feet as we speak. Michael's also has a lot of plain-old regular big-name designer goods that just keep on keeping on. Small sizes will do better than larger. Wedding gowns are now sold upstairs.

Open Monday through Saturday from 9:30am to 6pm, Thursday until 8pm. Closed Saturday in addition to Sunday during July and August. The sales staff is neither friendly nor helpful and can make a visit to Michael's less than thrilling. ***Best Bets:*** Michael's has a lot of Armani, Hermès, and Chanel. © 212/737-7273. www.michaelsconsignment.com.

A SECOND CHANCE
1109 Lexington Ave., between 77th and 78th sts., 2nd floor (Subway: 6 to 77th St.).

Located near other great clothing resources, this resale shop has the usual luck of the draw, with some designer names and some midrange names. You may find a Ralph Lauren, Mondi, or Adolfo label, or you may not. The store opens Monday through Saturday at 11am, Sunday at noon. *Web Tip:* A $5-off coupon is available on the website. ✆ 212/744-6041. www.asecondchanceresale.com.

Thrift Shops

Stores that specialize in upscale used merchandise consider themselves either resale shops or consignment shops; those that take whatever donations people choose to give in the name of charity are thrift shops, usually run for the benefit of a specific organization. As a result, most schools, hospitals, and disease-care and research organizations have their own thrift shops.

By definition, a thrift shop is only as good as you are lucky. It's impossible to review them, since the merchandise comes and goes, and one can never be sure. I've seen that over the years, the thrift shop has become very popular—aside from the young people who are into grunge, there are plenty of well-off middle-class people who are looking for high quality at a worn price.

Some shops offer new stock donated by some of the city's top designers. The **Memorial Sloan-Kettering Cancer Center Thrift Shop** recently had an entire rack of Carolina Herrera pieces, priced from $150 to $375. All in small sample sizes.

Do note that prices at these places can be high, especially if you are used to out-of-town thrift-shop prices. A few basic rules hold true for most thrift shops:

- Many thrift shops take credit cards; few will take checks.
- You can sometimes bargain a little if you buy a lot.
- Most stores open at 11am; Saturday hours may be strange. Few are open on Sunday.
- A lot of thrift shops are located on the Upper East Side; I've grouped together several that make the expedition worthwhile.

- If you are used to the high quality at stores like Encore and Michael's, you may be turned off after checking out a few thrift shops.

Some thrift shops specialize in home decor, including these:

Cancer Care Thrift Shop
1480 Third Ave., at 83rd St. (Subway: 4, 5, or 6 to 86th St.).
© **212/879-9868.** www.cancercare.org.

Housing Works Thrift Shop
143 W. 17th St., between Sixth and Seventh aves. (Subway: 1 to 18th St.).
© **212/366-0820.** www.housingworks.org.

245 W. 10th St., near Hudson St. (Subway: 1 to Christopher St.).
© **212/352-1618.** www.housingworks.org.

202 E. 77th St., between Second and Third aves. (Subway: 6 to 77th St.).
© **212/772-8461.** www.housingworks.org.

306 Columbus Ave., near 74th St. (Subway: B or C to 72nd St.).
© **212/579-7566.** www.housingworks.org.

Memorial Sloan-Kettering Cancer Center Thrift Shop
1440 Third Ave., between 81st and 82nd sts. (Subway: 6 to 77th St.).
© **212/535-1250.** www.memorialthriftshop.org.

Spence Chapin Thrift Shop
1473 Third Ave., between 83rd and 84th sts. (Subway: 4, 5, or 6 to 86th St.).
© **212/737-8448.** www.spence-chapin.org.

1850 Second Ave., between 95th and 96th sts. (Subway: 6 to 96th St.).
© **212/426-7643.** www.spence-chapin.org.

SPECIAL-EVENT RETAILING

An event just wouldn't be special if you couldn't buy something, would it? Museums have gift shops, circuses have vendors, and New York City has all sorts of special events that revolve around the selling of something or other.

The best of these events are charity-related, such as **Seventh on Sale,** usually held in May and November (www.7thonsale.ebay.com), when designers donate clothing to be sold flea market–style, with income going toward AIDS research.

The shoe industry also does an annual bash, QVC FFANY Shoes on Sale. Usually held in the fall, this annual gala and television event is a 3-hour QVC footwear program in which 100,000 pairs of designer shoes are sold at half their retail price. During the month of October (Breast Cancer Awareness Month), QVC carries a "Shoe of the Day" segment each weekday until it sells out. All proceeds go to breast cancer research. www.bcrfcure.org.

Some events are food-related—in May, the **Ninth Avenue International Food Festival** is a big block party that allows you to roam through throngs of people as you explore a variety of ethnic-food stands. In Chinatown, there's **Chinese New Year** in January or February. There are similar festivals in Little Italy, including September's **Feast of San Gennaro.** Check with your hotel concierge or *Where* magazine to find out if such events will be held when you are in town. NYC & Company also puts together a quarterly list of all special events in Manhattan; check out www.nycvisit.com.

Also investigate traditional charity events: For antiques and furniture, there's the twice-a-year **Seventh Regiment Armory Antiques Show,** at Park Avenue and 67th Street, as well as the Pier Shows.

For clothes, try the **Posh Sale,** a benefit for the Lighthouse for the Blind, also held at the Armory. Once a year, in May, the great ladies of New York society clean out their closets (designers do this as well) and send their tired, their poor, their wretched excesses to the Posh Sale, where we yearn for them to be free, but will pay $30 to $50 for them. Check www.light house.org for details. You can also stop by the **Lighthouse Store** (111 E. 59th St., near Park Ave.), a very nice boutique with a combination of types of merchandise. Some are related to large-type or large-size print for those who don't see very well, but many other items are more along the lines of what you would find in a museum store.

SPECIAL VISITORS

For a clothes encounter of the bargain kind, check for magazine and newspaper listings about special visitors from international retailing establishments. The British are particularly adept at flying to New York for a week, taking a suite in a Midtown hotel, and visiting with private customers, to whom they sell at wholesale or rock-bottom British prices.

To become a private customer, one needs only sharp eyes—ads usually run in newspapers or select magazines such as *New York* or *Time Out*. Tailors often employ this method, but so do manufacturers.

My tailor from Hong Kong, **W. W. Chan & Sons Tailors Ltd.**, sends a team to New York twice a year; contact sales@wwchan.com to get on the mailing list. They make both men's and women's clothing.

TRADE-SHOW SHOPPING

Inveterate shoppers usually shun the standard shopping services and go on the prowl themselves, and trade shows are one of their favorite haunts. If you are prepared to do your Christmas shopping in July, your Halloween shopping in May, and your kiddie birthday shopping by the dozen, you can get some great bargains. You'll also save a lot of time in future months when all your friends will be frantic, and you'll be cool as can be.

Manhattan hosts almost 1,000 conventions a year. Not all of these will interest you, but events such as the **Gift Show, Stationery Show,** and **Linens Show** are not only fun to attend (you get a sneak preview of next season's wares) but also fun to shop. On the final day of the show, company representatives will often sell the samples right out of the booths rather than pay to truck the merchandise home. You'll pay wholesale, sometimes less. You may also get a lot of small-time freebies. Trade-show shopping takes organization, storage space, and extra cash resources, but it's the best way to save money and time and still give fabulous gifts.

To shop a trade show:

- Get a list of the week's trade shows from your concierge, a magazine such as *Where,* or NYC & Company.
- Find out the last day of the show and the hours.
- Some shows require preregistration, either by mail or online. Once you're signed up, go to the convention hall to pick up your badge. Attendance at a trade fair may be free, or there may be a charge ($10–$25); either way, you must have some business credentials. This is what business cards are for.
- Your business card should be related to the business of the trade fair whenever possible; it should have some kind of company name rather than anything too cute. Your name should also be on the card. Have other ID, including photo ID. I recently had a very hard time getting into a trade show; they wanted all sorts of extra ID and business letterhead or checkbooks, and so on.
- Be prepared to answer a few innocent questions about your business, such as what you do. Having a gift-buying service or being in the party-planning business are two good entrees to just about anything.
- When you see something that interests you, introduce yourself—with your professional demeanor and company name—and ask if samples are being sold. If the answer is yes, pay in cash. No one wants your check. No one will change a

traveler's check. No one has American money for euros. Cash and carry.

- Every now and then, before the last day of the show, you can get a maker to let you buy items for your own use— but you still must meet a minimum order. Sometimes this is only $100. Shipping will be extra.
- Bring a rolly-roller.

CORPORATE DISCOUNTS

Many regular, traditional retailers offer corporate discounts. **Tiffany & Co.** has one of the most famous corporate plans; if you qualify (you must be incorporated), you can get a discount (usually 10%) on all merchandise.

Some corporate discounts are based on location: A fancy jeweler on Madison Avenue gives a discount to businesspeople who work in the neighborhood—he wants their business. A certain camera shop offers a discount to photographers who work for Time, Inc., because he likes to tell his regular customers that all the *Life* magazine photographers buy from him. And so it goes.

If you are visiting your corporate headquarters, it pays to ask a local company representative which retailers offer corporate benefits. You just may be surprised by the choices.

INDEX

FROMMER'S® COMPLETE TRAVEL GUIDES

FROMMER'S® DAY BY DAY GUIDES

PAULINE FROMMER'S GUIDES: SEE MORE. SPEND LESS.